C000231758

What If?

What If?

A CLOSER LOOK AT COLLEGE FOOTBALL'S GREAT QUESTIONS

_____

Matt Brown

© 2017 Matt Brown
All rights reserved.

ISBN-13: 9780692878569
ISBN-10: 0692878564
Library of Congress Control Number: 2017905999
Matt Brown, Hyattsville, MD

Table of Contents

Introduction

I'VE BEEN WATCHING COLLEGE FOOTBALL games nearly all of my life. I've watched them in my basement. I've watched them at crowded fraternity parties. I've watched them from my office at SB Nation. I've watched them from the very top row of Ohio Stadium, so far removed from the action I might as well have been in Akron rather than Columbus. I've watched them from a nearly empty press box at Middle Tennessee State, and from no press box at all at the University of Chicago.

Heck, I watched one from an airport bar while I was a Mormon missionary—nametag, suit and all. It was the 2006 Ohio State/Michigan game. Don't judge me.

But my favorite place to watch a college football game? My couch, with my wife. It isn't because my wife shares a rooting interest with me, since we went to college 2,000 miles apart. It isn't because of her detailed schematic insights either. In fact, she isn't even really that much of a football fan. She grew up just north of Chicago in Evanston, Illinois, a town best known for puritanical local zoning regulations that prevent bowling alleys from being built, and for Northwestern University, a school with a proud research tradition, a fantastic journalism school, and a long history of lousy football and indifferent fans. While other high schools across the Midwest went crazy for Friday Night Lights and fall prep football games, my wife's high school got excited for drama club.

My life experiences couldn't have been more different. I grew up in Licking County (please don't laugh, that's the real name), outside of Columbus, Ohio. My mother, who immigrated to the United States from Brazil when she was a kid, used Cleveland Browns games to help acclimate to her new country. Although to be fair, she later, and wisely, decided to give up on professional football.

"Why should I get emotionally invested in the Browns?" she told me, quite logically. "They stink, and they'll always stink."

In my formative years, Columbus wasn't nearly as big or as influential of a city as it is today, and the outlying suburbs were rural and mostly empty. The Blue Jackets didn't arrive until I was in middle school, and nobody I knew ever paid much attention to them, because they stunk. There were no other games in town. Just Ohio State football.

And in my community, Ohio State football reached an importance level just barely behind God, and maybe in some congregations, a little bit ahead. Just like for kids who grow up near Starkville, or Norman, or Auburn, even if you don't like football, you're going to pick up some understanding of the game, just to have a baseline of cultural literacy. A person who completely rejected football would be regarded as somewhat alien.

Our disparate backgrounds make my wife the perfect football-watching companion. She's picked up enough of the game by virtue of being married to a sportswriter, but since she wasn't completely baptized by the game as a kid, she tends to notice things that I miss, and ask about things that I completely take for granted.

Some of these questions were relatively easy to answer, like when I grabbed a bunch of our toddler's toys to try and diagram what, exactly, a wheel route was. *See, if the alphabet blocks hold off the pass rush, and the sheep sells his route here, then the farmer can hit this wee little pig for a touchdown and everybody on Twitter will scream about how awesome wheel routes are.*

Others didn't have easy answers, like, "Who thought Beavers would be a good nickname for a college football team?" or "What in the blue hell is Wyoming wearing?"

The longer I watched college football games for my job, the more complicated the questions became. In a sports world where the premier franchises are often in places like New York or LA, why is college football's in Tuscaloosa, Alabama? Why is a place like Nebraska good at football? Why does a place like Rutgers, in talent-rich New Jersey, stink? Why does Wake Forest get to be in a major college football conference? Why doesn't Houston?

Those questions are hard to answer in glib tweets. In reality, they go back decades, sometimes longer, as the seeds for today's college football dynasties were often planted in the turn of the twentieth century, when a thick sweater was your protection, the entire sport was little more than a lightly supervised brawl, and a win over Western Reserve or Dartmouth would be worthy of front-page news coverage.

Despite what some hyper-partisan fans might tell you, there were no stone tablets passed down from Mt. Sinai that said the South must always reign supreme in college football, or that a Catholic school in northern Indiana should become a college football powerhouse. Don't let a Notre Dame graduate lie to you. I even checked Deuteronomy twice before I started writing this.

Rather than divine fiat, much of what has determined the pecking order of current football powers stems from historical events, often very long ago, that could have easily gone a different direction. Maybe your school decides to hire their fourth choice for a head coaching vacancy, and he launches the program to unprecedented heights that they never should have enjoyed due to their demographics. After all, that happened to Nebraska.

Maybe a sports-skeptical university president decides to undercut a potentially promising program, locking you out of high profile matchups and unforeseen television opportunities. That happened to Chicago seventy years ago.

Maybe your program comes *this close* to being a part of a revolutionary conference realignment shift that would have catapulted your budget and exposure to the front of the country, only for it to fall apart at the last minute, and you never get another chance like it again. That happened to Southern Miss and East Carolina, among other schools.

There's a litany of these stories, many unknown to many college football fans, or at least, taken for granted. We tend to know the backstory and lore behind our own college football teams. Growing up where I did, I knew the stories about Woody and Bo, Earle, Cornelius Greene, Eddie George, and Chic Harley about as well as I knew anything I learned in Sunday School. But how USC became a superpower? Or how the SEC became so dominant? Or what a Sewanee was? Those were mysteries.

I started to dig into this history after my curiosity was piqued from writing what felt like 200 stories about Big 12 conference expansion and realignment for SB Nation. Between some of that historical digging, and my wife's questions, this book was born.

In each chapter, I'll pull back the curtain and try to explain what actually happened around a particular event, be that a coaching change, a conference realignment plan, an NCAA decision, or a single play on the field. Then, using advanced stats, newspaper records, history books, expert interviews, and some good ol' fashioned blogger-type speculation, I'll take a stab at projecting how our crazy sport would be different if things broke just a slightly different way.

These projections are not meant to be ironclad. I am not beating down my gavel, proclaiming a gospel truth. They are launching points of a discussion. After all, I can't predict the future. If I could, this would be a very different, and much more commercially successful, book.

Each of these individual questions is vast enough to fill a book by themselves, so they should not be taken as exhaustive histories of each subject. But in framing each scenario, I have tried to provide ample context and information to those who may not be intimately familiar with the details.

It is my hope that by reading this book, you will be a little more informed about some fun episodes of college football history, and a little better armed for the great debates of trivia night, tailgates, and Twitter feeds. I can't attempt to answer all of the great questions in college football. But by taking a closer look at history, we can try to explain some of the other weirdness.

Well, except Wyoming's uniforms. Sorry, Cowboys. Y'all are on your own there.

Glossary Of Terms

————

ONE OF THE RECURRING THEMES of this book involves evaluating and comparing teams from the past. That's a much trickier task in college football than it might be for some professional sports. After all, there are dozens and dozens more programs to keep track of, who don't play uniform schedules, and who face wildly different playing styles. A cursory glance at the standings may not come close to telling the full story.

To try and alleviate this, a few tools are used throughout this book. In order to make the reading a little easier, they've defined here.

SRS: This stands for Simple Rating System, a tool used by the invaluable Sports-Reference.com, and others. SRS is a value that combines Strength of Schedule with Margin of Victory. A 0.00 rating would be considered average, while negative ratings would be below average, etc. SRS is a predictive value, meaning that if team A had an SRS rating of 5.00, and team B had an SRS rating of 10.0, team B would be considered five points better than team A. For our purposes, SRS is used as a quick and dirty way of providing context for how "good" or "bad" a team might be, independent of its record. It's also useful because it is one of the few metrics that goes all the way back to the early 20th century, allowing some semblance of comparison between teams and conferences during seasons when intersectional play was more rare. For more information, check out Sports-Reference.com.

S&P+: S&P+ is a metric developed by my friend and SB Nation colleague Bill Connelly, who also writes for our college football analytics blog, Football Study Hall. S&P+ seeks to provide statistical comparison that adjusts for quality of competition and tempo, something that would be lacking when looking at data like total yardage.

Here's an example. Let's say one football team played against Texas Tech, a squad that runs an Air Raid system involving throwing the ball on nearly every play, and at a high tempo, where a defense might expect to face 90 plays or more over the course of a game. Another team plays against Navy, a triple-option team that might run the ball on virtually every play, and one that will seek to run a much lower number of plays, perhaps 60. The team that plays against Texas Tech will probably give up very few rushing yards, while the team that plays against Navy will likely give up few passing yards. But could one make a conclusive statement about the quality of those units? Could you compare them to each other? It's apples and oranges.

S&P+, or Success and Pace, assigns value to teams based on how they perform on a per-play basis, adjusted for opponent, garbage time, etc. While not perfect, it also provides another data point to compare not just teams against each other independent of their record, but also can help suss out what specific parts of the game historical programs excelled in. More details can be found on Football Study Hall.

What if Michigan never rejoined the Big Ten?

———

FOR A SPORT THAT TREASURES tradition as much as it does, not a whole lot remains the same in college football. The sport dominated and revered January 1, until it didn't. It refused to join the 20th century with a playoff, citing student welfare and logistical problems, until it did. The Southwest Conference was a powerhouse, until it vanished. The ACC clung to the edges of power football, until it raided a few other conferences and established itself as a heavyweight. Texas and Texas A&M don't even play each other anymore, deciding to settle their squabbles on Twitter, sniping about how they don't even miss each other since they aren't even rivals. You get the idea.

If there is one institution that has stood for tradition, the establishment, and for resisting change, it's been the Big Ten. Sure, it's still different from where it was back in the 1960s. It's a 14-team conference, for one, adding Penn State, Nebraska, Maryland, and (to my chagrin) Rutgers. It was the pioneer in conference television networks, championing perhaps the single biggest innovation in conference's ability to earn more revenue over the last twenty years. But historically, culturally, schematically, and maybe even spiritually, the Big Ten is proud to be a throwback of college football's past, when Men were Men, and when Bo and Woody battled under grim, gray Midwestern skies, with nary a forward pass in sight.

While everything else in the sport changes, the Big Two of the Big Ten have remained constant and stable. Ohio State and Michigan still fight every year in college football's best rivalry, for supremacy in the conference, the region, and often, the country.

But that rivalry nearly didn't happen. Michigan, who helped found the conference to begin with, briefly left the Big Ten, either because they were kicked out or forced out, depending on where your sympathies lie. And the aftershocks from their departure could have changed the trajectory of the conference, as well as the very organizing rules of the sport.

But that's a long story. Let's try and start at the beginning.

While almost everything else in college football has changed over the years, the crises in the sport have remained remarkably constant. The biggest issues in college football now—from concerns over player safety, to questions over how to define or enforce amateurism, to how to square the idea of merging large-scale athletic entertainment with research universities—have been debated for virtually as long as college football has existed. If anything, things used to be a lot worse.

After all, today, there's some sort of consensus that schools should at least *try* to enforce rules regarding eligibility and amateurism, and we have a decent idea what those rules should be. But back in the late 19th century, there wasn't anything close to a national consensus about how to manage this crazy sport. College football became very popular very quickly, which established a strong pressure to win, and win big. But anything resembling administrative organization had yet to be established.

As a result, the early years were marred by all sorts of chaos. One report from Illinois recalled those days when "conditions were far from satisfactory to students and most repugnant to the faculty. There were no codes of [eligibility] rules and no organizations to enforce any. [...] the one purpose was to win. Games were repeatedly broken up because of some savage quarrel as to a team personnel or playing methods, and the athletic departments (of competing institutions) were frequently on bad terms."[1] It wasn't uncommon for major athletic departments, from Ivy schools like Harvard and Yale to Midwestern ones, to suddenly sever athletic relations over foul play, allegations of cheating, and more[2].

Without monitored eligibility standards, "tramp" athletes flourished. Sometimes these were players who weren't college students at all, offering their services on a pay-to-play basis. Sometimes they were students at other universities who would mysteriously show up at another school for a few weeks, a category that included future Michigan head coach Fielding Yost, who transferred from West Virginia to Lafayette in the middle of the season, only to return two weeks later. He played in exactly one game for the Leopards, a key 6-4 win over Penn.[3] Sometimes those tramp athletes were even members of the faculty, which was allegedly the case at North Carolina, when a professor scored a touchdown against Virginia.[4] The North Carolina tradition of faculty and staff going the extra mile for their athletes isn't new, but that's another story.

One particularly illustrative example of not just "tramp" athletics, but the general disorganization and craziness that often occurred at early college football games comes from an early matchup between Georgia Tech and Georgia in 1893. On Tech's roster was a 33-year-old former army surgeon named Leonard Wood, a veteran of the Indian Wars and a man who was very much not enrolled at Georgia Tech or any other institution of higher learning. Wood dominated the game at guard, much to the chagrin of the partisan fans in the crowd, who began to yell at officials, and then later, Tech players[5].

Those insults turned to violence, as Bulldogs fans chucked rocks and other debris at Georgia Tech's players. One rock smashed Wood in the face, opening a three-inch gash. Instead of leaving the game, Wood simply wiped his bloody face on an opposing Georgia player. Georgia Tech won the game[6]. Paul Johnson would have loved this man.

Fast and loose definitions about eligibility weren't the only problem vexing college football. There was also the much more important matter of player safety. Cheap shots, hard hits, and crushing mass-momentum plays were badly injuring players, and occasionally, even killing them, perhaps most famously with Richard Gammen of Georgia dying from injuries he suffered against Virginia in 1897, a game which almost lead to the sport being banned in the state of Georgia. Rule innovations like the forward pass, or a standardized line of scrimmage hadn't gone into effect by the late 1890s, turning many games into grueling slogfests that trampled players.

Those risks, amplified by the new sporting press eager to splash reports of carnage across front pages across the country, threatened the very existence of the sport. Without some sort of action to clamp down on the excesses of college football, the whole sport would be in jeopardy. Some colleges, such as

Georgetown, Columbia, and Trinity (which we now know as Duke), temporarily canceled their football programs[7]. Others, like Northwestern, investigated doing the same[8].

Eventually, many of the leading football programs in the Midwest got tired of waiting for Yale and Harvard to take the lead in reform efforts, and decided to try and address some of these problems themselves.

In 1895, at the behest of James H. Smart, the president of Purdue, seven schools met at the Palmer House Hotel in Chicago to discuss a new organization: Purdue, Northwestern, Chicago, Lake Forest, Wisconsin, Illinois, and Minnesota. Lake Forest withdrew the following year (the Foresters now play in D3 against schools like Grinnell and Beloit), and was replaced by Michigan. Indiana and Iowa would join a few years later. This would become the first true athletic conference in the country, what would eventually be known as the Big Ten.

But they didn't call it that at first, since there were only seven programs. Instead, they went with the title on the minutes, the substantially less catchy "Intercollegiate Conference of Faculty Representatives." When that became a bit mouthy, they went with the "Western Conference." The group didn't officially change its name to the Big Ten until 1987.

It was impressive to get such disparate institutions to agree to cooperate with each other, since even though the schools were relatively close geographically, they were very different. Northwestern, after all, was sponsored by the Methodist church (their athletic teams actually went by 'Methodists'. Wildcats didn't pop up until much later). Chicago was private and still a relatively new institution, and one that placed a bigger influence on athletics than the others. Unlike the other institutions, the Maroons' faculty representative was the legendary Amos Alonzo Stagg, who worked in athletics. Plus, the schools differed substantially in size. Northwestern, after all, had just 317 "men available for athletics" in 1897, and Purdue had just 569, while Chicago boasted over 1,300, and Michigan over 2,000[9].

The early focus on the Big Ten was to solve eligibility problems. Rules emanating from the 1895 meeting included a statement restricting athletic participation to "bona fide students doing full work in a regular or special course as defined by the curriculum of his college", and also prohibited transfer students from participating unless they had been a student for at least six months, a rule that would have prohibited a player like Yost from flipping squads.[10]

Other early rules prohibited players from accepting gifts or payments for playing college athletics, playing under assumed names. It also prohibited college programs playing against professional teams and playing games at neutral locations. Off-campus games were often perceived to attract additional hooligan-type crowds, especially in the Northeast, and college administrators hoped they could better reign in the excesses of the games, and better control the revenue, if games were held a bit closer to campus.[11]

Several different schools fielded strong teams in the early days of the conference, like Wisconsin, who dominated thanks to the league's most unlikely early superstar, legendary Australian kicker Pat O'Dea. But the two true early superpowers of the Big Ten were the Chicago Maroons and the Michigan Wolverines, especially once Michigan hired Fielding Yost in 1901.

Yost was a controversial and domineering figure in the Big Ten virtually as soon as he stepped foot on campus. One of the first places Yost applied for work, Ohio State, threw him out, with a faculty member screaming "get this madman out of here!".[12] Yost's previous employer, Stanford University, passed a rule requiring that the coaching position be filled by a graduate of the university, forcing him to look elsewhere[13]. Having already successfully coached at places like Nebraska and Kansas (where he was not above using the occasional ringer to win a big game[14]), Yost first reached out to Illinois about possible employment, but since they had no opening, his information was referred to Michigan, who quickly hired him over their other candidate, former Brown football player Dave Fultz.[15]

Yost made no bones about being a professional football coach, a role that was still somewhat unique and controversial in an era where not every university administrator believed teams should pay outsiders to coach a team. Harvard coach Bill Reid echoed the thoughts of many in the football community when he said that "the man who coaches as a regular thing is likely to be a man of trifling ambition and small ideals, very often not a college graduate, and often lacking in the finer instincts.[16]" Having a professional not only potentially invited scandal, it was *uncouth*.

On a related note, it sure is nice that Harvard and Yale don't run college football anymore.

When Yost arrived at Michigan, he boasted that the Wolverines wouldn't lose a game.[17] And basically, they didn't. In his first season, bolstered by transfers brought via Yost's contacts across the country[18], Michigan not only finished 11-0, capturing what would be their first national title, but they didn't even give up a single point, outscoring their opponents 555-0 over the course of the year. Immediately, Michigan established themselves as the new class of the Western Conference, unseating previous conference heavyweight Chicago.

The 1901 campaign was the first of what was known as Yost's "point a minute" teams, so originally named because they did, in fact, average at least a point per minute. This was helped by Michigan's breakneck pace; they once ran 219 plays in a single game, an outrageously high number by today's standards, where 100 is a lot[19]. Their dominating defense likewise gave their offense plenty of possessions.

The next season featured even more blowouts. Once again Michigan finished undefeated, although they gave up a touchdown against Minnesota in the last game of the season. Before then, Michigan trounced their opponents by margins they would never approach again in history, like an 86 point win over Ohio State, a 107 point win over Iowa, and a 119 point win over Michigan State. Sure, Ohio State and Michigan State weren't close to national powers in 1902 (in fact, Ohio State was still struggling with teams like Oberlin), but *still*. Even beating high school teams by margins like that would be an impressive accomplishment. The Wolverines weren't exactly making friends, but they were dominating box scores and headlines across the Midwest.

In the Midwest, the most heated battles, even if they didn't always show up that way on the scoreboard, was with Stagg's University of Chicago. The Maroons were the second best team in the Midwest, boasted a larger-than-life coach with another larger-than-life ego, and battled bitterly with the Wolverines over recruits, especially in Chicago.

By 1905, Michigan had compiled an astonishing 55-0-1 record over Yost's tenure, with the lone non-win a 6-6 tie with Minnesota in 1903. Rarely would a team even come within 30 points of Michigan, let alone seriously threaten to upset them. The biggest worry of Michigan fans wasn't that some other football team might actually beat them, but that Yost might leave Michigan, either for Princeton, as newspapers had rumored[20], or another institution where he might regularly get a crack at the elite Northeastern programs. Apparently, whooping Western Reserve may not have been sufficient for his competitive juices.

A focus on the Northeast would be understandable for an ambitious college football coach, since that's where the center of college football was at the turn of the century. Even as Michigan barbecued absolutely everybody in sight from 1901 to 1905, they still shared national title honors with multiple Northeastern programs: Yale in 1902, Princeton in 1903, and Penn in 1904. This wasn't completely the imagination of biased New York sportswriters, although that probably did play a role. While they still played regional schools of lesser renown, the Ivy League institutions were still playing stronger schedules than Michigan.

The 1905 Michigan team didn't face an especially difficult schedule, but it was making another serious run at the record books. The Wolverines won their first 12 games by a combined 495-0, including their biggest blowout in school history, a 130-0 dispatching of West Virginia. Michigan also padded their stats against schools like American Medical (72-0), and Physicians & Surgeons (72-0)[21]. But Michigan was upset by Chicago 2-0, thanks to a careless Michigan safety, breaking the streak and any sense that Michigan was, in fact, invincible.

Even with the loss, Michigan made it clear that exceptional football was being played outside of the Northeast, as they laid an unimpeachable claim as one of the nation's elite. Strong intersectional showings by Wisconsin and Chicago furthered the Big Ten's reputation as an excellent football league. With those three programs, along with Minnesota, it looked like the Big Ten would easily continue their massive growth as one of college football's elite, if not *the* elite, league.

But then the administrators got involved.

1905 was an especially traumatic year in college football, as concerns over the especially injurious style of play continued to gather steam. 18 players died across the country that season, as previous reform movements to slow down mass momentum plays had proven ineffective.[22] College football in the early

1900s still resembles a Hobbesian state of nature, where games were nasty and brutish. Thanks to a rush of media attention, from national magazines to front pages everywhere, the public was made increasingly aware of football's problems.

Things got so bad that the president, Teddy Roosevelt, a noted football fan himself, brought officials from the biggest Northeastern football programs together to try and find solutions to the excesses of the sport[23]. While the actual impact of these meetings has probably been exaggerated a little bit, these meetings did eventually lead to the creation of the Intercollegiate Athletic Association of the United States, which would become the NCAA in 1910. If nothing else, it shows how seriously even the most important leaders in the country were taking reform of college football.

While much of the focus on football reform centered on colleges in the Northeast, the Midwest—and the Western Conference specifically—were not immune from negative press and concerns about the state of football. An article in popular *Collier's Weekly* accused multiple conference institutions, from successful ones like Chicago to less-than-successful ones like Northwestern of multiple recruiting improprieties[24]. The negative press spurred internal discussions at multiple schools about how to not only eradicate the abuses of the sport, but how they could attempt to control the tightening grip football had on the campus community.[25] Michigan's president James B. Angell called for a conference, and leaders in the Big Ten met in Chicago after the 1905 season to try and solve some of those problems.

The exact motives for what happened next depend on who you ask. If you're a Michigan fan, you probably think that Chicago, led by their faculty rep, Amos Alonzo Stagg, who just so happened to also be their football coach, pushed for a series of exceptionally strict rules that were specifically targeted at Michigan's football program. Stagg was the only member of the group that was affiliated with his school's athletic department, and stood to gain the most from any relative decline in Michigan's fortunes. Certainly, some of the proposed rules, like a rule to mandate that football coaches be members of the faculty, seemed specifically targeted at Fielding Yost. [26]

It probably isn't totally fair to say that the entire operation was engineered to "get" Michigan. After all, there was a powerful national movement to enact reforms around college football. Some representatives at these discussions, like Frederick Jackson Turner at Wisconsin, wanted to abolish football completely, or at least, temporarily. Michigan's president was heavily supportive of the strict measures as well. Angell didn't see eye to eye with Yost on the future of the football program, as Angell would have preferred that Michigan avoid big time football entirely, wishing to abolish a campus culture that celebrated "men of brawn rather than men of brain."[27] He would clash with Yost numerous times in the future, especially over Yost's goals for a large, on-campus, Michigan football stadium.

Basically, if there was a massive, anti-Michigan conspiracy afoot, Stagg was especially devious, and found a way to not only involve administrators who couldn't care less who won a Chicago/Michigan game, but some of the highest ranked leaders at Michigan themselves.

That Yost wasn't winning Most Popular Man on Campus awards with the faculty or administration isn't a big surprise, despite his massive football success. Many professors across the country viewed the entire football enterprise with skepticism, given how its popularity came to dominate energy and oxygen on campus, and how its unseemly side dominated headlines.

Yost was also paid more than most professors, even though he didn't even stay on campus full time. College coaching as a profession was still in its infancy, and during the offseason, Yost would head to Tennessee to attend to business interests there.[28] The idea that a non-academic, part-timer could earn more than a professor inspired no small amount of jealousy or ill feelings on campus. Stagg had to deal with similar concerns at Chicago, and he was technically part of the faculty.[29]

Yost probably could have smoothed over some of those concerns if he was the type to keep a low profile. But he wasn't. His ego would even get him in trouble with future Michigan coaches once Yost took over as athletic director. If you combine his penchant for running up the score, his relentless drive to succeed, his big salary, and his inability to just shut up for like, five minutes, and you can see why others may have been happy to humble him a little bit.

Whether the reform campaign was orchestrated to knock Michigan down a peg, to try and save the sport, as a dramatic power play by jealous academics, or some combination thereof (it's probably that), the leaders left with a new slate of rule changes for conference institutions.

Conference teams would be limited to only five games a season, and would no longer play on Thanksgiving, ending the highly popular Michigan and Chicago battles on Turkey Day. Athletes would only have three years of eligibility, training tables and preseason practices would be abolished, and ticket prices would be capped at fifty cents in an attempt to fight price gouging and profit-seeking in the game. Prices varied wildly across the conference at this point, but at least one historian says Michigan often charged around three dollars for good tickets[30]. If you adjust for inflation, that's about $80 per ticket.

Also especially detrimental to Michigan was a reform that limited athletic eligibility to undergraduates, so that law students, graduate students, and even transfers would be prohibited. Transfers and graduate students were important parts of the Michigan recruiting pipeline at the time.

Michigan actually agreed to several of the reforms, paring their schedule down to just five games in 1906. But they couldn't agree to everything, especially the requirement for coaches to be members of the faculty. Unwilling to submit to the wishes of the rest of the conference, Michigan withdrew (or was kicked out, depending on your partisan leanings) from the conference to start the 1907 season. There would be no more showdowns with the Maroons on the Midway. At least, not for a long time.

Students, fans, and alumni at Michigan expressed their displeasure at the reforms, even holding a mass meeting of thousands to protest the recommendations of the committee, but they were hardly the only group who wasn't thrilled with the proposed reforms. Students at Wisconsin were particularly incensed, as they worried the group would actually move to abolish or suspend football, like Northwestern had decided to do. Given the increasingly hard-line anti-football stances of the Wisconsin faculty, led by Frederick Jackson Turner, these fears were not entirely unjustified.

The frustration at Wisconsin came to a head on March 27, 1906, when a group of protesting students marched all the way to Turner's house, not just armed with angry shouts, but with rifles and revolvers, yelling "death to the faculty!" According to Dave Revsine's account in *The Opening Kickoff,* the protests eventually dispersed without violence, but not without Turner and two other Wisconsin professors getting burned in effigy.[31] Turner would eventually help broker agreements to keep football at Wisconsin[32].

So Michigan departed the conference, without bringing guns or death threats into the equation. Suddenly, the Wolverines needed a new rival. Actually, they needed more than that. They needed some teams to play, period. Early on, Michigan tried to supplement their suddenly independent schedule with teams from the Big Ten, adding Minnesota to a two game slate in 1908 and 1909, so they could continue their rivalry showdown for the Little Brown Jug.

A quick aside, just to demonstrate the kind of person that Yost was. The Little Brown Jug started in 1903, when the Wolverines were slated to play in Minneapolis. Afraid that agents of the Golden Gophers would somehow contaminate their water supply, Yost ordered his student manager to buy some sort of jug to carry their own water from Michigan. The manager, Thomas B. Roberts, picked one up from a local store for thirty cents[33].

The 1903 game ended up being one of the most exciting of the "point a minute" squads. The Gophers held the vaunted Michigan offense to a single touchdown, but their own offense struggled. With two minutes left, Minnesota plowed into the end zone to tie the score, causing a pandemonium, with fans rushing the field.[34] The game was called, ending in a 6-6 tie, Michigan's only non-victory from 1901, until their 2-0 defeat to Chicago in 1905.

In the ruckus after the game, Michigan accidentally left the jug behind. Minnesota's equipment manager recovered it and turned it over to the school, which promptly gave it a new paint job to celebrate Minnesota's "win" and hung it in the office of the athletic director. When Yost wrote, asking for the jug to be returned, Minnesota allegedly replied, "If you want it, you'll have to come up and win it."

Thus started the tradition of the oldest rivalry trophy in the country, and the Big Ten's curious habit of then assigning a traveling trophy for virtually every conference game—from jugs, to pigs, to my personal favorite, the recent "bits of broken chair" trophy, fought for between Minnesota and Nebraska, thanks to a parody Twitter account.

Anyway, after the two game series between Michigan and Minnesota had concluded (with two thrilling games that featured some early usage of the forward pass[35]), the conference passed a rule prohibiting member institutions from playing any former member of the Big Ten. In what was surely a coincidence and in no way a measure to specifically isolate Michigan, the only team to have ever left the conference was... Michigan.[36]

Since long-distance travel was expensive and impractical, Michigan couldn't simply haul off to play West Coast or Deep South squads multiple times a season. But the Midwest alone didn't have the quality of teams to challenge Michigan. With new space on the schedule, the Wolverines centered their attention towards the power center of the sport, the northeast.

Over the course of their independent era, Michigan added multiple games with Syracuse and Cornell, along with eastern power Penn, who took over as Michigan's chief rival now that Chicago and Minnesota were off the schedule. These games were well attended, but unlike their Western conference foes, Michigan didn't dominate them. The Quakers knocked off Michigan in 1907 and 1908, and the Wolverines only managed a 4-5-1 record against them from 1907 to 1917, which, given how badly they were stomping everybody else, constitutes some serious struggling. Cornell, Harvard, and Syracuse were able to pick up wins over Michigan during this era as well.

The Wolverines entered those games at a disadvantage, though. While Michigan adamantly believed they should be able to retain their professional coach, and were happy to play more than five games a season, they actually continued to uphold most of the Western Conference reforms, such as limiting eligibility to three years, and prohibiting freshman from playing. Cornell, Syracuse, and Penn, along with most of the Eastern powers as well as independent programs elsewhere, did not share those strict eligibility rules.[37] So expecting Michigan to run roughshod like they were against the Purdues of the world wouldn't have been realistic.

Michigan also couldn't play just Northeastern teams. While independent schedules were dotted with the occasional squad from the South, like Vanderbilt and Kentucky, the bulk of Michigan's opponents were still Midwestern. Many of these teams would be considered non-major opponents, like Case in Cleveland or Marquette. Later in independence, Michigan would be forced to scrape even lower in the proverbial barrel, adding games against squads like Lawrence, Kalamazoo, Wabash, Mt. Union, South Dakota, and Marietta. The Wolverines won all of those games, often by large margins, but it's not like any sportswriter or discriminating fan was especially impressed by it. These games were scheduled early in the season for a reason. Nobody recognized them as anything more than tune-up games.

A few of those regular games against less-than-impressive opponents would go on to become exceptionally important for Michigan and college football history. One of those regular opponents was a school named the Michigan Agricultural College, whose teams were nicknamed the Farmers.[38] Today, it's known as Michigan State, one of the chief rivals to the Wolverines. They should have stuck with the Farmer nickname.

Michigan's single biggest rivalry, if not the biggest rivalry in all of college sports, owes some of its roots to this era. Unlike Michigan, the Ohio State Buckeyes were not immediately successful as a college football program, and weren't even considered a major opponent during some of the early games in the series, games that Michigan won without fail.

Ohio State and Michigan first played back in 1897, only about 50 years after the Toledo War, when Ohio and Michigan actually fired guns at each other over a dispute over Toledo, which gave additional emotional fuel. Michigan's football program was far superior to Ohio State's in these early battles, although the games were still valuable for the Buckeyes. After Michigan won by eighty-six points in 1902, a backup defensive end on the squad wrote the school's Alma Mater, 'Carmen Ohio'.[39]

For the Buckeyes, these games with Michigan were important measuring sticks for what they wanted their program to be, since even by the early 1900s, Ohio State lacked a true peer institution within the state of Ohio. And for Michigan, they became important schedule inventory after independence created a need for regular, and stronger, regional opponents. This shared history helped create a true rivalry once the Buckeyes formally joined the Big Ten themselves.

Another rival during Michigan's independent era was Notre Dame. The Wolverines literally taught Notre Dame how to play the game in 1887, essentially launching the program. The Wolverines returned to play Notre Dame twice the next year, and even though Michigan won both games, the

Wolverines were booed once they returned to campus for having committing the unpardonable sin of allowing the Irish to score.[40] The two teams played several times before 1908, with Michigan winning every time.

But the series became a true rivalry in 1909. Michigan had won the first eight games in the series by a commanding 121-16 margin. Once Notre Dame hired a former Michigan Man, Frank Longman, as their head coach, the Wolverine's fortunes declined. Notre Dame sprung the upset, winning 11-3. Longman, who still lived in Ann Arbor, made a sweater for his dog with a big 11-3 on it, and walked it around town, which undoubtedly made him a lot of friends.[41]

A sportswriter at the game, E.A. Batchelor, described the men from South Bend as "Fighting Irish". As folklore goes, Batchelor apparently got the idea after overhearing a Notre Dame player yelling at his teammates, "What's the matter with you guys? You're all Irish and you're not fighting worth a lick."[42] Whether that's true, or whether Batchelor invented the nickname out of whole cloth, it was soon wildly popularized, giving what would become the most famous program in the country their iconic nickname.

The two teams were slated for a rematch the next season, but it never happened. Yost believed that Notre Dame was using two players that he thought should have been ineligible. A coach protesting a player wasn't uncommon, as there was no NCAA to create, or enforce, some sort of uniform code of eligibility. The two sides were unable to reach a compromise, and right before the game, Yost canceled the game[43].

Yost's fury didn't end there. A notoriously sore loser, Yost refused to schedule Notre Dame again, and the two schools would not meet again until the 1940s. [44]Yost was also instrumental in preventing Notre Dame from joining the Big Ten, insinuating that the program was dirty and insufficiently academic, while also playing off latent anti-Catholic feelings within the group. Yost was hardly the most enlightened man, after all. An unabashed racist, Yost also never had a black player on any of his teams, and was furious when other Michigan coaches did so while he was athletic director[45].

Compared to their lofty run of 1901-1905, Michigan football certainly declined during their independence era. They weren't competing for national titles and only went undefeated once, in 1910, an accomplished sullied a bit by their three ties. Was the decline simply a matter of a schedule dotted with better teams?

Not entirely. For one, there's a good chance Yost wasn't giving Michigan his complete and undivided attention. During this era, Yost's business interests in Tennessee multiplied, as he served as the director of four different companies in Nashville, in industries as diverse from banking, to cement, to furniture[46]. Given that these ventures paid Yost significantly more than he made as a football coach, it seems reasonable to conclude they were occupying a fair amount of his time.

But it's clear the schedule had something to do with Michigan falling behind a bit. A slate that featured multiple road games to strong squads with different eligibility rules, plus a part-time and potentially distracted coach, coupled with a decrease in talent, and it all adds up to Michigan falling from the true elite of the sport. Not like Michigan was bad or anything, (they never had a losing record during the Indie era), but they weren't in the conversation for national titles anymore.

The Big Ten didn't need to wait very long to find a replacement member for Michigan. In 1912, the conference added Ohio State, who had finally begun to outgrow their regular competition against squads like Ohio Wesleyan and Kenyon. The Buckeyes quickly established themselves as at least an average team in the conference. The Buckeyes won the league for the first time in 1916, a year when they beat Oberlin 128-0.

The Wolverines rejoined the Big Ten the next year, for the 1917 campaign. The concerns over various reforms had been mitigated, and the national conversation wasn't quite as dire in 1917 as it had been in 1905 and 1906. By 1918, Michigan was undefeated again, and as well on its way to national success. Only now, it had built up additional rivalries with Ohio State, now a conference-mate, and Michigan State, who would join the conference a few decades later, despite some resistance from Ann Arbor.[47]

But what if Michigan hadn't come back? What if those bridges had stayed burned?

I asked Greg Dooley, a historian and proprietor of MVictors.com, about what he thought about Michigan's ability to succeed without re-joining the Big Ten. He wasn't particularly bullish.

"The most likely outcome is that interest in Michigan football wanes, Yost loses influence and the anti-football academic forces at UM gain power.

If Yost is even still around in the early 1920s, he definitely doesn't get the support [from the university or from boosters financially] to build Michigan Stadium. Then you have the stock market crash in 1929 and the Great Depression, and you have to wonder if Michigan football slowly fades away like Chicago. So Michigan doesn't win the national titles in the early 1930s or the late 1940s."[48]

Everything would center on Yost. With Yost's blood feud with Notre Dame, and with the rest of the conference essentially blacklisting the Wolverines, Michigan couldn't recruit and retain the same level of elite talent, couldn't get enough quality local games, and perhaps most importantly to a man with such an immense ego, probably couldn't have competed for national titles or national acclaim, at least not with the East.

Because of that, it isn't hard to imagine him deciding to work elsewhere. Tennessee, a job that would have allowed him to keep a closer eye on his business interests, would open up for the 1921 season, and that may have been an attractive spot for Yost. Of course, that would have prevented Volunteer program father Bob Neyland from taking over in 1926, so perhaps we'd have a massive Yost Stadium in Knoxville instead.

Outside of Tennessee, Penn would need a replacement for John Heisman after the 1922 season. If Yost wanted to ply his trade at a more prestigious program, he would have had plenty of options. A Yost departure could have been devastating for Michigan, given the timing, and campus political situation. Yost was a major proponent for the construction of the Big House, but he faced opposition from key campus partners, some who worried that bringing a throng of 80,000 or more to campus would distract from the school's key mission.[49] Yost's power of personality and immense social capital at Michigan won the day, facilitating the creation of one of the great landmarks in all of college football, and cementing the tool that would allow it to generate revenue needed for a large athletic department. Had virtually anybody else been Michigan's football coach near the 1920s, Michigan Stadium probably doesn't happen, and the Wolverines' next stadium after Ferry Field would almost assuredly be more modest.

But the most interesting question about an independent Michigan, to me, is what happens with Notre Dame.

Perhaps the most recognizable trait about Notre Dame football beyond Touchdown Jesus, the Golden Domes, and their 4-8 record in the 2016 season[50], is their independence. But playing a national schedule, unbeholden to a conference, wasn't Notre Dame's original plan. The school tried to join the Big Ten multiple times before 1920, only to be rebuffed, due to concerns about their eligibility policies, and good ol' fashioned snobbery[51]. Among academic circles at the turn of the century, there was a feeling that religious schools couldn't possibly provide the same level of academic rigor that a secular school could produce, a feeling that has yet to be totally eradicated, even in modern times.

Notre Dame would seek closer ties to Big Ten schools, and even conference admission, again in the early 20th century.[52] But Michigan, led by Yost, helped wage war against the Irish, even convincing conference institutions to boycott playing the school at all.[53] Without Yost leading the charge in Ann Arbor, it's probable that other conference institutions would have realized that Notre Dame was actually playing by very similar eligibility standards by the 1920s, and had already established itself as a solid program. If Michigan wasn't in the Big Ten in the early 1920s, Notre Dame probably would be.

Such a turn of events would completely change the trajectory of Notre Dame and Michigan. With the comfort of regularly scheduled, high-quality opponents in the Midwest, Notre Dame would no longer need to travel across the entire country looking for games, (and also wouldn't have room on their schedule for them). Regular intersectional games with USC, Stanford, or jaunts to places like Texas and SMU couldn't happen at the same clip, if at all. That would make it much harder for Notre Dame to build up the "national brand" mystique it eventually would enjoy.

Being a college football pariah in the early 20th century certainly made life difficult for the Irish, but by weathering it, they unquestionably became a stronger program in the middle and later part of the 20th century. While Notre Dame would still have appeal outside of the Midwest, thanks to their status as the flagship Catholic university in the country and popular standing with New York based sportswriters, we would not be living in a world where Notre Dame has a special TV contract, or where Notre Dame enjoyed the same level of mystique in Hollywood that it enjoyed.

That means instead of fighting the NCAA and pushing for reform of a centrally controlled TV package, Notre Dame is in lockstep with the Big Ten, the closest thing to "the establishment" throughout NCAA history. Notre Dame doesn't jump ship and scuttle the College Football Alliance TV deal, since they never would have participated in the first place (perhaps it never even forms as a result). Any innovation or major decision tied to independence over the last several decades would vanish. Maybe the world is never subjected to *Rudy*.[54] We can dream of this world.

Michigan, on the other hand, would essentially be swapping places. With the Big Ten boycotting the school, and with Yost's bad blood preventing games with Notre Dame, there were almost no quality opponents in the Midwest for the Wolverines to play. Prolonged independence would force Michigan to not only play strong teams from the Northeast, but eventually, even farther away. Perhaps the Wolverines would end up pursuing a more national schedule, securing rivalries with Stanford (where Yost used to coach) and USC, instead of say, Minnesota and Illinois.

There's plenty of precedent for an independent program to be successful, even in the 1930s. Most of the eastern powers like Penn, Princeton, and Pittsburgh were independents, and other programs like Santa Clara before World War II, and Penn State and Miami produced excellent teams without conference affiliation. Even without Yost, and without some of the palatial facilities the Wolverines would enjoy after the Yost building boom, Michigan probably wouldn't stink unless they made horrid coaching and administrative hires, or found the department completely gutted over decades by anti-athletics administrators (which, given the proliferation of alumni who cared about sports, may have been hard to sustain). There were enough smaller local programs to fill out a schedule, especially if Michigan was able to continue their rivalries with Michigan State and Ohio State as they later joined the Big Ten.

But it would be structurally difficult for Michigan to enjoy truly elite success. After all, programs like Pitt, Syracuse, and Temple built rivalries with plenty of other big-time independent programs playing relatively nearby, making building rivalries and getting home and homes easier. Michigan wouldn't have that luxury. Notre Dame could count on its Roman Catholic affiliation to help expand its brand beyond its borders. As a state school, Michigan would have no such advantage.

Michigan was one of the largest universities in the country, even by the 1920s, and had a strong fanbase and football tradition. But expecting it to reach Notre Dame levels of success without conference affiliation seems unlikely, barring transformational coaching hires. Michigan's best case scenario seems to be achieving what Penn State did before joining the Big Ten, a few seasons of being in the conversation for national titles, and regularly in the mix for bowl games. Miss a few hires, and they're looking more like pre-Big East Pitt.

There would be one potential positive side effect of Michigan playing outside of the Big Ten: postseason flexibility. The Big Ten stubbornly refused to allow members to participate in any bowl game outside of the Rose Bowl, wouldn't allow teams to play in the Rose two seasons in a row, and would occasionally pick who got to go to the Rose by arbitrary means, like in 1973, where the 10-0-1 Michigan Wolverines were denied a postseason bid after the conference voted to send Ohio State instead.

Free of those rules, Michigan would be free to play in whatever bowl game would take them, and as a reasonably successful independent team they would find invites forthcoming. The Michigan teams of the 1950s and 1960s would likely get cracks at opportunities like the Sugar and Orange Bowls, which would help recruiting, along with the department's bottom line.

So the Wolverines would be more of a fixture in the postseason. Their annual game with Ohio State may have become a heated non-conference showdown earlier in the season. And they would likely play a more national schedule, depending on how willing other Big Ten schools would be to schedule them.

A big potential winner in this move? Ohio State. The two biggest regional rivals to the Buckeyes, Michigan and Notre Dame, are both likely diminished a bit by the Wolverines going independent, which would improve Ohio State's own recruiting. The Ohio State-Michigan rivalry probably takes a bit of a backseat to Ohio State-Notre Dame, likely the biggest Big Ten battle for Rose Bowl spots. Still, unless the Wolverines completely went into the tank for decades, the rivalry would maintain at least some of its prestige.

It's probably best for everybody that Michigan was able to patch up its differences with the rest of the conference. When they rejoined in 1920, the Wolverines, armed by an impressive building program, dogged alumni, and ambitious athletic director, quickly re-established themselves as the class of the conference, giving the league historic heft and prestige that would help translate into massive riches in the future, not to mention influence in NCAA decisions. It pushed Notre Dame out of the conference and into a world of independence, a move that harmed the Irish at first, but later would be the catalyst for their institutional identity, giving college football some important, regular rivalry games, and a new voice in NCAA policy.

Michigan and Notre Dame are rivals. They're two of the most successful programs in all of college football history. And if you asked their fans, I don't think many would want to switch places. How things worked out ended up being a good deal for them both.

What if Chicago stayed in the Big Ten?

———

I SPENT MY MID-TWENTIES LIVING in Chicago. Every morning, when I left my apartment in Avondale to walk to the subway station, I could look out and see a big billboard over the highway. Sometimes it had a picture of a smiling Pat Fitzgerald, sometimes just a basketball. But the text was always the same: "Northwestern. Chicago's Big Ten Team."

Everybody understood the rationale behind this advertising campaign, even if few in the city really believed it. Sure, Northwestern was technically the closest Big Ten program to the city of Chicago, with Evanston just a short jaunt on the Purple Line away. But their athletic program lagged far behind their Big Ten conference peers. Plus, the school's enrollment was already far below more conference institutions, and Northwestern has basically no sidewalk alumni or fans, even in Evanston. Chicago has more alumni from Illinois and Michigan than Northwestern, and the only place where the Wildcats would be a primary rooting interest would be at a newspaper staffed with Medill grads. (If you aren't sure if your newspaper is full of Medill grads, don't worry. Their reporters will tell you.)

You can run an advertising campaign like this because Chicago doesn't actually have a Big Ten football team. It's a city full of folks who moved from other Big Ten states, and their allegiances, along with Notre Dame, get all mixed up together. It's one of the few places within the Big Ten footprint that may be up for grabs.

But that wasn't always the case. Once upon a time, Chicago actually *had* a very, very good Big Ten team. During the peak of their run, they claimed two national titles, multiple Big Ten titles, owned the critical Thanksgiving real estate for the biggest end of season game in the conference, and won the first Heisman Trophy. They're inarguably a more successful football program than Indiana, and they haven't played D1 football in over 70 years.

We're talking about the Chicago Maroons, the city's original Big Ten team. And their rise, fall, and what-could-have-been is worth a closer look. To understand it, we need to go all the way to the beginning.

Back in the 1880s, when John D. Rockefeller looked to found a new Baptist university in Chicago, he tabbed William Rainey Harper, a young prodigy of languages at Yale, to be his first university president. One of the very first, if not the first recruitment meetings Harper set up for the school was with a young former divinity student named Amos Alonzo Stagg. Rather than looking to Stagg to help head a divinity department, Harper wanted Stagg to chair a department in physical education and to coach the football team.[1]

That Harper would look to Yale for a football coach wouldn't be a surprise. After all, in the early days of college football, the beating heart of the sport was in what would later become the Ivy League, and specifically at Yale. Many of the early giants of football, from Walter Camp, who helped guide the rulemaking process of the sport and would produce the first All-American list, to William "Pudge" Heffelfinger, who would be considered the first professional football player and would later coach at Cal and Minnesota, were Elis. As college football became more popular and schools in the Midwest, South and West looked to start programs, Yale alumni, along with other Ivy programs, were popular hires.

Stagg's background might have made him a unique fit to serve in a dual administrative and academic role. The son of a poor family in New Jersey, Camp spent time at Phillips-Exeter academy, a popular prep school and later recruiting pipeline into Ivy League football programs, before enrolling in Yale. On campus, Stagg excelled primarily as a baseball player, earning notoriety in eastern newspapers for his pitching prowess, along with his Christian values and ethics. Stagg turned down offers to play professional baseball thanks to his sense of loyalty to Yale, and concern about the moral values of professional baseball players.[2] He would later lead the campus YMCA and give speeches on Christian values. Basically, he was an 1880s version of Tim Tebow, if Tim Tebow was also actually a good baseball player.

Stagg would later achieve prominence on the football field though, start-ing at end for the 1888 Yale Bulldogs, a team that finished 13-0, outscoring its opponents 698-0. That year included wins like a 54-0 win over Penn, a 65-0 trouncing of Rutgers, and a 104-0 thrashing of Wesleyan. Stagg stood out on a team full of standouts, including George Woodruff, who would later coach Penn and become attorney general of Pennsylvania, Heffelfinger, and cele-brated American painter Frederick Remington, who was said to have "dipped his jersey in blood before the game to make it more businesslike."[3] Don't let anybody tell you that turn of the century college football wasn't hardcore. And also a bit crazy.

After earning All-American honors at Left End in 1889, Stagg finally left Yale, without actually finishing his divinity degree. He went to work for the Young Men's Christian Training School (now known as Springfield College), along with James Naismith, who would invent a little game called basketball while on campus. At YMCYS, Stagg would coach the school football team (named, what else, the Christians), and traveled the country extolling the virtues of being a Christian athlete. After two years in Springfield, building his administrative and recruiting skills, Stagg was ready for his next chal-lenge. He interviewed with Harper and accepted a radical new position at Chicago, although not without being sorely tempted by competing offers at Pennsylvania, Johns Hopkins, and his alma mater, Yale.

Stagg's new job title was Associate Professor and Director of the Department of Physical Culture and Athletics, and came with a salary of $2,500 a year, which would be a little more than $70,000 in today's money. This made Stagg the first tenured PE administrator in the country, and the first tenured coach of an intercollegiate team. The entire concept of a "pro-fessional college coach" wasn't really in existence at this point.[4] Even Walter Camp, the head of powerhouse Yale, had a day job at a clock manufacturing company[5].

So why was Chicago the first? Harper understood, better than any other college administrator at the time, that college athletics had the potential to be a powerful marketing tool for the university, not just as a leisure activity. In addition to launching the Midwest's first annual Thanksgiving football rivalry (a showdown with Michigan), Harper and Stagg also essentially launched the idea of a college football bowl game, with a West Coast trip featuring multiple games with Stanford, along with YMCAs and athletic clubs in California and Utah. One of those early Chicago/Stanford matchups included a fistfight between a referee and a Chicago player. Allegedly, the Chicago athlete called him a "cheesy sort of referee" after a disputed call.[6] Again, pre-1900s college football. A different world.

The Maroons quickly became a successful program. Between the large number of high schools and the Chicago Football League, a local youth program, Chicago was able to set up a talent system similar to the prep school pipeline teams like Yale, Harvard and Princeton had built, in part by pushing ex-Maroon athletes to work at high schools in Illinois and Indiana. Stagg and Harper were also creative in how they recruited prep stars, without appearing to actually recruit athletes. They would set up a massive high school track competition on campus that attracted players from all over the Midwest, or establish regular tours to Japan for their baseball team, a squad that would just happen to also feature many football players.

When you combine this with Chicago's location in one of the most talent-rich areas in the country, an administration unified in creating a quality football program, and a great coach, you get a quality football team in a hurry.

You also get a team that upsets the power dynamics in the Midwest. The ascension of Chicago threatened Michigan's recruiting dominance in the region, giving their Thanksgiving rivalry games even more spice, matchups that included two indoor matchups in the Chicago Coliseum, in 1896 and 1897. The most notable of those Thanksgiving games was arguably the 1905 contest. The Wolverines, under head coach Fielding Yost, had built the most powerful dynasty in the Midwest, if not the entire country, over the last few seasons. Heading into the game in Chicago, Michigan had not lost a game in four years, and had outscored their opponents by an impossible 2,821 to 40 over the last four seasons (or an average margin of victory of around 50 to 1 each game), averaging nearly a point a minute.

But the Maroons weren't stiffs themselves. They had outscored their opponents 269-5, and carried an unblemished 10-0 record into Thanksgiving. Most of those games were blowouts, with one of the rare close games, a 16-5 win over Indiana, only so close because Stagg underestimated his opponent and rested his starters.[7] They were led by their three All-American quarter-back, and one of the most famous college football players in the country, Walter Eckersall. A native of nearby Woodlawn, Eckersall nearly committed to Michigan himself, but Stagg admitted to dragging him away from the train platform before he could head to Ann Arbor.

The Thanksgiving matchup was hard-fought and exceedingly low-scoring. The two teams were completely deadlocked, but the Maroons found the winning points in an unlikely source. Wolverine halfback Dennison Clark made the poor decision to try and run a kick out of his end zone, only to be thrown back for a safety. That proved to be the only scoring of the game, as Chicago upset Michigan 2-0, and claimed their first national title. A despondent Clark would commit suicide at age 46, and reportedly expressed hope that his "final play" would atone for his mistake during the game. [8]

The Maroons would continue to be one of the stronger teams in the Midwest, if not the country, over the next fifteen years. They went 19-2 over the 1911-1913 seasons, with their 7-0 mark in 1913 good for the school's second claimed national title. From the program's first season in 1892 until 1924, Chicago would not have consecutive losing seasons. But such dominance couldn't last forever. After a 4-0-3 campaign in 1924, the wheels started to fall off the great Chicago train. The Maroons would have only one more winning campaign, a 7-3 season in 1929.

There are several reasons for the sudden decline of Maroon football, but perhaps the biggest would be administrative. The Stagg era began with an exceptionally supportive university president, but subsequent administrations after Harper's untimely death slowly chipped away at Stagg's athletic department fiefdom, leaving a bit more vulnerable when an openly antagonistic president took charge.

That man was Robert M. Hutchins, who became president of the university at the ripe age of 30, in 1929. While other leaders in higher education may have believed in a more muscular, holistic education of body and mind for undergraduates, Hutchins was decidedly more single-minded. If he were alive today, Hutchins would probably have an absolutely insufferable Twitter account.

Football was too powerful and popular at the start of Hutchins' presidency to remove immediately, but circumstances would change to make it more vulnerable. Stagg, due to both old age and internal politics, was eventually forced out, and Clark Shaughnessy, a Minnesota graduate who coached at Tulane and Loyola of Louisiana, was hired for the 1933 season.

While Shaughnessy didn't stop the struggles in the standings, it wasn't because he was an inferior coach. On the contrary, Shaughnessy was a Hall of Famer who saw huge success with Stanford, Maryland, and also the NFL. As perhaps the foremost authority on the T-Formation, a major innovation from the dominant single wing offenses of the era, Shaughnessy helped the Chicago Bears absolutely obliterate Washington in the 1940 NFL Championship game, 73-0.

So any struggles with Chicago can't be blamed on a lack of schematic innovation. In fact, the opposite was probably true. The T-formation was more complicated than single wing strategies and required additional practice time, not to mention quality athletes. But thanks to changes in Chicago's academic calendar, along with university prohibitions on spring practices, the Maroons had dramatically less practice time than their Big Ten peers. A complicated offense, with inferior players, against teams with a bigger commitment to football, lead to struggles on the field.

Perhaps the only bright spot during this era was the play of Jay Berwanger. A prep athlete from Dubuque, Iowa, Berwanger turned down Purdue, Michigan, Iowa, and several other major programs to head to Chicago, where he quickly dominated[9]. He was an outstanding halfback, but also passed, returned kicks, and tackled at a high level. Chicago's teams weren't very good while Berwanger suited up for the Maroons, (their best record was 4-4 during his tenure), but that doesn't mean his tenure wasn't memorable.

For example, Berwanger is (probably) the only college football player to ever scar a future president. Former Michigan lineman Gerald Ford later recalled, to the *Chicago Chronicle*, that "When I tackled Jay in the second quarter, I ended up with a bloody cut and I still have the scar to prove it."[10]

His actual football exploits were even more celebrated though, as Berwanger was the first player to win what would become the Heisman Trophy. While such an award would be a huge deal on campus now, Berwanger said "It wasn't really a big deal when I got it. [...] No one at school said anything to me about winning it other than a few congratulations. I was more excited about the trip than the trophy because it was my first flight."[11]

Later, Berwanger would be the first player selected in the NFL draft. He never played in the league though. After the Chicago Bears turned down his contract demands, he would instead take a job selling foam rubber.[12] This is not a joke.

The Maroons were highly fortunate to secure a recruit like Berwanger, and others even close to his level were few and far between, as Chicago's great institutional advantages, like their commanding demographic position, began to wane. The construction of Soldier Field and the founding of the popular Chicago Bears professional football team cut into Chicago's dominance of the football market, to say nothing of growing Northwestern teams, and Notre Dame, which played many of their home games in the city during the 1920s. Chicago was passed by many other Big Ten institutions in the facilities arms race, as the school declined to build a new stadium to replace Stagg Field, electing to make cheaper renovations instead.[13]

Plus, an administration that had so often looked the other way when it came to academic eligibility suddenly started to take a harder line, just as other Big Ten peer institutions were recruiting more heavily. Chicago took many steps to make their undergraduate departments more selective and rigorous in the 1920s, and declined to create physical education majors that were popular among other peer universities as easy places to stash athletes, much like communications, sports management, or general studies programs have been used recently.

The curriculum also changed dramatically under the Hutchins administration, with a new system called the "Chicago Plan" or the "New Plan". Now, all students would take standardized courses their first two years, followed by specializations in their junior and senior years. In practice, this meant huge exams while other schools were practicing, and it became impossible to "hide" promising athletes in less rigorous majors. Recruitment, as well as player retention, became substantially more difficult.

When you factor Chicago's diminished advantages, the improved competitive scene around them, and lack of institutional support, the stage was set for a decline in Chicago Maroon football. And if the Maroons weren't good at football, they weren't selling tickets. That meant they weren't making any money, which made the entire athletics department apparatus a harder internal sell to an increasingly skeptical administration.

Soon, Chicago football went from "run-of-the-mill bad" to "shockingly bad". In 1938, the school decided to schedule a game against tiny Pacific College, who was being coached by none other than Stagg himself, who was 76 years old at the time. What might have been a fun turn down memory lane[14] and a way to honor a university icon quickly turned embarrassing, as the Pacific Tigers absolutely demolished Chicago, 32-0[15]. The Maroons finished 1-6-1 on the season, with their win and tie coming over non-majors Bradley and DePauw, respectively. Big Ten play was ugly, as they lost to Michigan 45-7, to Ohio State 42-7, to Illinois 34-0. To add insult to injury, they lost to out-of-conference Harvard 42-7.

Chicago football soon got even worse, as they opened the next season with an embarrassing 6-0 loss to tiny Beloit. They managed to beat overmatched Oberlin and Wabash teams out of conference, but were absolutely steamrolled in every other game. They lost to Harvard 61-0. They were also shut out by Ohio State (61-0), Virginia (47-0), and Illinois (46-0). And in perhaps the biggest insult, Michigan demolished the Maroons, 85-0, the worst loss in Chicago history, in front of 5,000 dejected spectators who didn't have the good sense to leave early.

You couldn't even blame Michigan for running up the score, since the Wolverine starters only played 20 minutes. The *Chicago Tribune* opened their game story by saying "Thirty-five young men from the University of Michigan gave an interesting exhibition of a game sometimes described as American intercollegiate football," called the score "all too brutally correct," and joked that the Chicago scoreboard operators had to go to the hospital due to overworking.[16]

Years of below average football, along with changing undergraduate demographics, had sapped undergraduate and community support for Chicago football. Combined with a president that became openly hostile to the sport, and an absolutely catastrophic final season, everything was now in place for Chicago to finally kill the sport on campus. Hutchins saw his opportunity and moved swiftly. Chicago played their last season of big time football in 1939, and withdrew from the Big Ten in all sports in 1946.

The fitting end of the story of the Chicago Maroons happened in 1942, when the most important event occurred in the history of Stagg Field. No longer being used for football games, researchers found a new use for a space under the stands, the location for Chicago Pile-1, the world's first artificial nuclear reactor, integral in the completion of the Manhattan Project. The full stadium was demolished in 1957, with a historical marker and a library standing in its place.

Hutchins had hoped that the end of Chicago football would start a run of other institutions phasing out their football programs, but it didn't happen quite like he hoped. Chicago did enjoy mostly favorable press coverage for their decision, as they were depicted as making some honorable sacrifice in the name of academic progress, but no peer institutions followed their lead. After World War II, there was a run of schools dropping out of big time football, like Georgetown, George Washington, Marquette and St.Mary's[17], but the driving force was mostly financial rather than academic. Few of the departing programs had anything resembling the prestige or football success of the Maroons.

Even schools that might have wanted to downgrade or eliminate their programs would have struggled to do so, given that most schools had significant stadium debt to pay off after the stadium construction boom of the 1920s. Had Chicago decided to build a new field instead of simply renovate Stagg Field, Maroon football might have remained for a bit.

Chicago plays football today, only on a completely different level. The Maroons compete in D3, which they joined in 1973, against teams like Case Western Reserve, Millsaps and Carnegie Mellon. The new Stagg Field has a capacity of less than 2,000 students, and current players often note that it is smaller than where they played in high school. And rather than capturing the hearts of football fans, and media members across Chicago, the Maroons toil in near total anonymity. It is possible that many Chicago students do not even know the school has a football team now, let alone one that just to be a historical powerhouse.

So, what if Chicago hadn't disbanded their football team? What if they hadn't decided to punt on big time football?

If we assume everything else in Chicago's history remained the same, only with the school simply electing to continue their football program, it's hard to see how the Maroons would have been competitive in Big Ten play. Academic restrictions and university policy put them at a significant recruiting disadvantage compared to their conference peers. They had lost control of their biggest institutional advantage—the city of Chicago—to Northwestern, the Chicago Bears, and even Notre Dame, thus diminishing the powers of their sidewalk alumni. Chicago was also at a facilities disadvantage, from their stadium to their field house. The longer Chicago lost, the harder pulling themselves out of their funk would have become.

Plus, Chicago was a much smaller school than its Big Ten peers. By the mid 1930s, it had less than a thousand male undergraduates, a number more comparable to Oberlin, than Indiana[18]. Ohio State and Michigan, for example, had over 10,000 male undergraduates at the time. Based on this trajectory, it's easy to see Chicago developing a Big Ten history similar to Northwestern or Indiana, with occasional spurts of competence intertwined with long years of being a doormat.

But with a few possible tweaks to Chicago's history, the decision to shutter the program appears a bit less inevitable. The first would have been the untimely death of President William Harper. The founder of the university and the one to hire Stagg in the first place, Harper was a substantial supporter of Chicago football, and was willing to do what was needed for the Maroons to field a competitive football team, including recruiting and providing subsidy for the sport. Harper contracted cancer and died at age 49 in 1906. Had he lived a more normal life expectancy, it seems reasonable to believe his continued support of football, and larger-than-life influence of other university constituencies, would have continued, preventing institutional anti-football factions from taking root as firmly as they did.

On that note, it seems also possible to assume that Harper would have been willing to make a few administrative changes to Chicago's curriculum that would have helped the football program. Establishing an agricultural school, which produced popular majors for football players in the 1930s, seems a bit of a stretch given the rest of Chicago's academic offerings, but working with Stagg to produce a more robust physical education department would have made recruitment and retention of possible football players dramatically easier. Chicago also did not have an engineering program in the 1930s, which reportedly also was a detriment in recruiting, a sentence that would not make any sense in 2016.

The goal here would not be to make Chicago a football powerhouse in the late 1930s just like it was in the 1900s, just to prevent a total breakdown of the sport's fortunes, which helped convince others affiliated with the university that it was time to close shop. If the bottom hadn't completely fallen out of recruiting by the mid 1920s, that may have happened, allowing the team to take hold a little more with the student body and the surrounding community, and leaving the school to better figure out it's place in the national football landscape.

So if Chicago made just a few changes and decided to stick around, how good of a team could they become?

Chicago's biggest football advantage was geography, and it was one they used ruthlessly during their glory years. In the early days of the Big Ten, regular home and home conference schedules didn't exist, and the Maroons insisted on playing nearly all of their games, conference or otherwise, at home. Other schools may have grumbled about this, but financial realities trumped any sense of fairness. After all, Chicago sat in a huge city, had a big stadium, and had a ton of sidewalk fans, so games at Stagg Field would be more profitable than games in say, Ann Arbor or Iowa City, even for the visitors, since they'd get a share of the gate receipts. Some visiting schools even helped pay for improvements to Stagg Field, since a bigger home field for the Maroons meant bigger shares of the gate for them. The Maroon's insistence on wielding it's demographic advantages didn't win them friends within their conference (things got so bad that Wisconsin severed athletic relations with the Maroons, and other schools occasionally threatened) but it did pay the bills.

As professional football became more established and popular (to say nothing of Notre Dame and Northwestern football) and Chicago's administrative changes made them less of a recruiting powerhouse, the sheer advantages of their Chicago location diminished a bit, but that doesn't mean they didn't exist. And those advantages likely would have carried into the 1940s and beyond, had Chicago remained committed to Big Ten football.

Today, the most fertile territories for recruiting high level football players are mostly in the South, along with Texas, California, and Ohio. But in the early days of college football, Chicago and the surrounding suburbs were a very important, if not the most important, recruiting battleground. In 1940, the first year without Chicago football, 30 players who would appear on NFL rosters came from Chicago's Cook County. The next highest, Pittsburgh's Allegheny County, sent 16. In fact, Cook County produced more NFL roster players every single season until 1956, when LA County topped it, 38-36. Even into the 1970s, Chicagoland was the most important recruiting territory in the North, and while a few other metros in the Midwest have arguably passed it, there are plenty of really good high school football players there even today, certainly enough for a team to build a competitive program by focusing on local kids.[19]

How many of those kids the Maroons would be able to get, of course, would depend on their coach, and also how the school would decide to navigate academics and athletics. There are schools with similar profiles to Chicago—academically-oriented, private research universities—that have produced quality football teams over time. Some of those schools, like Notre Dame and USC, have a long, institutional history of prioritizing football success, and have made no bones about recruiting players who would otherwise not fit the undergraduate academic profile. During their glory years before 1920, Chicago also fit this profile.

Given the administrative strife and feelings from president Hutchins, that model wouldn't have been realistic for Chicago. But other schools, like Stanford, Boston College, Rice and Duke, have also achieved sporadic football success without recruiting the same pool of players. Especially in modern times, selective undergraduate academics, along with a robust and well-connected alumni base, can also be used as a major recruiting tool, helping broaden Chicago's appeal beyond just Cook County and nearby suburbs. This approach has helped Northwestern become a program that regularly battles for bowl bids.

One interesting question would be what the continuation of Chicago football would mean for Big Ten membership. With the Maroons departing in the 1940s, the Big Ten expanded back to ten by inviting Michigan State in 1949, although Pittsburgh and Nebraska were also strongly considered.[20] Would the Big Ten decide to stick at ten teams, without inviting Michigan State, forcing the Spartans to toil as an independent? Given how hard Michigan fought against State's admission, that seems likely.

What about their North Side brethren, the one's who now proudly claim to be Chicago's only Big Ten team? Northwestern has dealt with rumors they might drop football, or at least big time football, pretty much since they started playing it. The team was so terrible in the early days of the Big Ten that Wisconsin proposed kicking them out altogether. Prior to the early 1920s, Northwestern's only winning records were padded by wins over high schools, or small-college opposition. That's right; college teams used to play high school teams to pick up wins. Sometimes, they even lost!

But that all changed around the time that Chicago football began to fade away. Northwestern president Walter Dill Scott, a former Northwestern football player and a major advocate for athletics, helped establish a large recruiting ring run by alumni, similar to what Chicago had established in the decades prior. Coupled with Scott's prodigious fundraising, and an occasional fast and loose attitude towards the occasional academic indifference of star athletes, Northwestern's football fortunes began to turn around. The Wildcats upset Michigan in 1925 by a 3-2 score, and finished 3-1 in Big Ten play. They were even better in 1926, going 7-1 on the season, clobbering Chicago. Suddenly, in the eyes of Chicago sportswriters and local fans, the Wildcats were now Chicago's team, a development Stagg did not take so kindly to. Stagg accused Northwestern of recruiting violations, and never played them again.[21]

But Northwestern's success in the 1930s and 1940s was short-lived compared to the long history of Wildcat football. In 1955, the *Northwestern Daily*, the school's newspaper, ran a front-page editorial urging the school to drop out of the Big Ten, saying it didn't have the athletic resources to be competitive[22].[23] The 1955 Northwestern football season certainly helped that argument, as the Wildcats finished 0-8, complete with a 42-0 thrashing at the hands of Ohio State.

Calls for Northwestern to drop out, or rumors that they would, persisted. After a popular rumor persisted in 1969 that Notre Dame would replace Northwestern in the conference, Wildcat AD Tippy Dye told the AP "every time we lose three football games, somebody says we're dropping out of the Big Ten."[24] In the early 70s and 80s, there were reports the school was considering leaving the Big Ten, perhaps to join the Ivy League, which was interested in adding the Wildcats in an effort to remain in D1-A.[25]

Things were dire at this point, with Northwestern agreeing to play some league home contests on the road in order to make more money, since attendance in Evanston was so low. "I don't think too many people remember how very close it came at that point," said Frederick Hemke,[26] Northwestern's faculty-athletics representative to the Big Ten and NCAA from 1982 to 2003. It was even something Northwestern's coaches had to fight against in recruiting. Even in the late 1980s, some Big Ten columnists were calling for the school to leave the conference.[27]

One reason Northwestern was able to stave off constant calls for them to give up was the successful run by head coach Ara Parseghian, hired in 1956 after a winless campaign. The former Miami (OH) head coach quickly helped rebuild the Wildcats from a moribund squad to one that briefly sat #1 in the AP Poll in 1962. Parseghian coached five different Northwestern teams to winning records, but left for Notre Dame in 1964 without an AP Top 20 finish.

Parseghian admitted in a newspaper interview that he felt that he had accomplished everything he could at Northwestern when he made the switch[28]. He hinted that the program had a low ceiling, but Northwestern administrators didn't care. This era was held up as a shining example of what Northwestern was capable of—recruiting restrictions, poor facilities and lackluster campus interest and all.

Of course, the Wildcats wouldn't come close to reaching those heights again for years, appearing in the AP Poll just twice from 1964-1995. From 1976-1981, Northwestern won exactly three games. These may well have been the worst power conference football teams ever.

Without that shining example of the height of Northwestern football, I suspect the administration would be less enthusiastic about remaining in the Big Ten in the face of embarrassing losses, strained relationships with conference-mates over poor games and wore gates, and negative press coverage. Having one private, smaller, academically-selective university in the

Chicago area playing Big Ten football was hard enough for Northwestern. If they suddenly had to compete with another one, a pathway to plausible success becomes even more unlikely.

If another school had hired Parseghian away from Miami—Chicago, for instance—I think Northwestern eventually drops out of the Big Ten. And when they do, Michigan State would be the favorite to replace them. It would be difficult for Chicago to replicate their success near the turn of the century, though, especially as we get more and more into modern times. Chicago's enrollment is a hair under 15,000 in 2017, less than Northwestern's 20,000. 15,000 would be one of the smallest schools playing major college football entirely, comparable to Duke or Rice, other schools that struggle to find regular gridiron success.

But that doesn't necessarily mean they wouldn't be an important addition to the Big Ten. Like Northwestern, Chicago's alumni base isn't just in Chicago (a critically important TV market) but across the country, which would help make the conference even more attractive for television. Chicago's pristine academic and research reputation would be a boon for Big Ten schools that are conscious of their academic associations. And the second they became good again, a horde of sportswriters would descend to the South Side to write their Heisman Trophy history articles. It would be a very media friendly environment.

So if the Maroons never left the Big Ten, my best guess is that they'd achieve a level of success comparable to what Northwestern achieved, with a few Rose Bowl bids, some historic upsets, respectability when they hire a great coach, and crummy teams when they don't. The Wildcats would be free to pursue football at a level when they wouldn't be regularly crushed by Ohio State or Michigan every season, and the boys at the Manhattan Project would have had to finish their working atomic pile somewhere else, since those grandstands would have been occupied.

But even though that didn't happen, Chicago still has a football legacy to be proud of. They have the first Heisman Trophy. They have multiple national titles. And even though their program hasn't been in the Big Ten for 80 years, they still have more Big Ten football titles than Indiana.

That should count for something, in my humble opinion.

What if Maryland kept Bear Bryant?

———

IF YOU ASK FOLKS WHO the biggest sleeping giant in all of college football is, you're probably going to hear a lot of people tell you it's Maryland.

It isn't hard to see why. Maryland's College Park campus sits just a few miles away from Washington D.C., a large, fast-growing metro region that lacks an entrenched college football power to suck away attention and eyeballs. One of the best high school football programs in the country, Dematha Catholic, is a short jog away from campus, and numerous other programs that produce multiple D1 caliber players a season are just a short distance away. Outside of Navy, which doesn't exactly present a challenge in recruiting, there isn't another FBS program in the state.

With their affiliation in the Big Ten, and all of the TV access and money that comes with it, along with proximity to recruits, deep-pocketed alumni, and a region basically all to themselves, sure, it isn't too hard to talk yourself into the idea that Maryland could become a very good football program.

Of course, the trouble with sleeping giants is that they tend to be asleep for a good reason. Outside of runs in the 1950s and 1970s, Maryland football has been mostly unimpressive, toiling in second-tier power conferences like the Southern or ACC, where a good season might be a win over Virginia and a trip to the Gator Bowl. It's not like Maryland is Rutgers or Northwestern, but the program hardly garners the level of national acclaim befitting a possible "giant."

That's especially true in recent history. Even though there isn't another major college football team locally (sorry, Georgetown), DC residents have no shortage of other sporting distractions, from the plethora of professional options, along with any football fandom the large transplant population may have carried with them. I live just a few miles from Maryland's campus myself, and I don't think it's a stretch to say that Maryland is barely the most popular college football team in its own county. Both of the Ohio State-Maryland games I've covered in College Park were completely dominated by Buckeye fans, and not just ones who drove all the way from Columbus.

Demographics play a huge role in football success, but they aren't necessarily destiny. A team that has a difficult demographic situation can overcome it with a transformational coach. And a school in a favorable demographic situation can struggle if they fail to make the right administrative moves, like, say, Rutgers.

The funny thing, of course, is that Maryland actually had a transformational football coach. Even though his career is much more tied to Alabama, Texas A&M, and to a lesser extent, Kentucky, the Maryland Terrapins were the first school to hire perhaps the most successful and legendary coach in all of college football history, Bear Bryant.

But Bryant's stay was a short one. He left after only one season in College Park, departing for Kentucky, where he'd build the first of his many dynasties across the South.

Why did he leave? What if he had stayed? Would Maryland still be a sleeping giant, or a more established program, capable of taking advantage of its geographic and demographic advantages?

Let's take a closer look, starting at the beginning.

Maryland was a little bit of a latecomer to college football, compared to programs like Alabama or Georgia Tech. The Terrapins were usually good, occasionally bad, but never an elite program. They would typically fight for spots near the top of the Southern Conference, which lagged behind the Big Ten and elite Northeastern programs like Yale when it came to national recognition and prestige. But any ascent into the upper echelon of the sport was halted once World War II broke out, throwing all of college football—and of course, the rest of the country—into chaos.

Schools across the country switched to abbreviated schedules as travel restrictions and a decreased player pool made longer seasons impractical. Many other schools shut down their teams entirely. But one entity that wasn't afraid to make a large and public investment in football was the Navy.

Naval officials felt that football was not only important to sustaining morale, but that it taught many of the lessons they hoped to instill in their future leaders like courage, discipline, and leadership under duress.[1] Many of the great coaches of the 1950s and 1960s would end up coaching squads on naval bases—men like Darrell Royal, who would become a successful head coach at Texas, and Paul Brown, who coached at Ohio State and would later have great success in the NFL. But perhaps the most influential of them all was the head coach at North Carolina Pre-Flight, Bear Bryant[2].

The Bear, so nicknamed because he allegedly wrestled a bear as a kid (a childhood friend of Bryant recalled the incident, saying "I don't remember who won, but I do remember half the crowd was pulling for Paul, the other for the bear"[3]), already had quite a bit of football experience before he entered the service. An accomplished college player at Alabama, where he made second-team all SEC, Bryant had served as an assistant coach at Tennessee, Alabama, and Vanderbilt all before the start of the 1941 season. He clearly looked to be on a trajectory towards becoming a head coach in the South very soon, despite his young age.

In fact, Bryant was actually offered the head coaching job at Arkansas, but world events prevented him from actually accepting the position. The Japanese bombed Pearl Harbor, and Bryant left to join the Navy in 1942, along with other players and coaches from across the country.[4] While in the service, he ended up joining the coaching staff at Georgia Pre-Flight, and then later at North Carolina Pre-Flight in 1944.

North Carolina Pre-Flight, known as the Cloudbusters (a truly excellent nickname), was one of the most successful base football teams during World War II. One reason for that success? An excellent coaching staff. Future Hall of Famer Johnny Vaught, who would later achieve great success at Ole Miss, had served as an assistant in 1942, and the 1944 squad, under Hall of Famer Glenn Killinger, included Glenn Parsnell (Nebraska, Eastern Kentucky), John Ronning (Utah State, Denver), and Bryant, coaching the lines. The Cloudbusters finished that 1944 campaign with a 6-2-1 record, beating Navy the year after they won the national title and climbing as high as #2 in the AP Poll. North Carolina Pre-Flight was also fortunate to have future NFL Hall of Famer Otto Graham throwing passes.

Back in the civilian world, Maryland hadn't expected to be in the market for a new head coach, but Clark Shaughnessy surprisingly left to take the Pitt job in 1942, taking his complicated Split T offense with him. Maryland decided to hire Clarence Spears from the University of Toledo. Spears had a strong record himself, having coached winning teams at schools like Minnesota and Dartmouth, but the Terrapins would have struggled no matter who was coaching. Maryland football was a strictly civilian outfit, meaning they were trotting out a roster of 17 year olds and a handful of vets. The Terps went 1-7-1 in 1944, and Spears left coaching altogether to pursue a career in medicine. The Terrapins needed to make another hire[5].

Bryant was slated to be the head coach for North Carolina Pre-Flight in 1945, but then the war ended, and he was told that the base wasn't going to have a team next season. He'd need to find a new job.

Fortunately for Bryant, he had some powerful friends. While in Chicago to watch a college all-star game, Bryant ran into George Preston Marshall, the owner of the Washington Redskins, and a man who used to pay Bryant to scout players in the Alabama area. Marshall offered Bryant a job working as an assistant for the Redskins, to which Bryant replied that he was holding out for a head coaching job.

Marshall shot back, "Why the hell didn't you say so?" He immediately brokered a phone call with Maryland's Curley Byrd, who offered him the job on the spot[6].

Bryant told his Cloudbusters squad that he would coach wherever they decided for the next season, either at Alabama or Georgia Tech as an assistant coach, or at Maryland as a head coach. The players voted for Maryland, so Bryant accepted the $9,000 a year offer and went to College Park[7]. Thanks to liberal transfer rules following World War II, 15 of his players (including two who had played previously at Duke), as well as his team manager, were able to go with him. Coupled with the fact that Maryland would return some talented younger players from the previous season, the Terps looked to be in good shape to significantly improve from the year before.

Because of a late discharge date from the Navy, Bryant missed the summer at Maryland. In fact, he wasn't able to arrive on campus until eight days before Maryland's first game, a showdown against Guilford College. His players from North Carolina didn't show up until then either. They are all dead broke, with only their training uniforms as clothes.[8] But it didn't matter. The Terps plastered Guilford 60-6, thanks to strong performances from their military veterans.[9]

They followed that up with a surprising 21-0 win at Richmond. A year removed from a season when Maryland lost to something called a Hampden-Sydney and won just a single game, Maryland suddenly earned a top 10 vote in the polls, and talk among fans and beat writers was that a New Year's Bowl wasn't out of the question[10].

The run wouldn't last. The team was upset by Virginia Tech the week after, in a game where Bryant admitted they probably underestimated the Hokies. They later lost badly to William & Mary, blowing a 14-6 lead they held late in the third quarter thanks to a slew of turnovers and poor tackling. That nipped any major bowl talk in the bud[11].

But Maryland was excellent the rest of the season, obliterating VMI by 38 points the following week, knocking off nationally ranked archrival Virginia (a game where Cavaliers coach Frank Murray accused Bryant of playing "the dirtiest game I've ever seen"[12]), and then winning at South Carolina thanks to a reverse to conclude the season. Maryland finished 6-2-1, the lone tie against West Virginia, and had to feel good about their future prospects, given how young the team still was.

Bryant's coaching style was dramatically different from anything Maryland had seen over the last few years. Still a young guy at thirty-two, Bryant wasn't afraid to get off the sidelines and physically demonstrate how to block or tackle in practice. Like other young coaches, Bryant brought a very high intensity level, occasionally too high. He referred to his stint at Maryland as his "upchucking days", thanks to his habit of puking before a contest out of stress. He would later say that Maryland "would have been undefeated if it wasn't for my bad coaching."[13]

Growing pains or not, anybody would have felt positive about the future of Maryland football. Byrd himself said he thought the program would be set for years to come, and told attendees at a football banquet that Bryant had a lifetime contract with the school. In reality, Bryant didn't actually have a contract at all, let alone a lifetime one.[14] And thanks to Byrd's own screwup, he'd soon be looking for yet another new coach for the program.

Following the season, Bryant took a trip Alabama to visit some family. While he was there, Byrd made the executive decision to reinstate a defensive lineman, Larry Cooper, that Bryant had suspended earlier for missing curfew thanks to a late night trip to the bar.[15] Bryant was a bit of a taskmaster, forbidding smoking, drinking, and staying out after 10 PM during the football season. Breaking two of those rules at once would certainly merit a response.

A possible reason for Byrd jumping in? This particular lineman was the son of a Maryland politician, and Byrd, ever cognizant of the impact state funding would have on his ability to grow the school, wanted to make as many friends as possible. Byrd was also a bit of a meddler by nature. He was, after all, a former coach of the football program, before taking the unlikely career jump to university president. If Dennis Dodd had been writing back then, Byrd would have made him furious.

A single episode of administrative meddling might have been forgiven, but that wasn't the only one. Byrd was also trying to fire one of Bryant's assistant coaches, Herman Ball, a holdover from the Cleaver staff. This was the final straw. Bryant liked and admired Byrd, but he also wanted to be able to run his own program, without meddling or interference from administrators. So he decided to answer a telegram from the University of Kentucky and quickly accepted a five-year contract.

The news shocked everybody. Kentucky had won just two games the previous year and had never won more than six games in a season. Maryland looked loaded and could have competed for a major bowl appearance in 1947. His players cried. Bryant reportedly cried, too.[16]

The student body did not take the news well. Students across campus skipped class (well, *most* people skipped class; a *Baltimore Sun* report indicated students still showed up to a dance class "because they enjoyed it"[17]), and staged a protest march, with 2,500 students building a bonfire at Byrd's residence, demanding that the school retain Bryant. Only after Bryant himself appeared[18], days after the protest started, telling students he was leaving out of his own free will and that they should return to class, did the demonstrations disperse[19].

Bryant quickly turned Kentucky into a winner. The Wildcats won seven games in 1946, and then won their first bowl game a year later—the Great Lakes Bowl in beautiful Cleveland, OH—knocking out Villanova. Kentucky improved year and after year, before legitimately threatening to win the national title in 1950, climbing as high as #3 in the AP Poll, and winning the Sugar Bowl. Bryant would leave Kentucky after the 1953 season for Texas A&M (after turning down offers from programs like USC, Minnesota, and Arkansas[20]) and would build powerhouse programs there and at Alabama, en route to becoming one of the most, if not the most, celebrated, successful, and influential coaches of the modern era. And none of it happened at Maryland.

The Terrapins, instead, turned back to former coach Clark Shaughnessy to replace Bryant for the 1946 campaign. Shaughnessy coached at Maryland in 1942, leading the Terps to a 7-2 record, before surprisingly departing for Pitt after just a single season. Shaughnessy regretted the decision, and Byrd was willing to let bygones be bygones, in part because of a unique arrangement both parties worked out with the Washington Redskins, who would help pay for his salary in exchange for Shaughnessy providing some consulting[21].

Given Shaughnessy's successful and innovative T-Formation offense, and the returning serviceman talent that Bryant had brought in, it looked like Maryland would be able to build on their success and contend for a bowl bid. But instead, Shaughnessy was distracted between his professional work and college job. He fostered internal disputes, too; the *Washington Post* quoted him calling some of his serviceman players "bums", which for some reason, didn't go over very well.[22] All of that kept his players from reaching their full potential[23]. Maryland struggled to a 3-6 campaign, and just like that, Shaughnessy was gone again, leaving to coach the pros.

A potential dynasty slipped through Maryland's fingers, and they were left to find yet another coach.

But what if Byrd hadn't screwed this entire thing up? What if Bryant stuck around?

The biggest changes probably would have been at schools other than Maryland. Because fortunately for Terrapin fans, the program struck gold once Shaughnessy left.

Byrd kicked the tires on a few other targets, including Dick Harlow at Harvard, the first non-Harvard grad to lead the Crimson, before settling on two finalists, who both, curiously enough, coached at the same program.

Maryland centered their search at the University of Oklahoma, where Byrd hoped to bring in Sooner head coach Jim Tatum, provided he was willing and that Oklahoma's board was willing to release him from his contract. Failing that, Byrd would focus on his top assistant, line coach Bud Wilkinson.

In fact, Byrd would allegedly say that he "told them either one could have the job. Tatum wasn't sure he wanted to leave Oklahoma, so I said I'd take Wilkinson. We decided they should think about it overnight and decide among themselves who wanted it. Tatum called me the next day and said he did."[24]

Whether that's how it actually happened or not, Oklahoma did release Tatum, who accepted a $12,000 a year contract to head to College Park. Tatum would later say he didn't leave because of the money, which was comparable to what Oklahoma could give, but because he preferred to live in the East, where he was from, and because it provided "a wonderful opportunity for a young coach to grow with a program."[25] That may not have been entirely accurate, as Tatum's free-spending ways at Oklahoma led to the dismissal of the Sooner AD, and concerns over spending could have eventually reached him[26].

Grow is exactly what Maryland did, as the program experienced its greatest heights ever. Thanks to his focus on defense and a Split T offense that Tatum learned from Missouri's Don Faurot at Iowa Pre-Flight, Maryland quickly rebounded to 7-2-2, earning their first bowl appearance ever, a 20-20 tie with Georgia in the Gator Bowl. Running back Lu Gambino would finish 4th nationally in scoring with 96 points and rushed for 9.5 yards per carry.

The team would continue its rapid ascent from there, winning the first bowl game in school history just two seasons later (a 20-7 win over Missouri in the Gator Bowl), an undefeated campaign in 1950, where they knocked off Tennessee in the Sugar Bowl, essentially ending the popular usage of the single wing offense after shutting down Tennessee's attack, and the school's lone national title in 1953, thankfully awarded before bowl season, since the Terrapins lost 7-0 to Oklahoma that year.

From 1947 to 1955, Maryland was an excellent 73-15-4. They won a national title, conference titles in the Southern and the newly founded ACC, four bowl games, and a national coach of the year award. Tatum then left to coach his alma mater, the University of North Carolina, and Maryland never again competed for a national title. They would finish in the AP Top 10 just one more time in school history.

Tatum was charismatic and a strong recruiter, especially in Pennsylvania and along the East Coast. He also benefited from Byrd finally wising up and getting out of the way, allowing Tatum to serve as athletic director and coach without interference. Or at least, not as much interference.

Had Bear Bryant stayed at Maryland for a few years, given his later success, it's a good bet Maryland could have reached similar heights, although the final product may have looked different schematically. But it would have been nearly impossible for Maryland to keep Bryant around forever, especially if and when Alabama came calling. The pull of the old alma mater is strong, after all. Whether it was Bryant or Tatum, it seems safe to assume that Maryland would have fielded a very good football team in the 1950s.

It also seems unlikely that Maryland would be able to sustain their success into the late 1950s and beyond, as the school began to change dramatically. Byrd ran the school almost as a one-man fiefdom, showing the rest of the university little of the restraint he eventually learned for the football team, which helped the school grow quickly, but also attracted criticism.

Maryland's new president, Dr. Wilson Elkins, began to curtail Maryland's ambitious out-of-state recruiting efforts and budget, to try and bring football more into line with the rest of the school, and temper some of the critiques the school was facing for their emphasis on football[27]. That, along with the allure of coaching his alma mater, helped drive Tatum to North Carolina. By the mid 1950s, it's pretty easy to see Bear Bryant making a similar decision to bail.

But what if Tatum stayed at Oklahoma? What happens to Bud Wilkinson?

Let's take a closer look at Tatum's single season in Norman for some clues. He was unquestionably a master recruiter, bringing in perhaps the most storied class in Sooner history, with nine members of his 1946 recruiting class eventually becoming All-Americans.[28] He was successful on the field, leading Oklahoma to its first bowl victory ever, clobbering North Carolina State.

Even more importantly, Tatum's Sooners obliterated Oklahoma A&M (now known as Oklahoma State), winning 73-12, a victory made even sweeter by the fact that Oklahoma had lost that game two years in a row. All in all, that was a promising campaign.

But there were problems, too. Namely, financial ones. Tatum was determined to bring Oklahoma football into the proverbial "big time", and he wasn't going to do it on the cheap. Oklahoma's athletic department had a $125,000 surplus at the start of the season. By the end of the year, it had a $113,000 deficit[29].

Part of that may have been travel expenses (Oklahoma flew to West Point to open the season against Army, their first plane trip as a program), part of that may have been recruiting expenses, shady bookkeeping, or a bunch of other things. Tatum certainly wasn't opposed to sharing the wealth with his players, bylaws be damned. He asked his superiors if the school could give a gift to each player (he suggested golf clubs, or a shotgun[30]), only to be told no. Over the wishes of university officials, he gave everyone $125 instead.[31]

If you're expecting pearl clutching over the violation of the sacred concept of amateurism from me here, you won't get it. Given how hard the players worked, and how much money the school was taking in, even before the era of major television money, some college kids getting spending money doesn't seem like much of a big deal. But conference officials or sanctimonious rival presidents would have disagreed, even if they were partaking in similar practices themselves.

Tatum had a big ego and often won big games, but not always by making friends. At Maryland, he worked for a former football coach who wielded enormous power at the university, and one who wasn't enormously troubled by things like academic prestige. At a school without that structure, Tatum would have probably still won lots of games, but the threat of a power-struggle, or significant recruiting or financial scandal would have loomed. It's easy to see a longer-term Tatum era at Oklahoma not having the happiest of endings.

But fortunately for Sooner fans, it only lasted one year, as Oklahoma was then able to promote Tatum's talented assistant, Bud Wilkinson, a man that impressed Oklahoma regents so much that they insisted Tatum bring him to Norman as a condition of his initial hiring.[32]

All Wilkinson did was win three national titles (1950, 1955, 1956), completely dominate the conference, and roll off the longest winning streak (47 games) in the modern history of the sport. In an era of scholarship restrictions, I feel pretty confident no team, not even Nick Saban's Alabama or Urban Meyer's Ohio State, will win 48 games in a row.

Did Wilkinson run a squeaky clean program? No. Oklahoma was put on NCAA probation in 1955 for various recruiting violations. The list of programs that weren't handing out some variation of hundred-dollar handshakes in the SWC, Big Eight and SEC could probably be counted on one hand though. But Wilkinson didn't torpedo relationships with the Sooner fanbase, make outlandish demands of administration like Tatum did, and subsequently, was given a longer leash.

My guess, if Tatum didn't have a job offer at Maryland, he'd stick around at Oklahoma for a few more years before more or less getting chased out of town, no matter how many games he won, until he could find a spot with a sympathetic university administration who wouldn't be overly concerned about their team not being awash with academic all-Americans. Meanwhile, Wilkinson would head elsewhere, and the Oklahoma dynasty of the 1950s would have never launched.

Perhaps Michigan State wins the 1955 national title then. Perhaps Colorado breaks through and wins a conference title or two during the decade. Although maybe Oklahoma, still with some of Tatum's players, still wins the 1950 national title, only this time, with a Sugar Bowl victory to go with it. After all, their opponent, Kentucky, wouldn't have Bear Bryant coaching.

Given the historical trajectory of Kentucky football when coached by anybody other than Bear Bryant, it also seems like a safe assumption that the Wildcats wouldn't be competing for Sugar Bowl bids had Bryant decided to stay in College Park for a few more years. Even if Kentucky managed to steal away another great hire, something like the Great Lakes Bowl feels like a more realistic high bar for the program, especially given how tough the SEC was at the time.

It just goes to show how crazy and interconnected college football is, that perhaps the most celebrated coach of all time deciding to stick around a lesser-known program wouldn't shift a national title at Maryland (they probably still win one), or at Alabama (Bear probably still ends up at his alma mater eventually), but at a completely different program, Oklahoma, shifting the strength of an entire region of the country, and maybe beyond, depending on where Tatum and Wilkinson ended up. If Tatum didn't tragically die young at 46 of Rocky Mountain spotted fever, this entire scenario shifts even more.

Bear Bryant alone wouldn't have been able to wake up the sleeping giant at Maryland. But had he stuck around, he just might have put another giant back to sleep.

What if Tulane and Georgia Tech never left the SEC?

———

THE GLAMOR FRANCHISES IN PROFESSIONAL sports tend be the biggest and most powerful cities in the country, places like New York, Chicago, LA, Boston, or the Bay Area. But that isn't really the case in college football. While the sport's political power has historically been concentrated in the Midwest and West Coast (and before that, the Northeast), the cultural capital, with the most passionate fans, strongest recruits, and recently, the best programs, has been the South. And while other conferences have boosted strong individual teams, the best league, from top to bottom, has been the SEC.

Recently, the domination by the conference has been historic. From 2006 through 2012, an SEC team won the National Championship every single year. Since 2005, an SEC team has played in the championship game every year but once. They've captured five Heisman trophies since 2007, dominated the recruiting rankings over the last fifteen years, and launched an exceptionally successful conference TV Network. With the possible exception of the Big Ten, no other conference can match the SEC when it comes to institutional investments, football prestige, television exposure, and financial rewards. It's good to be the king. Or at least, in the same club as the king. (Sup, Vanderbilt and Kentucky?)

Affiliation in that kind of conference is an enormous advantage in college football, especially in an era of potentially uncertain television revenues. SEC membership means never having to worry about a bowl invite when you're 6-6. SEC membership means occasional home games against Alabama, Florida, Georgia, and other major heavyweights. SEC memberships means your team will not just always be on TV, but they'll always on a channel everybody has heard of. It means you'll have the money you need for your softball team, and that Nike will want to sponsor your uniforms, and that ESPN will talk about your program. As long as you have that SEC patch, all of those things are true, even if you're rarely actually good at football, like Vanderbilt, or Kentucky, or Mississippi State. If you lucked into SEC membership, you'd be absolutely crazy to leave.

But two schools did. Well, three, technically, but two major ones. And, like you'd probably expect, it didn't turn out very well for them.

Let's start at the beginning. By 1932, the sprawling Southern conference had grown simply too big to manage effectively, and the schools west and south of the Appalachian Mountains broke off to establish their own league: the Southeastern Conference, or SEC. Ten of the thirteen founding schools will be familiar to any football fan, as they included future powerhouse programs like Alabama, Auburn, Florida, and LSU. But three teams in the original league didn't stick around long enough to experience the league at its peak. Those three? The University of the South (known as Sewanee), Tulane, and Georgia Tech.

Sewanee was the first to leave, and if you're not from Tennessee or into the history of Southern college football, there's a good chance you've never even heard of the school, let alone the program. One of the very best teams in the South during the early 1900s, the Tigers' fortunes were already starting to wane before the SEC was established, and they got worse relatively quickly. In seven years of league play, not only did the Tigers fail to win more than three games in a season, they never won a single SEC conference game. Most of their battles weren't especially close. By 1940, Sewanee didn't have much in common with its peers in the league. A tiny school by comparison, with less than 350 students enrolled[1], they began downsizing their athletic programs as many other private colleges were doing at the time.

But Tulane and Georgia Tech continued on as the conference reformed with 12 members, and for a while, both fielded exceptionally strong teams. Tulane football may have peaked just before the SEC was established. From 1929-1931, Tulane compiled a staggering 28-2 record, against mostly SEC competition. The Green Wave finished 11-1 just two years before the SEC formed, clobbering many future SEC programs like Georgia, Auburn, and

LSU. The Green Wave played in the 1932 Rose Bowl, a game at least one newspaper was selling as a National Championship Game. (Tulane would lose, 21-12.)

A few years later, the Green Wave finished 10-1, going undefeated in SEC play (their only blemish was a 20-6 loss to Colgate in New York City), and topped off their campaign with a win in the first Sugar Bowl, a 20-14 triumph over Temple. They opened the 1936 campaign in the AP Poll, climbing as high as #9, before a late-season swoon with losses to Alabama and LSU knocked them from their perch.

After a return trip to the Sugar Bowl in 1939, Tulane's football fortunes dipped a bit, in part thanks to WWII. (You aren't going to believe this, but a massive world war had a negative impact on quite a few football programs.) The 1948 squad demolished LSU 46-0, beat a 10th ranked Mississippi State squad 20-7, and finished 13th in the final AP Poll with a 9-1 record, their only blemish a close loss to Georgia Tech. They led the SEC in attendance, drawing 37,058 fans a game[2], and were starting to pick up some serious media buzz. The *Sporting News*, after all, picked them as their preseason national champion pick.

The 1949 campaign started excellently, as Tulane knocked off Alabama to start the season, avenged their loss to Georgia Tech by dispatching the Yellow Jackets 18-0, and then clobbered Southeastern Louisiana by 48. Suddenly, Tulane was ranked 4th in the AP Poll, their highest ranking in school history. The next week, the Green Wave had a shot at Notre Dame, the top ranked team in the country. The combined score for their previous four meetings? Notre Dame: 158, Tulane: 12.

If there were ever a team outside the SEC that Tulane backers would have been particularly motivated to dispatch, it would have been the Irish. Before the game, a columnist with the *Shreveport Times* said, "There are some that say [Tulane] will beat Leahy's charges by three touchdowns."[3]

It wasn't clear who "they" were, but "they" certainly didn't have their pulse on the situation, because that very much didn't happen. Tulane did not win by three touchdowns. Tulane didn't even *score* three touchdowns. Notre Dame scored touchdowns the first four times they touched the ball, and when the smoke cleared in South Bend, the Irish were victorious, 46-7. The Wave dropped from 4th to 20th in the AP Poll, and then vanished completely.

In a vacuum, this season was still a successful one for Tulane. They finished 7-2-1, beat a top ten Virginia team on the road by two touchdowns, and won the SEC. But the season wasn't played in a vacuum.

First, Tulane did lose another game, and it was the one they absolutely couldn't afford to lose, a 21-0 upset at the hands of their hated rivals, LSU, on the last day of the season. Thanks to their embarrassing loss to Notre Dame earlier in the season when the entire country was watching, and their late season upset, the Sugar Bowl decided to pick LSU instead of Tulane. Despite finishing 10th in the country, Tulane didn't play in the postseason that year.[4] In fact, they wouldn't play in the postseason again until 1970.

Second, Tulane's administration was changing rapidly. In order to build a competitive program in the SEC Green Wave head coach Henry Frnka was engaging in just about every other recruiting process his peer institutions were using. That meant funneling players into less demanding academic disciplines and carrying a huge roster, which wasn't uncommon in the era before scholarship limits. In March 1950, for example, coach Frnka asked to fund 125 grants-in-aid for the season. Tulane often carried a roster near 100 players, just like other schools in the SEC were doing.[5]

Of course, it would be a little bit easier for a much larger, state-sponsored institution, like Louisiana State, or Georgia, or Alabama, to carry so many players, but Tulane was private, and had a much smaller enrollment than most other SEC schools. As GI Bill benefits started to wane after WWII, Tulane suddenly had to foot much more of that scholarship bill. The AP reported that Tulane's athletic department lost $46,000 in 1950 (over $460,000 in 2016 money) and was projected to lose even more money the year after. [6]And as the popularity of the program waned, combined with the declining academic profile of the team—the graduation rate for football players was under 36%[7]—a very academically focused administration decided to act.

In 1951, Tulane president Rufus Harris, a Yale law school classmate of Chicago president Robert Hutchins, who shut down the successful Maroon program, set an era of "de-emphasis" in motion. He proposed a wide-ranging proposal to the rest of the SEC, which would cap football scholarships at 75 and limit the number of coaches each school could employ. Harris also proposed substantially limiting practice time and moving popular physical education programs from a major to a minor, meaning that coaches would have one less easy home to hide academically challenged players.[8]

Other SEC schools, predictably, were less enthused about stepping away from the college football arms race. Florida's president H. Hillis Miller told the United Press that he thought the project was "too drastic", especially disagreeing with rules regarding the physical education degree program. Chancellor J.D. Williams of Ole Miss added that while he had some "sympathy" for the Tulane plan, but added, "It seems that we're trying to legislate fairness and honesty into football.[9] It looks like that is going to be a very difficult thing to do."

Even by the early 1950s, college administrators were expressing concern over whether trying to make every football program behave honestly was a bit of a lost cause.

The rest of the conference didn't follow suit, but that didn't stop Tulane from implementing the measures on their own campus. Shortly after the new regulations went into place, Frnka resigned as head coach. His replacement, Raymond Wolf, discovered that what was already a hard job had just become substantially harder.

Bob Whitman, an assistant coach during that era, described the predicament: "Some SEC teams like Georgia Tech and Ole Miss were recruiting twice the number of players we could, and then we were being asked to compete on an equal footing against them."[10] Under the best of circumstances, that would have been difficult for Tulane, who already boasted tougher academic standards than many SEC peers. With fewer scholarships, coaches (Georgia Tech had 11 coaches in 1951. Tulane had six[11]), and now fewer academically accessible academic programs, the Green Wave found themselves at a huge disadvantage.

It showed on the field. Wolf went 6-13-1 over two seasons and was replaced by Andy Pilney. The Green Wave cracked the AP Top 20 just once from 1952-1965, reaching #15 before losing to Georgia Tech by 40 points in 1956. They finished with a winning record just once during that time frame. Those close SEC losses started to become more and more like blowouts, which helped pave the way for some difficult conversations.

Georgia Tech football took a slightly different road over their history, but eventually reached a similar crossroads. Tech football struggled in its infancy, despite picking a truly excellent nickname, the Blacksmiths. After a 73-0 thrashing at the hands of Clemson's John Heisman (yes, *that* Heisman) coached squad in 1903, the program realized they needed to make an upgrade as coach if they wanted to win games in the rapidly more competitive South. So they hired John Heisman.

A quick detour here, if I may, since I can't write about pre-SEC Georgia Tech without mentioning the most bonkers box score in the history of college football. In 1916, tiny Cumberland College tried to back out of a scheduled date against Georgia Tech, using the reasonable excuse that they no longer had a football team. But Heisman, angry about Cumberland using non-student ringers to beat Tech in baseball the year before, refused to let them out of their contract. So Cumberland rounded up a few students and hoped for the best.

Their hopes were in vain, as Heisman was fueled not just by a desire for vengeance against a cheating program, but also to take a shot at sportswriters, who he thought, as a lot, were pretty stupid, and would simply go by who scored the most points to determine how good a team. As a sportswriter... well, I think that's probably fair.[12] When the dust settled, Tech beat hapless Cumberland by a historic margin that will never be bested in college football: 220-0. The Yellow Jackets didn't even throw a single pass. No wonder Coach Heisman got a trophy named after him.

Tech didn't beat everybody by two hundred points, but they did beat folks a lot, winning two national titles, in 1917 and 1928, respectively. By the time they entered the SEC, they could arguably boast more history and success than nearly any other program in the conference.

Tech started slowly in SEC, failing to finish above .500 in its first four seasons. Near the end of William Alexander era they found solid footing again, making three bowls in a row from 1942-1944 and finishing in the AP Top 20 every season. But the true golden era of Georgia Tech football really kicked off once Tech assistant coach Bobby Dodd replaced Alexander for the 1945 season.

Dodd was an amazing athlete in his own right, lettering in baseball, basketball, and track while with Tennessee, as well as leading the Volunteers to their longest unbeaten streak ever at 33 games. He fell into an assistant coaching job with the Yellow Jackets after a Georgia Tech scout asked Dodd for scouting information on North Carolina, and was so impressed with this game breakdown that he offered him a job.[13]

Dodd's philosophy went against the grain from conventional wisdom in the SEC, eschewing long, demanding boot camp–like practices (like Bear Bryant's famous Camp Junction), in favor of shorter, more tightly regimented practices. Former player and future Georgia Tech coach Bill Curry would say that Dodd told players early on that he "did not bring them there to kill them at practice."[14]

He was also unusual in his insistence that his students actually go to class and graduate, no small feat given that Tech's curriculum included coursework in calculus, statistics and physics for everybody, including members of the football team. Dodd boasted a truly impressive 90% graduation rate over his 22-year tenure as coach[15]. Even without the demands of being on a football team, there's no way in hell I would have been able to graduate from 1950s Georgia Tech.

But his approach worked, even without superior size or speed, a fact that sportswriters would sometimes attribute to "Dodd Luck."[16] Georgia's long-time coach, Wallace Butts, once quipped that Dodd was so lucky, "if Bobby Dodd were trapped at the center of an H-Bomb explosion, he'd walk away with his pockets full of marketable uranium."[17]

The Jackets saw major successes in the SEC. From 1945 to 1956, Georgia Tech finished in the AP Poll seven times, won two SEC titles, went 8-0 in bowl games, and won the 1952 National Championship. But Tech's run started to tail off after 1956, and two factors loomed to push Dodd and the Yellow Jackets, out of the SEC entirely.

The first conflict was more personal. Bobby Dodd and Alabama's Bear Bryant maintained a personal friendship over much of Dodd's early coaching career, but that ended abruptly over an ugly incident in a 1961 game. The two teams were playing in Birmingham, and Alabama held a 10-0 lead late in the game. Tech punted to Alabama, who signaled a fair catch. Tech running back Chick Granning, thinking the play was essentially over, relaxed a bit in coverage, only to be smashed in the face after the play by the elbow of Alabama linebacker Darwin Holt.[18]

Granning was badly injured. The full diagnosis included a broken nose, a shattered cheekbone, five teeth lost, and a concussion. These facial injuries completely ended Granning's football career. Given Granning's popularity with the team and fans—*Sports Illustrated* later described him as "basically too gentle to be a truly great football player"[19]—such a cheap shot demanded action, especially because Holt wasn't even penalized on the play. Much like today, the refs back then were clearly blind.

Dodd formally filed a protest to Alabama, alleging that this wasn't the first time that Holt had been involved in cheap shots after the whistle[20]. The SEC said it didn't have a mechanism to do anything about it, and Alabama did not suspend Holt or even formally apologize.[21] In response, Georgia Tech, already frustrated with Alabama's rough play, announced they would no longer play Alabama after their contract expired in 1964[22]. This was a big deal, considering that the team had played almost every season since 1902.

For what it's worth, conference schools deciding to not schedule each other would be impossible today, but wasn't unheard of before conference offices more rigidly defined league slates. Georgia Tech, for example, virtually never played the Mississippi schools during the 1950s, something both schools resented.[23] The SEC didn't even try to create a regular round-robin schedule until 1954, and virtually every school opposed it. In fact, the inability to agree on regular scheduling is one of the reasons the SEC did not expand during the 1950s and 1960s, despite considering adding Miami (FL) and Houston on multiple occasions.[24]

The second conflict arose over a rule that troubled Tulane greatly as well: SEC Rule 140. This conference bylaw allowed schools to keep up to 140 players on scholarship for football and basketball. Schools could sign up to 45 a year as well (today, FBS schools have a football scholarship limit cap of 85). The two limits, in theory, would prevent a team from signing 45 players a year.

But football scholarships were not guaranteed for all four years. If a player became injured (not uncommon given how brutal some coaches conducted their conditioning), their scholarship could be canceled. Heck, if the player just turned out to not be good enough to see the field, a coach could decide to replace them with a better player. On some level, this practice still occurs today, commonly referred to as oversigning.

Bobby Dodd hated oversigning. When Georgia Tech recruited an athlete, they kept him for all four years, even if he got hurt or was a bust. Dodd would famously say that if an athlete wasn't good enough for play for Georgia Tech, it wasn't the player's fault, but the coaches, for poor talent evaluation. So while his SEC conference peers would sign 40-45 players each season, Dodd would only add 30-32, keeping each player on the team until they graduated. Over time, that would give other conference schools a significant advantage in team depth, and Dodd felt that was unfair.[25] "Either love your players, or get out of coaching," he would say[26].

In fact, Dodd was an outspoken advocate against many of the excesses of recruiting, especially recruiting in the SEC during that era. In a 1957 profile from *Sports Illustrated*, Dodd went so far as to say "Recruiting has gotten too far out of hand, [...] the kind [of illegal recruiting] where a coach will go out and offer a kid the world with a fence around it—it's going to ruin football. It's bad enough now, and if it gets any worse I'll have to stand up and say, 'Let's get rid of intercollegiate football. Let's play on an intramural basis. But let's play it honest.'"[27]

At the 1964 conference meetings, Dodd proposed that the SEC limit the number of scholarships each school could give out to 32 a season, which would, in theory, dramatically limit oversigning. SEC administrators were split on the rule, and every vote was important. Alabama's Bear Bryant, easily the most important voice within Alabama's athletic department, reportedly assured Dodd that he would support the measure, making it dramatically more likely to pass. But when it came time for a vote, Bryant was nowhere to be found. Instead, Alabama President Frank Rose voted against the measure. The final vote was 6-6, not enough to overturn Rule 140, keeping the larger scholarship limits in place.[28]

Georgia Tech made it clear they wouldn't remain in the league without scholarship reform, and after the vote they announced their withdrawal from the SEC. Tulane would follow, two years later. As the Green Wave were already struggling to financially compete back in the early 1950s, a conference that doubled down on larger scholarship pools and rosters would make it even harder for them to compete.

Both schools spun their withdrawal from the SEC as part of their ambitions to schedule nationally. Tulane did schedule teams from all over the country, like Cincinnati, Boston College, Air Force and Virginia Tech, along with regular meetings against SEC competition, but trading dates with Alabama and LSU for West Coast squads was never the true reason for departure.

"That wasn't it at all," said Rix Yard, Tulane's AD at the time, to the *New Orleans Times-Picayune.* "The purpose was to lighten the schedule. [...] I remember going [SEC Commissioner] Bernie Moore and pleading to allow us to reduce our schedule. He wouldn't allow it."[29]

After all, Tulane finished 0-10 in 1962, and the Tulane's scholarship limits, plus their tougher academics and just plain bad luck, occasionally made the roster disparities enormous. In an era where some SEC teams may have had more than 90 players on a roster, Tulane once had as few as 38[30].

From 1952-1965, the "de-emphasis" era at Tulane, the Green Wave enjoyed a paltry 16-75-5 record in SEC play. They produced just two All-SEC players. They were uncompetitive in virtually every facet of the game.

Bobby Dodd had higher ambitions for Georgia Tech football as an independent, hoping to become something of a Notre Dame of the South. But the timing couldn't have been worse. After Dodd retired in 1966, Tech suffered three consecutive losing seasons. While they would occasionally enjoy some success as an independent, they never had access to top-tier bowl games, or won enough to become relevant nationally.

But it was the timing of that downturn that hurt Georgia Tech the most. For one thing, Georgia football began its ascent. Legendary coach Vince Dooley was hired in 1964, and the Bulldogs won the Cotton Bowl and finished 4th in the country the very next season. As Tech began to fade in the post-Dodd era, the Bulldogs became regulars as SEC contenders, AP Poll finishers, and contenders for top bowl games. Sidewalk alumni throughout the state, and even in Atlanta, who previously may have rooted for the Yellow Jackets, increasingly changed their allegiances to the team down in Athens. That robbed Georgia Tech of press coverage and recruiting momentum.

Plus, the state of Georgia was changing. After years of essentially being the only show in town, the Atlanta Falcons of the NFL began play in 1966. The Braves moved from Milwaukee that same year, and the Hawks joined in 1968. Suddenly, Atlanta residents were awash in sports options, robbing the Yellow Jackets of even more coverage and energy in the city. As Atlanta grew and became more of a powerful business center, fans from out of state would move to the city, carrying their old rooting interests with them, be that from other SEC schools, or elsewhere.

Under Dodd, Georgia Tech football was king of Atlanta. But without him, and without the lure of a possible SEC title, Yellow Jacket football didn't just slide to second or third place. It might have slid to fifth.

Tulane had similar bad luck. The Green Wave was lousy in the years before they left the SEC, and they were lousy right after they left. From 1966 to 1995, when they joined Conference USA, Tulane won only a single bowl game, and earned invites to just five. They did, in fact, start to play a more national schedule, adding squads like Michigan and Stanford to future slates, to go with the occasional SEC team and lesser-known programs like Cincinnati, to improve their chances at winning. But any momentum Tulane might have picked up by bringing some big-name, national programs to New Orleans was halted by a familiar problem.

The New Orleans Saints came to town and quickly sucked up some of the oxygen that previously went to the Green Wave. Over the next twenty years, sidewalk alumni, or fans who didn't attend the school, gradually tilted towards LSU, or focused on the NFL, as Tulane drifted farther into obscurity. Added Tulane AD Yard, "The impact of the Saints on Tulane football was tremendous. [...] the Saints came in and all of a sudden, we're the orphan on the street. All the publicity, all of the adulation went to the Saints. I think that was a blow to Pittman and more so to his players. They felt let down by all the attention given to the Saints."[31]

By the 1980s, the Green Wave had to deal with whispers that the university would consider dropping the football team.[32] Said Tulane's faculty representative at the time, Gary Roberts, "We probably had the worst Division I athletic program in the United States. It was just a mess."[33] Indeed, it was enough of a mess that Tulane seriously considered just getting out of the football business altogether. After the 1985 season, a 14-member committee voted on whether Tulane should just drop football, right before the Green Wave battled Southern Miss. The vote was a 7-7 tie.[34] The game? Southern Miss won, 31-19. That wasn't a surprise, since Tulane finished 1-10 that season, and gave up over 30 points a game.

For the most part, the football team has continued to struggle after leaving the SEC. There have been a few high points, like the dynamite 1998 team that finished #7 in the country after a 12-0 regular season, and then miscues, like not retaining Rich Rodriguez from that 1998 staff, or failing to hire Jim Harbaugh from San Diego when he expressed interest in the position.[35] (He would later go to Stanford, the NFL, and then Michigan.) And of course, Hurricane Katrina especially devastated New Orleans, and Tulane's campus, which was forced to close for the term.

Eventually, the logistical struggles of operating as an independent caught up to Tulane. The AP reported in 1989 that Tulane had made four different applications to rejoin the SEC[36], as Tulane athletic director noted that "the days are gone, with rare exception, where an independent can really compete in the television market."[37]

In 1990, Alabama athletic director Cecil "Hootie" Ingram told an interviewer that he hoped the SEC would bring back Tulane, along with adding Florida State, saying that former SEC Commissioner Dr. Boyd McWhorter made a great effort to bring Tulane and Georgia Tech back, only to have the proposal voted down.[38] Tulane also reportedly considered membership in the Southwest Conference.[39]

But Tulane football does have some things going for it. Now a member of the American Athletic Conference, it can claim membership in the premier non-power league in college sports, and thanks in part to its urban location and membership in the prestigious American Association of Universities (Rice and Buffalo are the only other members among non-power league schools), it was a candidate for Big 12 expansion in both 2011 and 2016[40]. If the schools are reshuffled again, it may find itself in a position they held back in the 1940s, when they were a member of a powerful league.

Georgia Tech's post-SEC history had higher successes, but struggled with similar issues. The independent era was often one of relative obscurity for

Georgia Tech. Pepper Rodgers, who coached Tech from 1974-1979, would tell the *Atlanta-Journal Constitution,* "It was a very, very tough schedule, and yet there was no incentive, except going to a major bowl, and at that time, there weren't 400 bowls like there are now." He also said he "never would have left the SEC."[41]

Fortunately, Tech wasn't forced to stay independent forever. The Yellow Jackets joined the ACC in 1978, playing their first football season in 1983. After struggling for a few seasons, Georgia Tech hit its stride, jumping from out of nowhere to win a national title in 1990 under Bobby Ross.

That elite level of success couldn't be sustained, however. Tech established a niche for themselves as at least "pretty good", making a bowl in 18 out of 19 seasons and finishing in the AP Top 25 eight different times. They might not be playing in a huge stadium, or achieving national adulation for their success, but regular bowl trips and semi-regular Top 25 finishes aren't nothing. All things considered, things certainly could have been worse.

Okay, but what if those schools never left the SEC? Or what if they came back?

Like Ingram said, that was a thing, at least for a little while. Some SEC administrators felt like the conference took an academic hit when the two schools departed, and would have been interested in reuniting. *The Tennessean* wrote that it would be nice to have Tulane back in the conference in 1989 as well.[42]

The *Atlanta Journal Constitution* caught up with former Georgia Tech coach Bill Curry and asked him how he thought things would be different if Tech had never left the SEC. He said that "Bobby Dodd Stadium would be 80,000 seats, and it would be packed almost every week."[43] Currently, Bobby Dodd has a capacity of 55,000, and it packed substantially less often, even when Georgia Tech is really good. But it wasn't just the stadium that isn't up to snuff. After leaving the SEC, Georgia Tech's athletic facilities, in general, were surpassed by other Southern institutions.

Looking at what SEC membership would have meant off the field, it doesn't seem like Curry's assessment is unreasonable. In 2015, the ACC distributed around $25 million a school, thanks to a large TV deal and distribution from bowl games and the NCAA Tournament. The SEC, on the other hand, distributed $34 million a year, with some schools getting as much as $40 million a year.[44] That disparity is likely to grow even more in the next few years, thanks to the SEC's wildly profitable SEC Network. That difference of 10-15 million dollars a year, coupled over decades, could have allowed Tech to make all kinds of important investments that they couldn't make in the ACC.

The difference would be even more dramatic for Tulane, as the financial gap between the proverbial "haves" and "have-nots" in college football only grows. Even though Tulane is currently a member of The American, the most prestigious conference outside of the Power Five, Tulane only took home about $2 million dollars in conference distributions.[45] When it comes to perks, facilities, coaching salaries, or virtually anything else, Tulane is completely non-competitive financially compared to the SEC or ACC. If the Green Wave stuck around and never won a thing in the SEC, they could at least take comfort in the fact that their checks still cashed.

Because of the scholarship disparity, it is difficult to imagine Tulane picking itself off the SEC mat until national scholarship reform took place in 1975. No matter how creatively the Green Wave recruited, if one team can stash 40 more players than you can, you're not going to win a lot. The best Tulane teams in that era still beat a few SEC squads, but imagining them in the week in and week out grind while facing teams with superior numbers would probably lead to disappointing results.

The question is, would the stakes of SEC membership have encouraged Tulane to make better administrative decisions? A larger budget might have lessened incentives to cut corners, or give expensive extensions for marginal coaches in an effort to convince the rest of the world you were sticking around. After all, if you're in the SEC, even if you stink, nobody will think you're actually going to cut football.

How would things look different on the field?

For one, the very membership of the conference would be different. If Tulane and Georgia Tech never left, the SEC wouldn't have needed to expand in the 1990s to get to 12 teams, and thus, a lucrative conference championship game. You could just throw Georgia Tech in the SEC East and Tulane in the SEC West, and you'd be all set. Given the rush to expand into different television markets later in the 2000s, assuming an eventual rush to 14 teams seems reasonable, but which ones? It's hard for me to see a world where Arkansas isn't in the SEC, but a compelling argument could be made for Texas A&M or Missouri to grab the other spot.

For the sake of geographical simplicity, and not having to spend another 2,000 words going into a deep SEC protected rivalry rabbit hole, let's just say it's Missouri.

How might that have impacted results over the last few years? It's hard to imagine Georgia Tech winning a share of the 1990 national title if they were in the SEC, for example. Tech's title that year was one of the most unlikely championships in the last 40 years, as they entered the season unranked and didn't meaningfully enter the national conversation until they upset Virginia, eight weeks into the season. Tech finished 11-0-1, beating a 19th ranked Nebraska squad with two losses in the Citrus Bowl to end the year. Without a swath of unlikely upsets, Georgia Tech never gets in the position to be in a national title conversation anyway.

They probably wouldn't finish a 1990 SEC schedule unscathed, given how strong Florida (9-2, 8th in final S&P+) and Tennessee (9-2-2, 11th) finished[46], and how fortunate Georgia Tech was to not lose to some relatively average competition, like their 13-13 tie with North Carolina (6-4-1, 40th), or a three point win over a 6-5 Virginia Tech team. While SEC membership would likely give them a more prestigious bowl slot by the end of the year, it seems likely that the Yellow Jackets would have been tripped up somewhere, knocking them down a bit in the polls.

But would Georgia Tech fans trade that for the money, fame, and attention that comes with SEC membership? Probably. Plus, it's not like there wouldn't have been other years Georgia Tech could compete. The 2014 Georgia Tech squad that won the Orange Bowl over a top ten Mississippi State also beat a top ten Georgia squad just two games before. They could have certainly competed for an East Division title. The 1998 team beat Notre Dame in the Gator Bowl and also beat a very strong Georgia team; they likely could have battled in the SEC, although eventual national champion Tennessee probably would have prevented them from winning the East.

In a 2014 interview, current Georgia Tech head coach Paul Johnson said he figured Georgia Tech would "probably be about .500" in the SEC[47], and if you plopped the current version of the program in there, that feels about right. Some years they'd catch a few teams by surprise and compete for an East title, some years they'd fall flat and win four games, but on the balance, .500 in the league seems reasonable.

But if you consider the possible multiplier effects of years in the SEC, without losing leverage and popularity in the city of Atlanta, with mostly sold-out home crowds, with more television money and fancier upgrades, Tech's potential seems higher. Not as high as Florida, or Alabama, or Georgia, but high enough to be a Top 25 contender, and almost certainly higher than it currently is in the ACC.

What about Tulane?

The Green Wave have mostly struggled on the field in recent memory, only qualifying for three bowl games since Mack Brown left after the 1987 season. The most memorable of those, of course, was the 1998 campaign, when the Green Wave finished 12-0, and 7th in the final AP Poll. Paced by the electric play of quarterback Shaun King, Tulane averaged 45 points a game, good for second in the country, and hung up 73 on Louisiana-Lafayette.

Tulane's schedule was terrible though. The closest thing to a power conference team they faced in the regular season was a 5-6 Rutgers squad in the Big East (who, to their credit, Tulane destroyed). Their SRS and S&P+ profiles didn't suggest Tulane was a truly elite team (Tulane was 23rd in SRS and 25th in S&P+[48]), and they had legitimate issues on defense, but they were certainly good enough to have beaten multiple SEC teams that season. They could easily be a Top 25 team that won nine games, playing an SEC schedule that year.

The easiest comparison to Tulane's fortunes would be Vanderbilt, another private, selective, research-focused institution in the SEC. Vandy has never won an SEC title, and mostly sits in the bottom half of the division, but with the right coaching and evaluation, they're a bowl team and can upset a squad or two. Since New Orleans produces better high school recruits than Nashville, perhaps Tulane's ceiling as a program might be a teensy bit higher.

But that, of course, is also projecting a multiple effect of years of TV revenues that would allow greater institutional investments. Today, Tulane would
probably be crushed in almost every sport outside of baseball.

An SEC with Tulane and Georgia Tech probably makes a little bit less
money than it does now, as Atlanta and New Orleans are already covered in
the league's TV footprint, and it's not like there's a massive Tulane fan dias-
pora that would open up a new market. But it would also make the league academically stronger, as both schools are respected research schools with AAU
membership. And it would be tighter geographically and historically.

And functional LSU and Tulane rivalries? Georgia Tech mixing it up
again with Alabama? Those would be pretty fun, too.

What if the PCC became the Airplane Conference?

————

THE IDEA OF A SUPERCONFERENCE, a football league with at least 12 teams, a championship game, and a collection of powerful athletic programs spanning more than one geographic region, feels like a modern notion. But if you want to define a superconference as just a league with a whole bunch of dang teams in it, then the idea is nearly a century old. The Southern Conference, one of the very oldest in all of college athletics, had over 20 teams in the early 1920s, including programs that would eventually spin off to form the SEC (Florida, Georgia and Alabama), programs that would eventually spin off to form the ACC (North Carolina and North Carolina State), programs that would eventually drop down to FCS football, (The Citadel), and programs that would depart major college athletics entirely (Sewanee).

Yes, friends: Once upon a time, Alabama vs. Sewanee was a conference game. The early days of college football were weird.

But the Southern Conference didn't expand to 20 teams out of a quest for athletic dominance. Many of those programs, even ones that would eventually become dominant names, were awful in the 1920s. These were the days when teams like Florida lost to Mercer, when LSU would struggle with Loyola and Rutgers, after all.

These moves weren't to consolidate television revenue either, since the TV didn't exist. Even monetizing radio rights was still in its infancy. This was a marriage of geographic and institutional convenience. You know, what used to be the basis for conference affiliation to begin with, before TV.

Well, what used to be the basis for *nearly* every conference affiliation. In the late 1950s, an idea started to take shape that would revolutionize the sport's organization forever. Why not form a conference not just in one geographic region, but across the entire country, complete with a possible championship game? This idea could have blown apart the conference structures in multiple other leagues, furthered a push for a playoff, changed the scope of the NCAA, and more.

It was called, colloquially anyway, the "Airplane Conference." And it started from the ashes of another major league.

In 2017, the major league of the West Coast is the Pac-12, but that wasn't always the case. The original power conference on the West Coast was the Pacific Coast Conference, founded in 1915, with Cal, Washington, Oregon and Oregon State as charter members. The league expanded relatively quickly, adding Washington State in 1917, Stanford in 1918, USC in 1922, Idaho in 1922, Montana in 1924, and then finally UCLA, a relatively late newcomer in college football, in 1928.

Things were relatively stable for a few decades, but in the 1950s, the entire enterprise fell apart. The University of Oregon was forced to fire their football coach after a conference investigation found them guilty of violating rules on subsidies[1]. Then, Washington football coach John Cherberg, who would later become Lt. Governor, was fired after three relatively lackluster seasons. After his dismissal, Cherberg alleged that boosters were operating a shady slush fund to pay players and turn them against him[2].

That paper trail led to Washington mega-booster Roscoe "Torchy" Torrance, a former Washington athlete who ran Greater Seattle, Inc., and who was indeed running a major payoff scheme that was very much against PCC regulations. Soon, newspapers were publishing stories of similar funds at UCLA. Next, a UCLA alum blew the whistle on slush funds and phony job setups at USC and Cal. The allegations amounted to everything about college football scandals that one associates with the message board era, with alumni of various schools frantically trying to out the others as ruthless rulebreakers. Suddenly, a good half of the conference had been outed in public as cheaters. The NCAA slapped several programs on the wrist, but the PCC's internal punishments were arguably worse—a Rose Bowl ban for USC and UCLA for three years.[3]

Things got ugly from there. The California schools, especially UCLA, resented the PCC's leadership under Orlando John Hollis, the law dean at Oregon and the presiding officer of the conference investigations. Regents from the University of California system openly disdained the schools in the Pacific Northwest, who they felt were academic and athletic inferiors.[4] Officials from UCLA and Oregon straight up refused to speak to each other. In such a dysfunctional environment, it was no surprise that USC, UCLA and Cal decided to leave the PCC in 1957. Washington would shortly join them.

Without the anchor California universities and scandal and administrative disagreements still swirling about, the PCC disbanded in 1959. Eventually, five of the PCC institutions (Cal, UCLA, Stanford, Washington and USC) would create something called the Athletic Association of Western Universities, a union that would eventually grow into the current Pac-12.

And the PCC? I think a headline from the Eugene Guard said it best: "Pacific Coast Conference, After Shaky Start, Gained National Prominence Only To Die In Near Disgrace."[5] Subtle.

But a similar Western athletic conference was not the only option for those institutions. Another, dramatically more radical plan, was also being considered. Why, after all, constrain themselves to another regional union, especially when you don't even like many of your neighbors? Why not look at something national? After all, technology was changing and giving schools more options. University administrators were wary of having athletes miss extended time for travel, something that was especially tricky for Western schools that comparatively lacked the number of nearby institutions like programs in the Northeast, Midwest, or Deep South. Oregon's *Bend Bulletin* broke down the logistical problems Western schools faced in the past[6]:

"For Stanford, as an example, it was over a 24 hour train trip to play the University of Washington at Seattle. The team left Palo Alto on Wednesday night to make it to Seattle in time to have one workout and play a Saturday afternoon name. Members arrived back on the campus late Sunday or early Monday by dint of close after-game scheduling."

But thanks to air travel becoming safer, more popular, and more affordable during the 1950s, programs weren't *necessarily* constrained to only regularly playing institutions within a short train trip away, especially if a longer road trip promised a big payday.

The Western institutions weren't the only schools thinking about starting a national conference. The idea, interestingly enough, first came from Notre Dame's President John Cavanaugh. Today, Notre Dame's football independence has become something of a treasured artifact that fans and alumni would be loath to give up, even if it was financially beneficial. But that certainly wasn't true for all of Notre Dame's football history, and in the early 1950s, some structure might have been helpful.

Cavanaugh's proposed grouping was curious, to say the least. His proposal called for a conference that would include Indiana, Iowa State, Navy, Michigan State, North Carolina, Notre Dame, Oklahoma, Army, Penn, Pittsburgh, SMU, Texas, USC, UCLA and Yale[7]. Such a grouping would have certainly been advantageous to Notre Dame, who would get regular opponents in all corners of the country and a few regular, local rivals.

But for many of those schools, the grouping didn't make sense. Even by 1951, Yale's prominence as a football program was fading dramatically, as most Ivy League schools were scaling back. Many of the other institutions shared no common history, or were already in comfortable conference situations. Plus, since Cavanaugh's stated reasoning centered on "reforming college athletics on such issues as financial aid to athletes and long-term coaching contracts"[8], trying to rope in disparate institutions like Yale—which didn't give athletic scholarships and didn't even really want to be in big-time college football anyway—alongside Oklahoma and UCLA would be nearly impossible. A grouping with the biggest programs, with all of the financial trappings that came with it, and schools that were not wholly committed to football was dead on arrival. Officials at places like Navy, USC and SMU listened politely, but there was never any serious interest.

But Notre Dame wasn't the only institution to start thinking in new, dramatic ways about conference affiliation. Tom Hamilton, the athletic director at Pitt, proposed joining the five Western institutions with six Eastern institutions: Army, Navy, Notre Dame, Pitt, Syracuse and Penn State[9]. The Air Force Academy was thrown in to make things even.

Other reported versions of this plan mentioned multiple other institutions, including higher-level programs such as Duke, Georgia Tech, Houston, West Virginia and Miami (FL) along with lower-tier schools such as Penn, Holy Cross, and Colgate.[10] It's not clear how many schools that were listed in newspaper reports were being seriously considered for such a venture, so for the sake of consistency, we'll focus on the plan that was reported the most often, including the above institutions.

Hamilton was the perfect man to propose a radical change. A former Admiral in the Navy, Hamilton had been a respected athletic director at both the Naval Academy and Pittsburgh, and coached at both schools to boot. In 1958, he left Pitt to become the conference commissioner for the AAWU. A man with ties to service academies, Eastern independents, and Western institutions would be the perfect person to create a national institution.[11]

This grouping began to be known to the press as the "Airplane Conference," since taking the train between UCLA and Syracuse was not a viable option. At least once, the AP referred to the proposal as the "American Conference."[12] (Sorry, 2016 Tulsa.) It also appeared in print as the Continental Conference or the National Conference. For the sake of consistency, we'll stick with Airplane Conference. (Also, that's a better name, because airplanes are cool.)

It wasn't hard to see the appeal of such an organization for the Western programs. Schools like Cal and Stanford could free themselves of what they perceived as academic, if not athletic, deadweights like Oregon State and Washington State. Bigger programs like UCLA would no longer have to travel to Oregon to play in front of tiny crowds[13]. And with Air Force in the fold, they'd benefit from association with the military, which was a nice thing to have in the late 1950s to early 1960s.

It's worth noting that the Airplane Conference would have used a different institutional structure than the AAWU. Speaking to the Pasadena Independent Star-News, UCLA athletic director Wilbur Johns said, "Primarily, the AAWU will be in association of universities equal in size and athletic facilities. Each institution will establish and enforce its own policy and will rely on the integrity of the other universities, thus it will be operating completely differently from the past. [...] We believe in the integrity of an institution, and therefore there will be no necessity for investigations such as the ones employed by the PCC."[14]

Embarrassed after institutional investigations a few years earlier, Airplane Conference members would then presumably be freed from the extra regulations they had in the PCC (such as a conference ban on coaches visiting prospects off-campus, which was allowed by the NCAA), and wouldn't have to worry about pesky snoops coming in to embarrass them if they decided they wanted to say, have more liberal interpretations of the rulebook.

The appeal for many of the Eastern schools was real, too. Even in 1960, few schools really recruited players on a national level. But Notre Dame, Army, and Navy certainly did, and a formalized national conference would make scheduling games in every region of the country that much easier. Syracuse and Pitt, operating as Eastern independents, would now have easier access to a potential big-ticket bowl game, as well as other lucrative opportunities. Plus, having Notre Dame as a conference-mate would certainly improve one's chances for getting on national television.

This entire operation wasn't just a back-of-the-napkin fancy from administrators either. Representatives from various institutions were talking about the idea to the press too. Notre Dame athletic director Moose Krause, in 1958, told the *Los Angeles Times*, "Yes, Notre Dame is interested in joining a National Conference. It would be good for college football."[15] Representatives from UCLA and Pitt were also on the record making similar statements.[16]

But it never happened. Why not?

Despite heavy interest, not every institution was on the same page. Cal, USC, and UCLA all underwent significant administrative change in the early 1960s, and the new school leaders were not as enthusiastically pro-football as their predecessors.[17] Without major support from the West Coast anchor schools, a national conference would never have a chance.

Internal politics surrounding the service academies seems like another possible reason. The *Pasadena Independent Star-News*, in 1961, reported that the plan "suffered a serious knock down" when Navy was passed over for a Rose Bowl bid in favor of Minnesota.[18] Others said that the Pentagon itself wasn't thrilled with the idea and killed service academy involvement. No matter who specifically killed it, without Army and Navy (and to a lesser extent, the Air Force), the Airplane Conference idea was, for better or for worse, grounded.

Before we dig into what this grouping might have meant for college football, let's try to answer another question first. Would this league have been any good?

Air Force probably would have had a hard time competing in the league. Falcon football is dramatically younger than Army or Navy, having only started full-fledged varsity competition 1956 (with head coach L.T. "Buck" Shaw beating out some guy named Vince Lombardi for the first coaching job[19]). While Ben Martin did lead the Falcons to a Cotton Bowl appearance in 1958 after a 9-0-1 regular season record, Air Force fielded relatively average teams during this period. Still, they did compile a 14-15-1 record against Airplane Conference foes from 1958 (the start of Martin's tenure) through 1968, and regularly held their own against UCLA, Cal, and Stanford. If the Falcons had to replace games against middling regional foes like Idaho and Colorado State with regular visits to USC and Notre Dame, they would have likely struggled even more.

If nothing else, the fact that Air Force would likely have been a below-average football program in something called the Airplane Conference would been a boon to shameless newspaper editors across the country. The pun possibility would have been endless.

What about the rest of the group? Certainly, a few teams were excellent. Washington finished in the AP Top 10 both in 1959 and 1960, winning the Rose Bowl both times. USC won the national title in 1962, and again in 1967. But for the first decade of the hypothetical Airplane conference, depth would probably be lacking along the Western side. Cal and Stanford struggled for the entire decade, and UCLA was hardly consistent either. While USC, and occasionally Washington and UCLA would have been nationally competitive, the strength and depth would probably have been in the East.

Let's take 1960, for example. Even though Washington finished 10-1 and won the Rose Bowl, Penn State finished with a higher SRS rating. Navy, Syracuse, Pittsburgh and Army all had SRS scores that would have been good for 3rd in the West, and last place Notre Dame, with a lowly 2-8 record, was just a shout behind USC for 4th. Cal and Stanford were well behind their Eastern peers.

That trend would continue into the 1960s, especially after Notre Dame hired Ara Parseghian in 1964 and rocketed up from a rare down stretch to third in the final AP Poll. While the Western side of the Airplane would have likely produced one or two excellent teams, one through six, the Eastern side would have been better, and programs like Stanford and Cal would have likely struggled even more if games against foes like San Jose State and Utah were regularly replaced with jaunts to face Army, Pittsburgh, and Penn State.

But even if things weren't equally balanced, who cares?

The Airplane Conference could have claimed 33 teams getting ranked in the final AP Poll from 1960-1969, a feat made even more impressive given that for most of that time the AP Poll only ranked ten teams instead of twenty. They would have claimed three outright national championships and could have easily swung a few others. After all, 1968 Penn State finished undefeated, but second in the final AP Poll behind Ohio State, who knocked off USC in the Rose Bowl.

If Penn State had faced teams like UCLA or Washington in the regular season instead of say, Kansas State or Maryland, maybe they get the juice to pass Ohio State. Plus, they might have gotten the Rose Bowl shot against the Trojans instead of an Orange Bowl against Kansas.

The Rose Bowl is an interesting variable here, since that would have been one of the biggest appeals for the Airplane Conference. When the PCC dissolved before the 1959 season, the Rose Bowl no longer had an official contract with the conference. The game still picked a Western squad (Washington) to face a Big Ten team (Wisconsin) in the 1960 game, but there was no agreement compelling them to do so.[20] By the 1963 Rose Bowl though, the AAWU and the Big Ten signed a new agreement obligating the biggest postseason game in the country to accept the Western champ, and the Big Ten champ.

But if the AAWU didn't exist then and was replaced by the Airplane Conference, all bets were off. In fact, the league proposed using the Rose Bowl to host the champion between their Eastern and Western divisions, instead of the Big Ten, whose faculty reps were already nervous about extending a Rose Bowl contract anyway, thanks to concerns about the event's overcommercialization.[21] Ohio State turned down the Rose Bowl in 1962, citing these same issues. This, of course resulted in the decommercialization of the bowl game and a return to—nah, I'm just kidding. It's even bigger now.

Given the status of the Airplane Conference, and the quality of teams at the top for the 1960s, this may have very well been the closest thing to a national championship game the sport would have had. Under this agreement, Penn State would have likely played USC instead of Ohio State, guaranteeing an Airplane champ in the 1968 season.

Locking down the Rose Bowl, along with a number of the biggest and most profitable teams in the country (USC, Notre Dame, Penn State, for starters) would have given the Airplane enormous clout, politically, and financially.

The television market for college football wasn't nearly as robust as it is in the 2000s, but it was starting to mature by the late 1950s. With the closest things to national programs in tow, along with heavy presences in major markets like LA and across the East, the Airplane could have become a dynamo, even under the draconian rules the NCAA enforced regarding who could sell TV rights.

Even if they weren't able to completely exploit their TV dominance, the size, scale and clout of the Airplane would have been advantageous in negotiating lucrative scheduling arrangements and other bowl appearances, perhaps locking them into regular spots in say, the Gator Bowl, the Bluebonnet Bowl, or the Liberty Bowl, if not other entirely new games. That leg up in exposure and revenue would have helped recruiting even for the least competitive programs in the conference like Cal and Stanford.

Could it have lasted forever? Who's to say? Once the TV market truly opened up after *NCAA v. Board of Regents of the University of Oklahoma* in 1984, which ended the NCAA's stranglehold on TV rights, broadcast revenues fell for several years, as the supply of televised football games suddenly outstripped demand. If Airplane membership pushed that issue into the courts sooner, for example, a drop in overall revenue could have made the significant travel costs hard to sustain over the 1970s and 1980s. Perhaps the logistical challenges involved for other sports, such as basketball or track, would have scuttled the project (the league was described in the press as attempting to be an all-sports league, after all). But it does seem safe to assume that for at least 15 years, and perhaps more, it would have been one of the very best, if not the best, league in all of college football.

So the Airplane seemed like a pretty good deal for the teams involved. But college football is, of course, a zero-sum game. Who would have been the losers in such an arrangement?

Perhaps the most obvious would be the West Coast teams that now no longer got to join the Pac-10, on account of it not existing. Washington State rejoined the conference in 1962, and Oregon and Oregon State came back in 1964. If the Airplane took off in 1960 or 1961, there wouldn't be much of an incentive to add those programs.

Being an independent in the West for a long period of time would have been harder than being an independent in the East, which had many more possible opponents in close proximity. Presumably, Airplane membership would make it harder, if not less attractive, for former AAWU schools to schedule Oregon and Oregon State. Eventually, the Pacific programs would have either needed to join the upstart WAC, which started in 1962, or the Big Sky. The WAC feels much more likely. And hey, Washington State, Oregon, and Oregon State were involved in the original WAC conversations anyway.[22] That would have given the WAC a nine-school membership, with Oregon, Oregon State, and Washington State joining Arizona State, Arizona, Utah, BYU, New Mexico and Wyoming. That isn't a great conference for the 1960s and early 1970s, but it would have offered improved depth behind Arizona State and Wyoming. The influx of larger programs may have made it easier for the WAC to get a bowl showcase before the Fiesta Bowl in the 1970s.

The other big loser would be the Big Ten, if the league wasn't able to hold on to their Rose Bowl affiliation. Without that, the conference would have to negotiate a spot for another large bowl, which might be difficult, given the segregation policies of several other bowl sites in the late 1950s, like the Sugar Bowl. It also would have removed a major cash cow that helped the league establish itself as a political and financial powerhouse in the college football hierarchy.

And even without the Rose Bowl, the Pac-10 served as a critical political ally for the Big Ten in NCAA political fights, from academics, to TV revenue allocation, to even battling against a possible playoff. Without another obvious ally, the Big Ten would need to evolve many of their positions, or face further isolation.

Plenty of excellent football was played outside of the Airplane during the 1960s and 1970s. Ohio State and Michigan, undoubtedly, would have continued to field excellent teams. Texas, Arkansas, Oklahoma, Alabama and others in the South would be been elite as well. But the balance of power would have been shifted dramatically had this confederation happened.

By the mid 1960s, conference configuration was relatively stable for the major leagues in the sport, like the Big Ten, SEC, Southwestern, Big Eight, and others. It wasn't until the early 1990s, with the financial reality of the sport changing dramatically thanks to TV and court battles, that old alliances began to shift in new directions.

The Airplane Conference was probably the last, viable proposal to unify many of the disparate Eastern independent programs, Notre Dame, and service academies, at least for several decades. It might have changed the course of bowl history, television history, NCAA administrative history, and more.

It was a move that was probably too radical, too daring, and too different for it's time. But man, it would have created some pretty great football games. And it would be decades before the collective college football world would fathom something like it again.

What if Penn was allowed to keep its TV deal?

———

So MOST OF THE STORIES in this book are about coaches or administrative decisions. That isn't to diminish the importance of players in college football history. After all, LaVell Edwards never threw a touchdown pass, Tom Hamilton never kicked a game winning field goal, and Jim Delany never ran for a touchdown. It's the players that make the plays, win the games, and go down in the record books.

But those administrative decisions play huge roles in determining where those players attend college and how successful they might be. Recruiting, stadium construction, training, coaching, all of those things cost money, and increasingly large sums of it. Your favorite team's ability to provide the infrastructure, support, and resources needed to win football games depends, in large part, on who they hire as their coach, what conference they play in, and their athletic department's ability to bring in funds. Those decisions make up some of the more interesting "what if" scenarios in college football history.

But there's one administrative choice in particular that is maybe the most influential, one that has shaped the NCAA into what it is today, helping establish it as a governing body capable of enforcing rules, rather than a toothless figurehead. It also changed the way virtually every college thinks about what has become, by far, the dominant revenue source, and perhaps the single greatest driver of change in college football: television revenue.

Our story begins in the Ivy League. Well, actually, not exactly. The schools that are commonly known as Ivy League institutions, schools like Harvard and Yale, have been playing football against each other forever. The early rules and organization of the sport sprouted from Yale, and virtually every major innovation, from the Bowl Stadium (Yale), to the marching band (Princeton), to the recruiting violation and drunken undergraduate riot (uh, everybody), can be traced to Ivy League football.

But there wasn't a formal Ivy League for years, not until 1954, well after other conferences, like the Big Ten, Southern, and Pacific Coast, had been established. Administrators at the "Big Three"—Harvard, Yale, and Princeton—were concerned that formal athletic affiliation with other Ivy schools might sully their academic brand, perhaps the single most Harvard concern possible.[1] The Big Three had no problem regularly scheduling teams like Columbia, Cornell or Dartmouth for football games, or working with them on other matters. But formalizing a conference? With mandated scheduling? That was a bridge too far for many years.

One of the schools that some Ivy Leaguers were worried about was Penn. There was always this sneaking suspicion that maybe Penn wasn't exactly on the same page as everybody else. Maybe their academics weren't quite as selective or elite, or quite as dedicated to the aversion of Big Time Sports as some of their Northeastern peers. Maybe they wanted to win at football a teensy bit too badly. Maybe they just resented getting stomped.

A future Penn athletic director would later remark, "Yale considered us part of the great unwashed. They thought they were too good for us."[2] They almost certainly weren't the only one of the Ivies to feel that way.

Whatever misgivings that other Ivy schools might have had about Penn came to a head over a critical and sometimes ugly battle over a newfangled technology that changed the very landscape of the sport. The first televised college football game was back in 1939, when Fordham defeated Waynesburg College, 34-7. A single camera was set up on a tripod near the 40-yard line, meaning the actual picture quality wasn't very good[3]. Not that enough people were actually watching to muster much of a complaint. An NFL broadcast between the Brooklyn Dodgers and the Philadelphia Eagles just a few weeks later had only 1,000 viewers[4]. Even in the Northeast, which had some of the greatest concentration of television sets listening on the radio was a far bigger draw.

But that didn't stop Penn from experimenting with the medium further. The Quakers began to broadcast some of their own games that season to tiny audiences. The next year, Penn entered into an arrangement with the Philco Radio and Television Corporation to televise all of Penn's home games, using an experimental license[5]. If viewers could get past the terrible picture quality, they saw some pretty good games. The Quakers finished 6-1-1 on the year, winning all of their home games, and finished 14th in the final AP Poll.

The Quakers made a commitment to get in on the ground floor of television broadcasting, getting their games on television before nearly anybody else. Penn broadcast nearly all of their home games over the next decade, working with multiple companies like RCA and DuMont, researching and perfecting the craft of televising a football game. But that didn't mean they were making any money off of it. Prior to World War II, televisions weren't nearly widespread, even in a city like Philadelphia that boasted a larger concentration of TVs than most other cities. Because of that, the market for television advertising was very shallow. Schools may have been able to make money off of radio broadcast fees, but the real bulk of the revenue came from ticket sales[6].

That started to change after WWII. If anything, live sports became one of the biggest reasons for anybody to buy a TV, as boxing and baseball games were increasingly broadcast in substantially higher quality. Notre Dame, one of the very few programs that could claim anything close to a national following, became the next major program to get a multi-game broadcast agreement, with their games appearing around the Chicago area in 1947, before an estimated 165,000 viewers a game, a number perhaps buoyed by Chicago area Catholic churches purchasing equipment to show Notre Dame games at parish halls. Better to have folks watching football in church than at a bar, right?

Notre Dame didn't get a major financial benefit from the contract, but they did get significant free publicity. They also were given the option to veto specific types of ads from being broadcast during their games, choosing to strike advertisements for alcohol, cigarettes, and surprisingly, laxatives[7]. This, of course, prevented the rest of the country from making the connection between being full of crap and Notre Dame football until the Charlie Weis era.

But the financial value of broadcast rights started to grow quickly. Notre Dame found itself with multiple offers for exclusive broadcasting rights, and sold them for $36,000 to DuMont[8].

The value of those TV deals started to increase with Penn as well, as their new administration was determined to make the most of it. In 1948, Harold Stassen became the new president at Penn, after failing to secure the Republican nomination for president. Stassen was an impressive man. A former governor of Minnesota, Stassen also helped write the United Nations charter, all before he turned 41. Stassen clearly wanted to be president (he would later run for the Republican nomination a whopping nine times, turning himself into a running joke in the process), but with immediate political movement unlikely, a stint in academia was inviting[9].

The match was a curious fit for Penn. The university was in the middle of an ambitious capital campaign and needed a strong fundraiser, a talent that Stassen certainly had in spades. But Stassen wasn't an academic. He wasn't a Northeasterner either, having earned his bachelor and law degrees at Minnesota, and he wasn't especially gifted at diplomacy between fellow Ivy institutions. The more elite institutions already distrusted Penn, and bringing in an ambitious, smooth-talking politician probably didn't help matters.

Stassen didn't care. He saw that the school needed to find ways to improve its financial situation, especially the athletic department, which was saddled with a mortgage of over $1.6 million on Franklin Field, where the Quakers played football.[10] And Stassen saw a solution that would not only help balance the books, but could provide additional university exposure, and by extension, exposure for Stassen. Growing Penn Quaker football, thanks to the powers of television.

Stassen's first major move was to hire Francis Murray as the new Quaker athletic director. A former All-American halfback at Penn back in 1936 who also played in the NFL, Murray was an outsider to athletic administration. He had spent the last several years working in the television and radio industries in promotion, sending another clear signal that Penn wanted to make these new industries a priority. Murray got to work trying to improve Penn football's image, from more aggressive scheduling, to expanding and promoting the school's marching band.[11]

Penn signed a $100,000 contract with ABC to broadcast all of the Quakers' home games in 1950, one that financially dwarfed anybody else in the marketplace outside of Notre Dame. Northwestern, another early adopter of televised games, was paid the same small amount the school earned in radio rights, and Oklahoma, a dominating team that just went undefeated, made a measly $3,000 from their TV rights[12]. Next, Penn decided to schedule a multiple game series with Notre Dame, along with other bigger, non-Ivy programs, like Virginia, Cal, and Wisconsin.

A product of the Big Ten himself, Stassen didn't see a disconnect between profitable, high-level football programs and academic excellence, and he made it perfectly clear that he intended to pursue both, calling his new athletic campaign "Victory with Honor." Such proclamations would have made a fan at say, Michigan, or Stanford, very proud. Stassen's peers in the Northeast did not share his enthusiasm. Victory with Honor, after all, still meant victory, which implied that Penn was going to actually try to win football games. And Penn's peer institutions were not entirely comfortable with that.

After all, Penn gave out more scholarships than schools like Harvard and Yale, a consequence of Penn's weaker ties to elite prep schools in the region and higher percentage of public school graduates on the team. Even though Penn was not a public school, state law also allowed state senators to nominate students for scholarships at the institution, a practice that rankled Harvard so much that the Crimson refused to schedule the Quakers, even though it provided only a marginal benefit to the football program (the scholarship program only produced seven Quaker lettermen)[13].

The Stassen push also came at a time when Penn was already crushing their Ivy peers in football, and as other Ivy schools were deemphasizing football even more after World War II. Under head coach George Munger, only Cornell and Princeton had managed to beat the Quakers, and Penn was a regular in the AP Poll. The scheduling of Notre Dame also brought out some good ol' fashioned racism, as one critic of Stassen wrote, to the Penn Board of Trustees, "Mr. Stassen is having difficulty in subduing his [...] wishes to ingratiate himself with the Roman Catholics.[14]" For what it's worth, Stassen was a Baptist.

Ivy League institutions weren't the only ones concerned about these television developments. Athletic directors all over the country were worried, as attendance had started to dip around 1950. Schools that were broadcasting on some level across the country, from Washington to Oklahoma to UCLA, reported losses in their weekly attendance. The impact was particularly pronounced along the East Coast, the part of the country that had the highest concentration of TVs. From 1947 to 1950, football attendance at Ivy League schools dropped by a whopping 25 percent. Between 1949 and 1960, ticket sales dropped by over 28 percent in New England[15].

Asa Bushnell, commissioner of the Eastern College Athletic Conference, warned that "television is the scientific method which has been developed to consign all athletic directors to the Smithsonian Institution and to make football stadiums of interest only to archaeologists."[16]

The Ivy League and Northeasterners weren't the only ones sounding alarms though. Bernie Moore, commissioner of the SEC, also worried about TV's potential to limit attendance, and somewhat ironically for the South, clamored for national policy to reign it in. Like the Big Ten, the SEC agreed to ban television broadcasting in 1950, although Georgia Tech ignored them and decided to show their games on Atlanta television anyway[17].

Athletic directors were wise to keep a close watch on attendance trends, since ticket sales still provided the biggest bulk of revenue. If revenue from radio rights was still relatively modest, and schools were often still paying off big mortgages from the last stadium boom, even smaller drops in attendance could have significant consequences.

But was it fair to pin those drops on television? Probably not. After all, it shouldn't be a surprise that attendance at Ivy League games dropped. Without athletic scholarships or commitment to higher level recruiting, the quality of Ivy League football dropped off substantially, and outside of Penn, nobody was really in a hurry to schedule interesting intersectional games. Who wanted to watch Penn demolish Brown, or watch Harvard punt around with Columbia, especially in a region with other professional sports options?

The simpler explanation would be that that college administrators simply didn't understand television at the time, which was understandable. Even if they weren't totally sure if television alone would negatively impact their attendance, they knew that having Notre Dame and Penn on TV everywhere could. Why would anybody head off to the stadium to watch Delaware, or Bowling Green, or Brown, the argument went, if they could stay at home and watch Notre Dame?

The NCAA didn't really have the capacity to do anything about it, though. Since it was founded in 1910, the NCAA operated on the principle of "home rule", meaning that individual schools and conferences had the authority to make regulations and penalties, not a national organization. Without sticking to this philosophy in the early days of the organization, the strongest programs in the country (including, ironically, many Ivy League schools) would never have joined. Far from the activist enforcement organization that exists today, one capable of enacting harsh penalties, the early NCAA was essentially a debating society and an advisory committee. It didn't have the standing to really tell anybody else what to do.

The first time they attempted to stray from that mission, it failed miserably.

For decades, there was no consensus as to what was appropriate for athletic aid. Under-the-table payments and subsidization had existed since virtually the formation of college football, after all, but different schools and conferences had different philosophies about what was appropriate to hand out officially. Big Ten and PCC schools favored a program that would focus on allowing schools to provide work-study options and financial aid, rather than open athletic scholarships[18]. Southern schools favored open athletic scholarships, claiming that job-focused athletic aid was biased towards schools in larger, more industrialized cities that had more possible employment opportunities. Plus, they would argue, the Big Ten and others were hypocritically subsidizing athletes on the down-low anyway, and trying to pretend that support was over some sort of principled conviction was silly. By contrast, the Ivy League programs would have preferred to just do away with this subsidy business altogether.

What followed was called the Sanity Code, which was passed in 1948. The Midwesteners got their way, as the NCAA prohibited athletic scholarships or direct subsidization for athletes, calling for students to only be admitted if they could earn admission as regular students, and for aid to be reserved for financial need. It was ambitious, difficult to enforce, and highly unrealistic, even for the late 1940s. It didn't take long at all for offenders to start popping up[19].

By 1950, seven schools, dubbed the "Sinful Seven" by the press, had been accused of running afoul of the Sanity Code, five of which played in the

South. It was a curious group, including just one actual, big-time program (Maryland), another with a reputation for running a clean program (Virginia), two military schools (VMI and The Citadel), and two Catholic schools (Boston College and Villanova). The NCAA membership voted on what to do with the seven offenders, who were hardly repentant. Virginia called the rule "hypocritical", and Maryland's colorful athletic director, Curley Byrd, loudly defended the Terps[20]. If two-thirds of the membership voted to actually enforce the Sanity Code, the seven schools would have been expelled from the NCAA, locking them out of championship opportunities. In fact, other schools in the South who weren't found to be noncompliant were considering leaving too, as they felt they couldn't follow those rules.[21]

Instead, the vote failed, and the Sinful Seven very much remained in the NCAA, badly damaging the organization's ability to be seen as an enforcement arm. The Sanity Code itself was quickly scrapped, replaced with legislation allowing for athletic scholarships later in the 1950s. After such a major embarrassment, it would take an enormous amount of political capital for the NCAA to attempt another enforcement action that would threaten expulsion from the group.

But the perceived television threat certainly qualified. Powerful Big Ten schools were worried about Notre Dame dominating the airwaves in the Midwest, hurting them from a recruiting and financial perspective[22]. Ivy League schools, whose administrators just so happened to dominate the NCAA's new committee on television, feared Penn for similar reasons[23]. Everybody else was worried about nationally televised games would do to their gates, or that a new trend was coming that they weren't in a position to take advantage of. Alabama athletic director Coleman specifically encouraged action "to keep Penn and Notre Dame from being on every week."[24] Thank God administrators were willing to make the tough decisions to spare America from being subjected to Ivy League football broadcasts.

In 1950, Michigan pushed for the NCAA to break the tradition of home rule and ban schools from televising games completely, like the Big Ten had previously done. That proposal eventually morphed into a marginally less strict national policy, which earned over 95% of the vote among member institutions[25].

The new NCAA television policy of 1951 was an experimental one, one that would limit how often teams would be able to play on television (twice a year, once at home, once away), would institute regional blackouts to try and test a relationship between television and local gates, and more importantly, remove the ability for individual teams to negotiate their own TV deals. Notre Dame and Penn would need to cancel their individual TV contracts, or face expulsion from the NCAA.

Penn showed no interest in following along, telling the NCAA it intended to not participate in the NCAA plan and would go ahead and sell their own TV rights. Penn's leadership, from Stassen to Murray, thought the NCAA's plan was a violation of the Sherman Antitrust Act and wouldn't hold up in court.[26] They were both right, as the Supreme Court eventually ruled the NCAA couldn't restrict individual school's ability to sell their TV rights in *NCAA v. Oklahoma*.

Unfortunately for Stassen, that case was settled in 1984, not 1954, and being right on the merits of law would be moot if the Quakers didn't have anybody to play. The ECAC informed its membership that member schools should only play against programs that participated in the NCAA TV plan, and almost immediately, schools like Dartmouth, Princeton, and Columbia dropped Penn from their schedules, although with other major programs, like California[27].

Even worse, the NCAA informed Penn that by not participating in the plan, they would no longer be a member in good standing, and that even scheduled a vote to kick Penn completely out of the NCAA[28]. A targeted boycott might be have been avoided had Stassen, the professional politician, been a slightly better politician, but nobody was going to give Penn the benefit of the doubt. Not even Notre Dame, who agreed with Penn, but opted against making a massive public display of their fight against the NCAA. Although they did so begrudgingly, Notre Dame participated in the 1951 TV plan. The Irish wanted to see how things went with Penn before making any moves themselves.[29]

Once the boycott was on, Penn was suddenly out of options. They could pursue a battle through the courts, but that could take years, and further alienate their peers. They could decide to just keep the contract anyway, but without anybody to play against, who would continue to pay for their rights? Penn wasn't going to stubbornly keep a devalued TV deal broadcasting games against D2 teams or something just out of spite. Or Penn could fold, abandon their TV deal, and try to change the system from within.

That's what Stassen ended up doing, in part due to pressure from local media and fans. Polls showed that Penn fans wanted to continue to play against teams like Princeton and Cornell, series that would be jeopardized if Penn was kicked out of the NCAA, or if the ECAA continued a boycott[30]. Plus, once some fans connected Penn's stubbornness with Stassen's political ambitions, his capital was all shot up.

The Quakers tried a few more options after public intransigence failed. Stassen floated a compromise plan that would move control of TV rights to individual schools, instead of centrally by the NCAA, but would also require teams to "voluntarily" refrain of broadcasting nationally or locally on four different Saturdays. That way, the NCAA could still get data on whether television negatively impacted attendance, but schools, namely schools like Penn, could still benefit from the financial and exposure benefits of broadcasting[31].

But nobody else supported the plan, not even Notre Dame. Without any additional options, and without any other friends in the fight, Penn was forced to fold. They returned their advance money, and played the next season without a single game being televised, unlike Notre Dame, or even other Ivy League schools.

The 1951 NCAA plan didn't produce conclusive evidence that television broadcasts actually hurt football attendance. In fact, college football attendance started to bounce back just a few years later.[32] But the precedent had been set, and for the next three decades, the NCAA would maintain centralized control over broadcast rights. Enterprising individuals schools would, to a large extent, find themselves out of luck.

So who were some of the losers of this deal?

Unquestionably, a major loser was Penn. The Ivy League may have been on its way out as a major player in college football, but it certainly wasn't completely irrelevant yet. Penn was playing in front of crowds as large as 60,000 at Franklin Field, finishing in the AP poll, and establishing themselves as one of the stronger teams in the East. In fact, it wasn't a stretch to say that Penn was a bigger name and a stronger program than Penn State, who wouldn't truly ascend until the Joe Paterno era began in 1966.

A chance at a lucrative TV deal would have given Penn a significant advantage financially and in terms of exposure. Depending on how hard Penn would be willing to exploit those advantages, those could translate into better recruiting, facilities, and more, further widening the gap between the Quakers and peers like Cornell and Princeton.

And had that gap widened too much for the Ivy schools, the Quakers probably would have been fine. Penn fans didn't have deep attachments to every school in the proverbial Ivy League (Harvard and Yale weren't on the Quakers' schedule), and fans were excited to face programs like Wisconsin, Notre Dame, and Ohio State. With the exposure benefit of television broad-casting all up and down the East Coast, what would have stopped Penn from becoming Penn State before Penn State? Only their own ambition.

But faced with an Ivy boycott and no schedule to sell, Penn folded. Stassen left Penn in 1953, and the school forced Murray to resign shortly thereafter, as he was too closely tied the school's dalliance with Big Time football for the next administration.[33] Penn decided to double down on their affiliations with fellow Ivy League institutions, which gave them a stable conference home, but also ended any shot of being a football power again.

In 1952, perhaps influenced by major academic scandals at schools like Army and William & Mary, Harvard and Yale pushed even harder for to de-emphasize football within the Ivy group, asking for all schools to ban spring practice. Despite Penn's football ambitions, Stassen cast the deciding vote in exchange for every school in the Ivy League to play each other at least one every five years, ending the quasi-boycott against Penn.[34]

With that move, the Ivy moved from an informal confederation towards eventually becoming a formalized conference. It gave Penn security in future schedules, and secured an affiliation with schools like Harvard and Yale for the future. But it also completely ended any shot at the school participating in big time football. By the late 1950s, Penn had regressed from a rising Eastern power to one that lost regularly to crummy squads like Yale and Columbia. Had they been able to keep their television deal, it's hard to see Stassen ever making that vote, and Penn football falling off so quickly.

Another one of the biggest loser was the DuMont Television Network. DuMont was the scrappy upstart battling against established giants like ABC, CBS and NBC in network broadcasting. Unlike the other three major networks, DuMont didn't have significant cash reserves they built up from success in radio broadcasts, nor did they have the sheer inventory of affiliated stations[35]. If they wanted to compete, they'd need to be lean, mean, and have some unique ideas to set them apart.

One of those was a focus on live sports. DuMont was the first network to broadcast a full slate of NFL games.[36] They recognized early on the potential power that live sports could have on television demand. This was the network that ultimately reached agreements with Notre Dame and Penn, and the NCAA's decision forced them to exit the potentially lucrative NCAA broadcasting market.

While there were other factors at play, like rival ABC's merger with United Paramount Theatres, DuMont's failure to establish a foothold in major college broadcasting led to the network itself shutting down in 1955. Had they been able to keep their contracts with Penn and Notre Dame, DuMont may have been able to secure the production expertise to allow it to win bids over larger networks, and the cash needed to continue to grow. This would have made the network television landscape more competitive, and could have increased revenue for other NCAA member institutions much earlier. Had Penn been able to keep their TV deal, the impact would have stretched far beyond the Ivy League and the competitiveness of the broadcast television industry. It could have changed the entire structure of the NCAA, and really, all of college football.

But let's take a look at the Ivy League first. Remember, before 1954, the Ivy League itself didn't exist outside of colloquial speech or in sportswriter generalizations. "Ivy" schools did not have an obligation to schedule each other; there was no tournament, no league office, no records kept. It was Penn who managed to secure the key vote to move the grouping toward the deemphasized route of Harvard, banning spring practice.

If Penn gets to keep the TV deal, there's almost no way an Ivy League with the original eight teams is created in 1954, if ever. Even then, there was hardly perfect unity among the eight programs regarding just how they wanted to pursue football excellence. Penn, and to a lesser extent Cornell, was willing to attempt big time football at level that Harvard and Yale were not. Playing major programs on national or regional television for real chunks of money would not have been compatible with Harvard's vision of the sport, which was closer to glorified intramurals.

Best guess on what happens next? Harvard uses the extravagance of Penn as an excuse for why they can't formalize relations with the rest of the group, and the eight Ivy programs are unable to agree upon shared standards needed for a league. Harvard, Yale, and Princeton draw closer together, Penn and Cornell aim for a bigger stage, and Columbia, Dartmouth, and Brown are left to wonder if they should hew closer to the Harvard model or simply get out of football altogether.

Considering how badly Columbia and Brown would struggle over the next several decades, the idea of either program simply electing to drop the sport doesn't feel farfetched. If Dartmouth joined them, it would rob the college football world of perhaps the last great Ivy League team, the 1970 Dartmouth squad that was the last Ivy program to crack the final AP Poll. Beyond that, I'm not sure fans outside of the Northeast would notice.

The implications from this decision extend far beyond just Ivy League membership, though. It also changed the nature and mission of the NCAA. Author Keith Dunnavant told me that without the NCAA membership pushing Penn to drop the TV deal, "the NCAA, as we know it, would not exist."

Prior to the consolidation of power around television rights and revenue, the NCAA was pretty toothless as far as enforcement was concerned. They could censure a member, the parliamentary equivalent of sending a mean tweet, or they could vote to expel, a measure that nobody was going to take seriously after the NCAA's first attempt at expelling failed. But the whole affair established precedent for the NCAA to take control, now the group was armed with legislative muscle, as well as a genuine carrot and stick, access to TV.

That helped create momentum for more of a centralized governing structure of the sport. Television access and money, after all, wasn't controlled by conferences, but by the NCAA, which included the wide spectrum of membership, from superpowers like USC and Michigan, to Ivy League schools, to tiny ones like Hofstra. That led to smaller schools, at least for a while, having an outsized role in decision-making and exposure. The NCAA TV deal forced TV networks to carry small-school games at the expense of bigger name programs, even when demand wouldn't have supported it. Later, legislation favored by smaller programs, like restrictions on coaching staff sizes, and even scholarship limits, would change the nature of the sport entirely.

Dunnavant argues that this can't happen without the NCAA controlling TV revenues, and that doesn't happen without Penn's TV deal getting smacked down. Had Penn been allowed to keep it, "We'd see legislation be driven more at a conference level."

In 2017, we're starting to see this a tiny bit, as the power conferences have been given additional autonomy in NCAA legislative affairs. but that wasn't the case in the 1960s and 1970s. Freed from having to care about what smaller schools thought, conferences like the SEC, Big Eight and SWC, and maybe even others, could have decided to keep unlimited scholarships even farther into the future.

The ability to recruit massive numbers of players was instrumental in the success of programs like Nebraska, Maryland, Oklahoma, and others across the South. Rosters of well over 100 were not uncommon. Scholarship reform dramatically increased the parity of the sport, freeing up talent that might have just gone to the top ten programs or so to play for dozens more. If you're a fan of, say, Kansas State or Indiana, and you're mad about college football already being a bit of an oligarchy, imagine if Texas could still sign 120 kids. Just making a bowl might be hard.

Projecting the financial impact of a slew of individual and conference-driven TV deals over decades feels like a bit of a fool's errand, but it is worth noting that after *NCAA v. Oklahoma* broke up the NCAA TV monopoly, TV revenue plummeted for several years. After all, schools enjoyed the benefits of NCAA monopoly pricing, and while a sudden proliferation of games on TV was great for the consumer (especially if they had cable!), it wasn't great for schools that depending on that revenue to fund large athletic departments.

I think it is certainly possible that once other schools figured out Penn could keep a TV deal in the early 1950s without football stadiums being relegated to the dustbin of history, the market for games would become very crowded, driving prices down. Non blue-blood schools that especially benefited from hefty rights fees may not have been able to enjoy as much of a financial windfall in a world without centralized TV control.

All in all, the early discussions about TV revenue may very well be the most important decisions in college football history that we don't think about much anymore. It brought to the surface many of the anxieties Big Ten schools still harbored towards Notre Dame, a jealousy that still hasn't completely gone away.

It helped create a tradition of centralized power in the NCAA, one that led to the negotiation and control of TV deals, investigations and punishments (from TV bans to Auburn in the 1950s, to the Death Penalty to SMU in the 1980s, to the aborted attempt to penalize Penn State in the 2010s), shifting power away from conferences and major powers throughout the 1950s through the 1980s. It helped end the national aspirations of Penn, formalized the Ivy League, and kept a door open for national greatness that Penn State would eventually waltz right through. And of course, it set the table for how the quest for TV money would drive nearly all major college football decisions in the future.

Were these decisions for good? Even now, it's hard to say, unless you happen to be a Penn Quakers fan who wishes they could make a run at the Rose Bowl. But you certainly can't ignore them.

What if Nebraska never hired Bob Devaney?

———

COLLEGE FOOTBALL REALLY MIRRORS AMERICA is lots of important ways. It informs us of our substantial regional differences, from north vs. south, urban vs. rural, legend vs. leader, and more. It's expansive, entertaining, corrupt, and everybody knows it, yet can't look away. And like in American society, class mobility is actually much harder than you'd think. There have been a few exceptions of smaller schools playing their way into major conferences and major paydays, most recently with Utah and TCU, and with programs like Arizona State and Florida State elsewhere in college football history.

But very generally, the mechanisms of the sport fight to make it even harder for underdogs to make lasting gains. With a smaller team from outside the power structure, like a Wyoming or a Marshall, any claim to true national recognition is drowned out with calls of "they ain't played nobody", while a lack of a true, inclusive playoff system make overcoming those objections nearly impossible. For every Utah that managed to get hot at the right time and get themselves into the Pac-12, there are plenty of Boise States in college football history, winning lots of games, but never really bettering their class. Personally, I blame the blue turf.

Many, if not most of the teams that were good at the start of college football are still pretty good today. A look at the AP Polls from the late 1930s provides many familiar names, such as Ohio State, LSU, Alabama, Washington, Notre Dame, Michigan, and more. There are a few schools that don't participate in FBS anymore (sorry, Santa Clara, Dartmouth, and Holy Cross), and a few that probably won't ever reach such a high station again (sorry, Northwestern and Texas Tech).

One of the big reasons for this relative inelasticity is geography. If a school is located near a major recruiting ground, and they were good in the early days of football, they're probably still pretty good, unless they actively messed something up, like with administrative de-emphasis, or years of horrendous coaching hires. If we look at a map of where the most high level college football players come from today, you'll see that the bulk of the recruits come from southern California, Texas, Ohio, Florida, and the Deep South. It shouldn't be a surprise then that many of the best college football programs are, in fact, in southern California, Texas, Ohio, etc. When other areas of the country produced more elite recruits, like western PA or Minneapolis, schools like Pitt and Minnesota were better as well.

There are a few examples of programs that have been able to overcome this, like Oklahoma State and Oregon, but they often involve massive influxes of donor money. If you're willing to write checks for hundreds of millions of dollars, you can overcome some of your disadvantages. Just like in America!

There have also been a few examples of programs enjoying sustained success over many years, despite not being blessed with administrative and geographical advantages. But perhaps no program has been able to rise above their perceived geographical disadvantages to reach enormous heights like Nebraska. Despite their location in a small state, without a major media center, and one that never produced a ton of great college football players, not only did the Cornhuskers rise to eventually dominate their conference, but they reeled off one of the greatest runs in college football history, and can stake a claim to perhaps having the very best single team in the modern era.

And if they hadn't hired Bob Devaney, it might have never happened. And they definitely almost didn't hire Bob Devaney.

Let's be clear about one thing up front. Nebraska pre-Devaney wasn't exactly bad. Nebraska was coached by Fielding Yost for a season before he left for Kansas and then Michigan, where he'd become a college football legend. The Huskers also didn't record a losing record from 1900-1918.

Of course, Nebraska was far away from the centers of college football power in those days, the Northeast and the Great Lakes (Nebraska unsuccessfully tried to join the Big Ten in 1901 and 1912[1][2]), and wins over programs like Grinnell, Lincoln High School and Omaha Balloon School[3] weren't likely to give Nebraska the proper respect from the college football media and establishment.

Not that Nebraska didn't try. The 1902 squad not only finished undefeated, but they didn't give up a single point and beat major programs like Colorado, Minnesota, and Northwestern. The 1905 team dropped 102 points on Creighton. In 1910, they crushed Haskell, 119-0. Those scores, in my humble opinion, are pretty good.

Almost as good, in fact, as Nebraska's early nicknames. Cornhuskers is a pretty great college football name, inflatable mascot aside, but it doesn't compare favorably to some of their early names, like the 'Antelopes', 'Rattlesnake Boys', and my personal favorite, the 'Bugeaters', which is apparently a kind of bat. But by 1900, the school decided to stick with Cornhuskers[4].

Slowly, Nebraska started to pick up more recognition. They upset Notre Dame in 1915, picking up praise in the *New York Times*, and had their first All-American shortly thereafter. Throughout the 1920s and 1930s, Nebraska continued to produce highly competitive, solid teams, firmly establishing themselves as one of the elite programs in the Big Six conference that featured Missouri, Oklahoma, Iowa State, Kansas and Kansas State. When the AP first introduced their poll in 1936, the Cornhuskers were ranked as high as sixth, and finished the season ninth, with a 7-2 record.

Under Biff Jones, Nebraska remained a mainstay in the AP Rankings, with their crowning achievement an appearance in the 1940 Rose Bowl. [5] The Cornhuskers lost to Stanford, 21-13, in part because they were completely unprepared for Stanford's T Formation, which wasn't used in the middle of the country[6], but hey, they still made the dang Rose Bowl. The reputation and trajectory of Nebraska football seemed to be on the up and up.

And then, after 1940, a funny thing happened to Nebraska that hadn't really been an issue over the last 40 years. They weren't consistently good at football anymore. In fact, they kinda sucked.

From 1941-1961, Nebraska finished in the AP Poll just once, and appeared in just one bowl game. They posted just three winning seasons over that stretch, never winning more than six games.

So why was a team that was consistently good for decades suddenly... not good?

There are a few possible reasons. One would be coaching attrition. The Cornhuskers were changing coaches every five or six years for decades, which isn't a problem if you're constantly able to hire another amazing coach. But by the 1930s, Nebraska's luck began to run out a bit. Dana Bible, who arrived in Lincoln in 1929 from Texas A&M, enjoyed quick success, winning the Big Six conference six out of eight seasons, and a true Cornhusker dynasty looked inevitable. But Bible left after the 1936 campaign, a year which saw a 7-2 Nebraska squad finish #9 in the final AP Poll. Bible returned to the Lone Star State, taking the job at Texas for a hefty raise, a move that rankled local sportswriters and administrators, especially since Nebraska was already a well paid position in the industry[7].

Bible was replaced by Biff Jones, a college football Hall of Famer who was so tough, he stood up to Louisiana Governor/Actual Tyrant Huey Long while coaching the LSU Tigers, resigning after an argument over whether Long should give a motivational speech at halftime in the locker room[8]. A West Point grad, Jones also had a distinguished military career, retiring at the rank of Major right before he accepted the Nebraska job.[9] On paper, Jones seemed like a perfect fit, marrying coaching experience at Nebraska's chief rival, Oklahoma, along with a military discipline and toughness. At first, things went quite well, with the Cornhuskers winning the Big Six in his first season, and then making the Rose Bowl in 1940, an achievement celebrated in Lincoln like a national title, even though the Cornhuskers lost to Stanford. Bob Devaney would later remark that he was in Lincoln for years before he learned they actually lost that game.[10]

But Jones' toughness and rigidity also alienated boosters and others in the Nebraska community. Following the 1940 Rose Bowl loss, the Huskers dropped to 4-5 in 1941, a year that included a near unthinkable five game losing streak, with losses to bad Indiana, Kansas State and Pitt squads. Whatever momentum had been gathered from the Rose Bowl trip had been immediately squandered.

Of course, right after the 1941 football season, Pearl Harbor was bombed, and what happened with Nebraska football suddenly became a teensy bit less important. Jones jumped back into the military service[11], even though he had just signed a contract extension[12], and Nebraska suddenly needed to replace not just a football coach, but administrators, players, and staff members, as men were needed for the war effort.

That leads to the second possible reason for Nebraska's demise. Unlike many other schools, Nebraska did not have a Navy pre-flight program on campus. So while other schools, like Notre Dame or Iowa, enjoyed access to a steady stream of athletes who were training on campus, Nebraska did not[13]. Their recruiting pipeline would subsequently be savaged by the draft. The Cornhuskers certainly weren't the only team to struggle because of war-time concerns (some schools simply stopped fielding teams, after all), but it did take them a while to bounce back.

Things got even worse after the war. Nebraska hired Bill Glassford, a former Pitt star and New Hampshire head coach, who sought to restore something of the culture of toughness that Biff Jones brought. Glassford pushed for a more aggressive recruiting program, especially in Ohio and Pennsylvania, but at the expense of local prospects. That meant the Cornhuskers missed on one local kid they didn't recruit particularly aggressively, some guy named Tom Osborne. (SPOILER ALERT: He becomes important later.) But Glassford's recruiting efforts never led to success on the field, and his players grew to resent his brutal training methods.

By 1961, Nebraska was in disarray. They weathered an embarrassing, and too-public, player revolt. They had an alumni and fan base that expected winning teams, but hadn't enjoyed them for the better part of two decades. They lacked top-level facilities, they had fallen badly behind their conference rival, and their demographic disadvantages looked only more stark. Husker coach Bill Jennings, dejected after years of struggling, said "I've been watching things closely, and I don't think this state can ever be great in anything."[14] This was not a program that looked to be on the precipice of decades of success, even dominance.

But then they hired Bob Devaney.

But first, they almost didn't hire Bob Devaney. He certainly wasn't the top choice of the administration, or maybe even the third choice. The Cornhuskers had a new athletic director, Tippy Dye (who, I am obligated to mention, was an excellent quarterback at The Ohio State University, defeating Michigan three times) and wanted to make a splash.

Dye was coming to Lincoln from Wichita, and it was assumed he would go after his old coach for the Shockers, Hank Foldberg[15]. Foldberg had just finished back-to-back 8-3 seasons at Wichita, both with Missouri Valley Conference championships, and took the Shockers to the 1961 Sun Bowl, which they lost to Villanova. Given his ties to the Midwest, recent success, and positive working relationship with Dye, nobody would have batted an eye if he ended up taking the Nebraska job.

But he didn't. A Texas A&M graduate and former player, Foldberg decided to return to his alma mater, where he took a job coaching football and serving as athletic director[16]. He told his players it was the only job he would ever leave Wichita for. Maybe he shouldn't have left, as he wasn't particularly successful, finishing with a dismal 6-23-1 record over three seasons at College Station. He was replaced by Gene Stallings, and left the college sports world for a career in real estate in Arkansas in 1965[17].

After striking out with Foldberg, Nebraska decided to shoot a little farther north. Working with Nebraska chancellor Clifford Hardin, who previously taught at Michigan State, the Cornhuskers tried to gauge the interest of successful Spartans head coach Duffy Daugherty. Daugherty indicated that he wasn't interested, but did offer some recommendations about where the Cornhuskers might look instead, mentioning a former assistant with the Spartans who was now working at Wyoming, none other than Bob Devaney.[18]

But Nebraska didn't immediately heed that recommendation either. Instead, they looked with option number three, the head coach of Utah State, John Ralston[19]. In his first college head coaching job, Ralston had done a nice job building a winner in a geographically isolated town like Logan, Utah, going 31-11-1 over four seasons, including two bowl bids and two Skyline Conference championships. His contract was up, and he was looking for another job. But the California native spurned the Cornhuskers and headed to Stanford instead.

Depending on which account you read, Devaney might not have even been the fourth choice for Nebraska. Another candidate in the mix was Utah head coach Ray Nagel.[20] He did admit to being at least interested in the job.[21] After stints working at Oklahoma and his alma mater at UCLA, he was named the head coach of the Utes at just 30 years old. For some perspective,

I am 30 years old, and I am overwhelmed against middle school kids when I play Madden on my Xbox. Fortunately for fans in Salt Lake, Nagel had a better handle on the game than I do.

Utah was a tough job in the early 60s, but even as a very young coach, Nagel enjoyed some success. He finished with a .500 or better record in three of his first four seasons in Salt Lake. Depending on which account you read, either Nagel turned the Nebraska job down, was simply a candidate, or was kept in the background in case Devaney was unable to accept the position[22]. Either way, Nagel stuck around Utah for a few more seasons, then left after the 1965 campaign (one where he finished 3-7), to take the job at Iowa.

So that leaves Devaney. On paper, it isn't hard to see why he would have been a candidate worth pursuing for Nebraska. In addition to the recommendation from Duffy, and some personal connections Devaney had with university administrators, he had also experienced strong success on the field. Wyoming wasn't exactly a gut and rebuild job when Devaney got to Laramie, but after an adjustment year in his first campaign the Cowboys won the conference four straight seasons, won the Sun Bowl over Hardin-Simmons in 1958 (this was a bigger deal in 1958, I promise), and cracked the final AP Top 20 in 1959.

But the fact that Devaney's career had reached this point at all was pretty surprising. Unlike other major coaches, Devaney didn't play college football at a big name program under a big name coach. He spent a few years after high school working in factories around Michigan before playing at tiny Alma College. He spent the next several years coaching high school football in Michigan and attributed his big break —joining the Michigan State coaching staff as an assistant—to his being home from vacation at just the right time.[23] Devaney didn't get a college coaching job at all until he was 37.

But Nebraska wasn't able to easily pluck Devaney out of Wyoming, even when both parties were interested in each other. Before coming to Wyoming, Devaney had reportedly been promised the job at Missouri, before things fell apart at the last minute[24]. And while coaching the Cowboys, Devaney also kicked the tires on openings at California and Maryland[25].

Even once the two sides had agreed, Devaney was still under contract, and Wyoming wasn't so sure they wanted to let him out, even after it was clear he wanted to coach elsewhere[26]. After all, Devaney had just signed a new five-year deal after the 1960 season, and a source at the school told the *Omaha World-Herald* that "Wyoming will live up to its bargain and expects Devaney to honor his obligation."[27]

Nebraska's intention to hire Devaney made the newspapers by early January 1962, but thanks to "serious objections" raised by some Wyoming trustees, the board decided to postpone a vote for a month, an action that surprised the coach. "It's just a matter of what the board decides to do," Devaney would tell UPI. "I told the people at Nebraska I would like to come there, pending my release, but it's up to the Wyoming trustees."

Devaney didn't just sit on his thumbs over that month, touring the state of Nebraska, visiting campus, talking to recruits, and generally acting as if he was coaching the Cornhuskers, even though his contract said otherwise. Finally, on February 2, the board voted 8-4 to allow Devaney to leave, but not without taking one final shot at Nebraska and Devaney in the press. The Cowboys then hired Wyoming assistant Lloyd Eaton.

Based on a reading of newspapers from Lincoln to Laramie to Salt Lake, it doesn't look like Wyoming was too serious about actually preventing Devaney from taking the Nebraska job. After all, forcing a coach to stick around who doesn't want to be there seldom works out. But after losing two consecutive coaches to bigger jobs once they enjoyed some success, they may have been in the mood to just act out a little bit.

On February 2, the Wyoming board voted 8-4 to allow Devaney to leave, but not without taking one final shot at Nebraska and Devaney in the press.[28] With the last bit of drama behind them, Devaney took to Nebraska, and at started to face the daunting rebuild job in front of him.

For starters, Nebraska had fallen dramatically behind their Big 8 peers when it came to football facilities. In his biography, Devaney was shocked at how much worse the facilities were when compared to Wyoming, a school that didn't even have a formal alumni or booster club (Devaney said "one old rich guy would just give us $10,000 a year[29]"). The last bit of advice Jennings gave to Devaney was to "get himself a real football office."[30]

Nebraska also needed a culture reboot, as players were burned out from the constant practices, scrimmages and internal competition from the

Jennings era. Devaney would occasionally stop practice not to chew players out (although he did do that occasionally), but to tell a joke. The idea that football, which allegedly is still a game, should actually be fun was a bit of a revolutionary concept in the coaching community at the time. Still is, to be honest.

Devaney was also worried about the initial talent he inherited. He wrote, "When we first saw the players, we were disappointed. We thought we were going to have a crappy team." Later, when asked why they thought jumping from Wyoming to Nebraska was a good idea, assistant Jim Ross quipped, "If we didn't win here, it'd be the dumbest thing we ever did in our lives[31].

Certainly, building a national powerhouse wasn't the initial goal. Said Devaney, "My goal was to have a winning program so I wouldn't get fired. I wanted to win just enough games to please the alumni but not so many as to draw an NCAA investigation."[32]

Fortunately for Ross and Devaney, their initial scouting report was a bit overly pessimistic, as the Cornhuskers began to rebound quickly. The coaching staff could focus on bigger goals than just trying to stick around until next season.

Paced by an offense that finished in the top ten in the country in scoring offense, Nebraska finished the 1962 season with a 9-2 record. They traveled to Ann Arbor, not far from Devaney's old high school stomping grounds, and beat Michigan, 25-13 (this win looked a lot more impressive in week two than it did by the end of the year, since the Wolverines would get shut out five times and finish with a 2-7 record). They scored on Missouri for the first time in four years (it was off an interception return, but those still count), and knocked off Kansas and Iowa State. Their reward? An invitation to the Gotham Bowl, marking the first time the Big 12 earned three bowl invitations.

The actual Gotham Bowl was an awesome football game, with Nebraska out-dueling a Miami (FL) squad quarterbacked by George Mira, one of the best in the country that season, 36-34, giving the Cornhuskers their first bowl win.

Everything else about that game was an abject disaster. Nebraska was a late addition to the game, as bowl organizers struggled to find an opponent for the Hurricanes. Newspapers in New York City were on strike, effectively neutering local interest, and there were concerns that the game would not be financially solvent enough to pay Nebraska a guarantee. In fact, the plane carrying the team was delayed, as the university wouldn't let them take off until the check from the game cashed.[33] Thanks to horrible weather and poor organization, only 7,000 people[34] actually showed up to watch.

It shouldn't be a surprise, but that was the last Gotham Bowl ever played. But Nebraska got a trophy, a chance to see New York, and some much needed momentum. Future bowl trips would go a bit more smoothly. And there were a lot of them in Nebraska's future. The Cornhuskers made bowl games in each of their next four seasons, and nearly won the national title in 1965, finishing undefeated in the regular season before losing to Alabama in the Sugar Bowl.

After back to back 6-4 seasons in 1967 and 1968, years that saw Devaney retool his recruiting and offensive schemes, the Cornhuskers came roaring back, hitting the peaks of his already illustrious career. But the best was yet to come. From 1970 to 1972, Nebraska won two national titles, and came within a whisker of a third, instead settling for an Orange Bowl win and a 4th place AP poll finish. They beat Oklahoma in one of the most celebrated college football games ever. They avenged their loss to Alabama. They won a Heisman Trophy (Johnny Rodgers, in 1972). And then Devaney left, at virtually the top of his game, handing the keys to the kingdom to his offensive coordinator and schematic braintrust, Tom Osborne.

When the dust settled, Devaney and Osborne transformed Nebraska from a pretty good program in flyover country, to a national title contending, elite program that could pull kids from all over the country. As Nebraska's athletic director from 1967-1993, Devaney pushed for infrastructure upgrades with multiple sports[35], helped expand Memorial Stadium (and launched its famous sellout streak), and cemented Nebraska as one of the premier athletic departments in the country. Devaney won eight Big Eight titles, finished 6-3 in bowl games, and had a winning record against every Big Eight opponent except Oklahoma.

Would that have happened if Nebraska hired one of the other candidates?

It's worth taking a closer look at why Devaney was successful. A former high school coach in Michigan, Devaney was able to work his Midwestern ties, along with those on his staff, to aggressively recruit in the Midwest and

Big Ten footprint. During the 1960s and 1970s, Big Eight (later Big 12) schools could offer more scholarship than Big Ten schools, sometimes dramatically more. In the early 1960s, the Big Ten passed legislation locking each recruiting class at 30 kids. But the Big Eight had no such rules, and Nebraska sometimes took as many as 60 kids in a class, giving the Cornhuskers an additional advantage on the trail. "We felt there was a lot of sense in signing a large number of players," Devaney said. "If you only sign a small number and you're wrong on a few prospects, you're in trouble. But the size afforded us a certain measure of safety." Other major programs, like Alabama, agreed.

Those recruiting pipelines were augmented with others established in California once Tom Osborne was elevated to offensive coordinator, and with a relentless effort to recruiting and selling Nebraska football across the entire state of Nebraska.

Devaney certainly wasn't an untalented schematic mind, but his biggest successes could probably be attributed to his skills as a recruiter, motivator, administrator, and developer of coaching talent. He also had the good sense to allow Tom Osborne to serve as a graduate assistant in 1964, even though he didn't have the budget for any additional coaches (Osborne's chief compensation at the time was the ability to eat at the training table[36]). While his coaching tree produced many important names, like Monte Kiffin, one of the most influential defensive coaches in the NFL, it was the grooming and retention of Osborne that helped continue the Nebraska dynasty after Devaney left.

It's difficult to imagine Nebraska being nearly as successful had they hired Hank Foldberg. Foldberg would have had a strong relationship with his athletic director, and it's possible that he would have been able to open up new recruiting territories for Nebraska, as he had previously worked as an assistant at Purdue, Florida and Texas A&M, along with his head coaching gig at Wichita.

But there's nothing in his head coaching record to suggest that he would have been ready for the uptick in difficulty the Nebraska job presented. He won only six games in three years at Texas A&M, and was out of the athletics profession entirely just four years after he left Wichita. It seems reasonable to think that if Tye had hired his old head coach, he would be looking for a new one again in a few years, if he wasn't looking for a new job himself.

Hiring Ray Nagel probably wouldn't have worked out for Nebraska either. Like Devaney, Nagel was from Michigan, but unlike Devaney, Nagel never coached high school or developed especially strong ties to the region. He went to high school in LA, quickly enrolled in UCLA, and outside of a brief assistant coaching stint at Oklahoma, spent his entire coaching career pre-Nebraska offer west of the Rockies.

Nagel enjoyed some success at Utah, a tough job, but if he took over at Nebraska in 1962, he would have been younger than Devaney was when he got his very first college assistant job. Nebraska's administration badly wanted to win, but given the high expectations of the fanbase, a tradition of involved booster clubs, and tricky schedules, Nebraska may have been a bit over Nagel's head.

His tenure at Iowa does little to convince us otherwise. Nagel reportedly had problems with his athletic director, Forest Evashevski (he wouldn't be the first one, as Evashevski was reportedly part of the reason the Iowa job wasn't very attractive to begin with, leading the Hawkeyes to hire a young coach who just had a losing season at Utah), and that was a program with lower expectations than Nebraska. Nagel wasn't Iowa's first choice, as the program was unable to lure Bob Blackman, an Iowa native, away from Dartmouth.[37]

Nagel never really managed to put a strong defense together with the Hawkeyes, even with their offense ranged from competent to record setting, and then would later struggle with racial unrest and student boycotts.[38] His temperament and skillset appeared to be better suited towards athletic administration, where he excelled. If the Cornhuskers hired him, it's probable they would have been looking for another coach by the late 1960s.

So that leaves two other, more exciting options.

John Ralston presents a very interesting hypothetical. He went to high school in Michigan, but his real roots are in northern California, where he was born, played college football (linebacker at Cal), and started his coaching career. Ralston had a lot of success at Utah State, compiling a 31-11-1 record over four years, including a conference title, but also did it with a relatively conservative, run-focused offense, one that probably wouldn't have looked too out of place at Nebraska or many other Big Eight programs.

But when Ralston took his next job at Stanford, that all went out the window. He adopted a more pass-focused approach, which he believed better suited his personnel. He was right, ultimately leading the Cardinal to back-to-back Rose Bowl bids after years of irrelevancy, and earned his quarterback, Jim Plunkett, the Heisman Trophy. Nobody would confuse those years with say, the LaVell Edwards era at BYU, or Air Raid teams of the 2000s, but for the early 1970s, it was revolutionary stuff. Ralston would leave for an NFL career in 1972.

Could he have been successful at Nebraska? Probably! Ralston is a College Football Hall of Famer, after all, and had experience winning in rural areas. He could also have carried potential recruiting pipelines to California and the West along with him. But what offensive system he might have used is a fun intellectual exercise. Would Nebraska fans, boosters and the media have been patient if he tried to overhaul their roster with new philosophies, especially if they struggled at first? And if he decided to continue his Utah State trajectory, what happens to the rest of college football history? After all, his assistant coach at Stanford, Bill Walsh, would become the father of the West Coast Offense, influencing the passing game at every level of football for years to come. If Ralston decided to play Woody Hayes football in the Big Eight, maybe Walsh never gets his big break, and the entire schematic history of the sport changes. That's probably a book right there.

That leaves Duffy Daugherty. There are plenty of similarities between Daugherty and Devaney. Both are former Michigan State coaches with Rust Belt ties. Both have similar personalities and were famous for their sense of humor. And while Daugherty didn't reach the professional heights that Devaney would in Lincoln, he had a very successful career in his own right, although his biggest years wouldn't come until after Nebraska offered him the job in 1962.

The Spartans were dominant in 1965 and 1966, finishing 19-1-2 over both seasons, culminating in one of the most famous college football games ever, a 10-10 tie with Notre Dame in 1966's Game of the Century, one that controversially led to the Irish earning the national title in the AP and Coaches Poll. One of the first Northern schools to heavily recruit African-American players in the South, Michigan State produced some of the most racially integrated teams of the era. Plus, they cranked out All-Americans and NFL Draft Picks.

But could Daugherty have replicated that success in Nebraska? That's hard to say.

Part of what made Duffy so successful at Michigan State was his ability to recruit a truly integrated team, something that was unusual even for a Northern college at the time. While Devaney certainly recruited players from diverse backgrounds over his tenure, building a comparable program in a place like Lincoln, which was more rural and substantially more conservative than East Lansing, may have been tough to pull off, especially for a coach that didn't have the institutional buy-in of somebody who had been around for a long time.

It's also worth pointing out that Duffy wasn't quite Duffy in 1962. The Spartans were a good team, winning seven games or more four times during his tenure already, including a Rose Bowl victory in 1955, but they also struggled with inconsistency. His true stars, like Bubba Smith, either hadn't enrolled or hadn't become rotational pieces yet, and the true peak of his career was yet to come.

Daugherty was a good enough coach that predicting him to achieve success at Nebraska doesn't seem like stepping out on a ledge. Perhaps if he leaves for Lincoln in 1962, Devaney then becomes the head coach at Michigan State, reaching similar heights in the mid-60s, while competing with Ohio State and Michigan in the top-tier of the conference. Which school would be more successful by 1970 is an interesting question, as Michigan State boasted more favorable geography and recruiting options, but played in a tougher league and with stricter recruiting rules than Nebraska.

The wild card for any non-Devaney option would be what would happen to Tom Osborne. Devaney probably doesn't deserve much credit for discovering Osborne, as he asked to serve as an unpaid graduate assistant. But Devaney had the good sense to retain him, promote him, and to enjoy enough success to make him want to stick around for the next several seasons. Had another coach, perhaps one that felt more strongly about filling GA or assistant roles with "his guys", run Osborne off, not only would he be deprived of a promising offensive mind, but the odds that Osborne would want to return to Nebraska after being disrespected a second time appear to be zilch. By retaining and developing him, Nebraska ensured a true dynasty between the two coaches, one that compares favorably to most others in college football history.

Because of Devaney's ability to hire and develop assistants, recognize his own weaknesses, work as a dynamic and dogged recruiter, and some good fortune, Nebraska won multiple championships, overcame their demographic challenges, and dominated in a way they're unlikely to ever again.

In fact, thanks to rule changes in everything from scholarship limits, to academic standards, and the way that television revenue dominates the power structure of the sport, it's possible no school located in a place like Nebraska will dominate like the Cornhuskers did from the mid 60s to the mid 1990s.

Because of that, Nebraska fans should be lucky they didn't end up with the school's first choice, or even third choice, for that fateful open position. Their fate could have turned out very, very differently.

What if Arizona State lost the 1975 Fiesta Bowl?

———

THE COLLEGE FOOTBALL POSTSEASON, LIKE so much about this glorious, stupid sport, doesn't really make any sense.

Sure, in 2014, college football joined virtually every other sport in the United States by creating a playoff system to crown a final champion (after arguing about it for over a hundred years), but the three-game playoff is also joined by dozens of exhibition games. As of 2017, there are over 40 of these mostly meaningless games we call "bowls," and there would be even more if the NCAA allowed it. As it stands there aren't even enough mediocre teams to fill the bowls we have, so some games have been forced to take squads that didn't even finish with .500 records.

Not every bowl game is equally important, and it isn't too hard to figure out the games a little lower on the proverbial totem bowl. The less important games are typically played earlier in December, featuring teams from lesser-regarded conferences like the Sun Belt or the MAC. Rather than in big cities or major tourist hotspots, they're played in forgotten outposts, like Shreveport or Boise, and under ridiculous corporate sponsors, like Quick Lane, TaxSlayer, or even worse, a defunct TV show that never actually paid up (the Duck Dynasty Independence Bowl), or a digital currency people use to buy drugs or avoid taxes (the Bitcoin Bowl).

These games don't exist because people want to watch them in person. Many of them are played in half-empty stadiums, after all. They don't exist because they bring glory, or even necessarily a meaningful financial reward for every team. Some teams actually lose money on bowl trips, after they buy back tickets and pay travel expenses.

They exist because ESPN knows that folks will watch basically any college football game in December so they can avoid doing things like Christmas shopping, or talking to family members, and the Birmingham Chamber of Commerce Bowl featuring Central Michigan and Louisiana Tech creates important television inventory.

And I don't know about you, but I'm not complaining. I'm going to watch it, too. Plenty of those lower-tier bowl games are fun, year after year. If you don't believe me, go look up the last few minutes of the 2009 Humanitarian Bowl on YouTube, with Bowling Green and Idaho. You won't be sorry.

But not every bowl game is some fly-by-night affair featuring forgettable teams on a high school field. A few bowl games, even ones not actually involved in crowning a national champion, have importance and cachet that still matters to fans, to coaches, to their community, to recruits, and more. They're played in January, usually on New Year's Day, the holiday that college football owns like the NFL owns Thanksgiving and the NBA owns Christmas. You've heard of these games. The Rose Bowl. The Sugar Bowl. The Cotton Bowl Classic. Most of these bowl games started before World War II. Most of them are in big tourist-magnet type cities, and they attract big name teams, playing for a big prize, and a big piece of college football history.

Bowl games don't move between social strata. It's hard to imagine a scenario where the second volume of this book talks about the historic Dollar General Bowl. Typically, if you're an undercard bowl, you stay an undercard bowl; and if you're a blueblood, you stay a blueblood. Heck, that's pretty much how college football works, in general.

But there's been one, very notable exception: the Fiesta Bowl. What originally started as a bowl for overlooked mid-majors outgrew its original expectations, eventually challenging the bowl hierarchy and competing for the coveted New Year's Day timeslot.

Now, not only has the Fiesta Bowl played host to some of the best and most important college football games of all time, it helped change the makeup of the Pac-12, helped change the way we thought about the postseason, and even the NCAA itself.

But we're getting a little ahead of ourselves here. Let's start at the beginning. Let's try to take a look at why these crazy games exist.

The first major college football bowl game was held in 1901, officially titled the "Tournament East-West football game", and was technically held as a fundraiser for the Tournament of Roses Parade. The game featured Fielding Yost's Michigan squad, the first of his famous "Point a Minute" teams that earned their nickname for well, being pretty good at offense. Yost wanted to play Cal, but the Golden Bears had the good sense not to accept.

Instead, Michigan played Stanford, Yost's previous employer. This might have been a bit of a mismatch on paper, as Stanford's best wins leading up to the game were Nevada, and something called the Reliance Club, which sounds more like a grocery wholesaler than a football team. Michigan did what they did to everybody else they played that season. They kicked Stanford's ass, winning 49-0. The drubbing was so complete that Stanford asked to end the game eight minutes early. Michigan agreed.[1]

Was this game a success? Was the public so captivated by Michigan's mastery that they clamored for more intersectional football games? Actually no. Michigan might have been amazing, but bowl organizers also decided they were boring, so boring, in fact, that they didn't invite any college football teams the next year. Or the year after that. Or the year after that.

Instead, fearing another lackluster blowout, tournament organizers switched to polo the next year, which was also a disaster.[2] Then, they switched to Roman-style chariot races as the headlining act. In a move that could have been predicted by absolutely nobody, letting amateurs race in chariots turned out to be really dangerous! In one race, a horse died when the tongue of a chariot broke and plunged through his chest.

So the Rose Bowl ditched the chariots. But the Michigan experience apparently still scared the committee, because they tried ostrich races instead, and, in 1913, a race between an elephant and a camel. In case you were wondering, the elephant won.[3] The camel probably wasn't properly prepared thanks to his horrible out of conference schedule.

Eventually, tournament officials decided that college football is better than an assortment of animal related amusements, and they restored football as a permanent fixture of the event in 1916, when Washington State beat Brown, 14-0. The annual game became so successful that the temporary seats were insufficient, and a permanent stadium was needed on the grounds. Modeled after the Yale Bowl, the Rose Bowl was built ahead of the 1923 game.

Other cities realized that if Pasadena could enjoy the tourism and publicity benefits of an annual intersectional bowl game, then maybe they could too. Some of those early games would become some of other most prestigious bowl games, like Miami's Orange Bowl, or the Sugar Bowl of New Orleans. Others, like the Gator Bowl, first held in 1945, didn't garner quite as much prestige. It's now called the TaxSlayer Bowl.

Years later, some schools would retroactively claim other exhibitions as bowl games during this era. Perhaps the funniest example of this was the 1912 "Bacardi Bowl", a two-game series Florida played against Cuban clubs in Havana. The Gators dispatched Vedado Athletic Club 27-0, but the trouble started when they faced off against the Cuban Athletic Club. After discovering that the official was the previous coach of the CAC, and after what they perceived to be a disastrously officiated first half, they decided to stop playing the game.[4]

This was a big mistake, since stopping the game was actually illegal, as Cuba specifically forbid the suspension of a game for which gate money has been charged. Cuban authorities arrested Florida head coach George Pyle, and he was "ordered to take his team and get out of town before [they] put them in jail."[5] So, Florida's first foray in postseason play nearly ended in an international incident. It seems crazy that after this, not only did teams continue to visit Cuba to play (Ole Miss would visit, and lose, in 1921), but that the Bacardi Bowl would later become an actual, certified bowl game.

International hijinks and possible boosts to local tourism aside, bowl games were slow to grow across the country. By 1960, there were only nine bowl games—the Rose, Orange, Sugar, Cotton, Sun, Gator, Citrus, Liberty and Bluebonnet. A few others, like the Pineapple Bowl, Delta Bowl and Harbor Bowl, had started up and failed.

Why was development slow? For one, just like they are today, bowl games are risky investments, ones that require a lot of initial capital and depend on good luck with infrastructure, weather, and team selection. These were the days before fat TV contracts and massive corporate investment, and sometimes these margins were tight.

School administrative officials also struggled with how they should treat bowl games, as it's difficult to reconcile the idea of amateurism with signing up their athletes for nakedly commercial, cross-country outings. Some programs, like Notre Dame and Army, refused to participate in them. Other groups, like the Big Ten, heavily regulated appearances, limiting schools to only accepting certain bowl bids. If the supply of quality, marketable teams was going to be limited, then the supply of actual bowl games was going to be limited too. And for some schools, that was a big problem.

Namely, it was a problem for the fledgling Western Athletic Conference. Founded from bits of the defunct Border and Skyline conferences, the WAC consolidated a few of the stronger programs in the mountains, but didn't have the clout to secure much national recognition, or bowl invitations. The league's champion in that inaugural season, a New Mexico squad that finished 7-2-1, didn't secure a bowl invitation. Arizona State performed even better the next year, going 8-1, including going undefeated in league play, but also did not get a postseason invitation. They didn't earn their first until 1964, when Utah beat West Virginia in the Liberty Bowl.

This wasn't a plight unique to the WAC. If a non-power conference team didn't secure a bowl bid from the Sun or Tangerine Bowls, a bowl invite wasn't going to happen. Strong teams from other leagues, like the Southern, Mid-American, or strong independent teams (like the 1963 Memphis State team that finished 9-0-1), also did not earn postseason recognition. And the bowl invitations that did go out weren't always to the best teams. For example, the 1947 Sun Bowl featured a 3-3-3 Virginia Tech squad over better opponents, thanks to a committee member who just happened to be a Virginia Tech grad.[6] The entire process was messy, political, and certainly not purely meritocratic.

Even when the WAC, or other mid-major conferences, were able to get bowl bids, they often weren't very great matchups. The 1966 WAC champion, a 10-1 Wyoming squad that also boasted the nation's top rushing defense statistically, finished 15th in the final Coaches Poll, but only earned a Sun Bowl appearance against a 6-5 independent Florida State team. Only the 1968 Wyoming team, who finished undefeated in the regular season and finished

6th in the final polls, earned anything approaching a major bowl bid, a close loss to LSU in the Sugar Bowl.

That frustration came to a head in 1968, when Arizona was picked over Arizona State for a trip to the Sun Bowl, even though the Sun Devils clobbered the Wildcats 30-7 in the final game of the season. ASU president G. Homer Durham said afterward, "Maybe we should start our own bowl game."[7].

Enough was enough. In 1971, community leaders in Tempe decided to launch the Fiesta Bowl (over other suggested names like the Boll Weevil Bowl and the Lizard Bowl[8]), and set up a deal with the WAC to host their champion, ensuring that the days of a conference champion being home for the holidays were over. The game would be played in Tempe, even though other bowl games in Arizona hadn't worked out so well. Tom Fridena, who would become the president of the Fiesta Bowl, recounted to the *Los Angeles Times* that the previous games were "disastrous attempts [...] Salad and Copper Bowl, never got off the ground. We even tried to start something called the Goulash Bowl."[9] Can't imagine why that one didn't stick around.

But the Fiesta Bowl benefited from advantageous timing, as Frank Kush was building a powerhouse program at Arizona State. Not only would the WAC champ be sure to get a bowl game, but they'd be essentially playing a home game over the next few years.

Looking back on the bowl in 1988, Executive Director Bruce Skinner noted that because the Sun Devils won the WAC so often back in the early days, "it was easy to sell tickets, which is often a problem for a young bowl."[10] Arizona State made the first three Fiesta Bowls, knocking off an unranked, 8-4 Florida State team in front of 51,089 fans in 1971. They beat mediocre Missouri and Pitt teams the next two years, after Tulane and Houston reportedly turned down a trip to Arizona[11].

Those are all fine bowl wins, but for a team that was regularly finishing in the top 10 and dominating conference opponents like Arizona State was in the early 70s, they probably also felt pretty hollow. This was a program that was probably capable of beating much better teams, but if they couldn't secure a better bowl arrangement, how would they ever get the chance to prove it? It's not like Ohio State or Alabama were itching to play a WAC team at home.

But their luck turned in 1975. According to *The 50 Year Seduction*, Big Eight commissioner Chuck Neinas set up a deal to send the loser of the Oklahoma-Nebraska game to the Fiesta Bowl, with the winner taking the Big Eight's spot in the Orange Bowl.[12]

The trouble was, that enthusiasm wasn't immediately shared by the schools. While Oklahoma accepted the Fiesta Bowl invitation ahead of their matchup with the Cornhuskers, Nebraska did not, under the guise of wanting to focus on Oklahoma. The move upset enough fans in Arizona that a group decided to mail a crate of chickens to Nebraska's campus[13], a move that the Fiesta Bowl committee had to formally denounce, and one that led to the excellent headline in the *Chicago Tribune*, "Fiesta Chicken 'Tasteless'"[14].

(Also, unclear from all the various media reports on the story...what happened to the chickens? Did Nebraska save them? Eat them? Set them free to build a new home for themselves, free from petty squabbles between bowl boosters?)

The Cornhuskers had been expecting a bid to the more prestigious Sugar Bowl to battle with Alabama, but organizers there, reportedly at the behest of Alabama head coach Bear Bryant, opted for Penn State instead.[15] So maybe that chicken gambit worked after all, because Nebraska changed their minds and accepted the Fiesta Bowl invitation after all, once they lost to Oklahoma. The game sold out, lifting a local television blackout, as fans wanted to see what Arizona State could do against a higher profile program. After all, Nebraska and Arizona State combined for the best record ever for a bowl game outside of the Big Four. Oddsmakers were a little more skeptical about the matchup, installing the Cornhuskers as a two-touchdown favorite.

Nebraska head coach Tom Osborne was much more cautious, complimenting Arizona State on their strong team speed, and told reporters, "We'll have our work cut out for us here when we come down here for the Fiesta Bowl."[16]

The oddsmakers, as it turned out, were wrong, and Osborne was right. The Fiesta Bowl was an absolute battle.

The two teams battled back and forth all day, but the Cornhuskers held a 14-6 lead heading into the fourth quarter. Facing a critical 4th and one at the Nebraska 13, Sun Devil head coach Frank Kush initially called for a field goal attempt, only for ASU QB Dennis Sproul to beg for a chance to get the conversion. His appeal was successful, and he ran for just enough to get the conversion, although he injured his wrist on the play. His backup promptly tossed the game tying touchdown[17]. Sproul would come back later in the quarter to lead a drive leading to a field goal with about four minutes to play. Danny Kush, the son of Frank Kush, booted the winning score.

Nebraska stormed back, but fumbled the ball on the Arizona State 22 on their final drive.[18] The Sun Devils held on to upset Nebraska 17-14 and finished the season a perfect 11-0, grabbing the #2 spot in the final polls. More importantly, they established themselves as a program to be taken seriously outside of just the West, and the Fiesta Bowl as a game worth paying attention to.

A few months later, CBS convinced Fiesta Bowl officials to change the date of the game, moving it to Christmas Day for the 1977 season[19]. Because Christmas Day was on a Sunday, the Fiesta Bowl wasn't able to secure what would have been their first choice, BYU, and had to invite WAC co-champion Arizona State instead. The game itself also wasn't especially close, as Penn State, who also unexpectedly landed in the game after thinking they were going to the Orange Bowl instead, defeated the Sun Devils 42-30.

Fiesta Bowl Executive Director Bruce Skinner described his rationale: "From the standpoint of local support, the move was a nightmare, but the move was done purely for television. We thought it would give us national exposure on a good day for football because of all the people at home.[20]"

Skinner was right. The game was a smashing success on television, ending with the 4th highest TV ratings of the bowl season, beating out every other "mid-tier" bowl game, along with the Sugar Bowl. An inter-regional showdown, on a TV night all to themselves, suddenly made the game a very attractive property. NBC decided to buy the rights to the game for $400,000, smashing CBS's offer and easily making the game the most profitable outside of the Big Four, even more than the Sun Bowl, which was decades older.[21]

If tweaking the date of a bowl game could make it dramatically more profitable, why not tweak it again? How big could the Fiesta Bowl get?

It turns out, much bigger. Throughout the mid-1970s, USC began to make noise about wanting to leave the Pac-8 and try life as an independent, as they were tired of being forced to make unprofitable trips to smaller, empty stadiums at schools like Oregon State and Washington State.[22] The balance of power in the conference, from population to quality of programs, had unmistakably shifted to LA, and without reform, it could have caused another disintegration of the league. Without USC, the Pac-8 could have lost the Rose Bowl, or even UCLA. It would have been a catastrophe.

In order to keep everything together, conference administrators decided to expand the conference in 1978, hoping that the addition of new teams with large, sold-out stadiums could increase financial opportunities in the conference, and placate USC.

While a few other teams were discussed, like San Diego State[23], the conference decided to extend invitations to Arizona and Arizona State, who were winning a lot of games, and more importantly, playing in front of big crowds that weren't that far away from LA.

Not everybody was in love with the move. A Stanford official called the whole affair "one of the crudest power plays I've seen in some time."[24] But it did ensure the stability of the Pac-8, and kept USC from bolting. Without the Fiesta Bowl giving Arizona State increased exposure, especially the huge upset over Nebraska, it is possible those invitations are never sent.

After the Arizona schools left the WAC, the Fiesta Bowl ended their relationship with the conference, opting to go totally independent. The 1978 edition, for example, featured a 10-10 tie between Arkansas and UCLA. The bowl would host multiple other big name teams, like Ohio State and Penn State, but Skinner and the rest of the Fiesta Bowl leadership weren't satisfied. They wanted more.

"Our goal was to put ourselves in a position to stage a game for the national championship," Skinner said later, "but the only way we could possibly accomplish that was to move to New Year's Day. You weren't anybody unless you played on New Year's Day, and we wanted to be somebody.[25]"

Of course, moving your bowl game to Christmas was one thing, but moving to New Year's was a much more controversial decision. After all, New Year's was the hallowed and exclusive ground for the Big Four bowls, which had been played on that date since the beginning. It would be encroaching on tradition, after all.

But a window of opportunity presented itself. Skinner learned that the Sugar Bowl was planning to shift to prime time in 1981, leaving only the Cotton Bowl as an early afternoon game. With the support of their broadcast partner NBC, the Fiesta Bowl petitioned the NCAA, who certified the bowl games, to move the Fiesta Bowl date.

The move was risky for everybody. Sure, the Fiesta Bowl had staged some memorable games and hosted bigger name teams, but it was still an upstart brand that lacked the history and longevity of the Cotton Bowl. There was the risk that they'd get crushed in the TV ratings, directly trying to compete with the SWC champion.

The NCAA wasn't thrilled about the idea either, but after checking with their lawyers the NCAA realized they didn't really have the standing to prevent the Fiesta Bowl from switching the date—at least, not without potentially inviting a costly legal battle.

"The attorneys advised us we'd be treading on thin ice to try and keep the Fiesta off New Year's Day,"[26] NCAA Bowl advisor Dave Cawood said. Bruce Skinner was more blunt, later telling a reporter "The NCAA legal counsel actually fought that battle for us. They knew they couldn't stop us."[27] So the NCAA capitulated, and allowed the 1982 game to be played in January.

The experiment was a success. Over 71,000 fans showed up to watch Penn State knock off a sluggish USC squad in Heisman winner Marcus Allen's last collegiate football game. Both teams walked away with over $630,000 each, and the Fiesta Bowl knew it could compete head to head against nearly any other bowl game. Television noticed, with NBC kicking in over $1 million in TV rights after 1984, more than doubling what they were making just a decade before[28].

To go from accepting the hometown mid-major and hoping for the best to bringing in top-ten squads and major money would be a remarkable success for any bowl game, but Fiesta officials weren't content to just squirm their way into the top echelon of bowl games. They still wanted more. They wanted to host a game with national championship possibilities, rather than just a fun game with two very good teams.

In the mid 1980s, that was almost an impossibility, no matter what kind of TV ratings you could pull or what kind of financial incentives you could provide to a possible team. After all, most conference champions were contractually obligated to play in a specific game. If you won the Big Ten or the Pac-12, you had to play in the Rose Bowl, even if the Orange Bowl offered you an enormous novelty check that doubled whatever the Rose was offering. If you won the Southwestern, you played in the Cotton Bowl. If you won the SEC, you played in the Sugar. If you won the Big Eight, you played in the Orange. And if you won the Mid-American, well, nobody was paying attention. You probably got a trophy.

So there often wasn't an actual national championship game. Instead, there'd be a series of almost-but-not-quite championship games, leaving everybody to holler about who was actually #1. If you were lucky, things broke just right to set up a #1 vs. #2 matchup in one of these bowls, like in 1982, when Penn State squared off against Georgia in the Sugar Bowl. But from 1936 to 1986, the #1 and #2 teams met in a bowl game just six times. Every other year, the matchups wouldn't line up evenly, and there wouldn't be an agreement over who the champ actually was. Thus, Alabama can at least half-plausibly claim a gazillion national titles.

This system sucked. The only people who liked it were bowl executives and crusty newspaper columnists who got paid to complain about it. And maybe Alabama, I guess. But as luck would have it, a perfect storm would arrive in the 1986 season to potentially change this system.

The preseason top team, the Oklahoma Sooners, tumbled out of the top spot thanks to an early season loss to the Miami Hurricanes, who took over and would not relinquish the spot. The preseason #2 team, Michigan, looked to be in excellent position with only two weeks left in the year, before they were upset by 25-point underdog Minnesota. Alabama, who also held the #2 spot for several weeks during the season, lost by 20 points to Penn State. By the end of the regular season, the Miami Hurricanes and Penn State Nittany Lions were both undefeated, and sat #1 and #2 in the polls.

Both teams were operating as independents, as Penn State had yet to join the Big Ten and Miami had yet to join the Big East. And both teams wanted a shot at each other for an actual national championship game. That knocked the all of the Big Four bowls out of contention, with their conference championship contractual obligations, and opened things up to other bowls to try and secure the arrangement.

The Fiesta Bowl had shown to the bowl world that upward mobility was possible, and now, they suddenly had competition to try and lock down Miami and Penn State. The Citrus Bowl, formerly known as the Tangerine Bowl, when it hosted teams from the MAC or other mid-majors, was also determined to make a splash and made it known they'd engage in a bidding war to secure a potential championship game.[29] Before the prospect of hosting a potential title bout, the Fiesta Bowl planned to give out roughly $1.2 million a team. But with the Citrus getting involved, the going rate jumped to around $2.5 million, and that didn't include perks like hotel rooms or other arrangements.

Officials at the Fiesta had to get creative. They weren't going to get any additional television money from NBC, and they couldn't simply raise ticket prices enough to allow them to outbid anybody else for a premier matchup. And without comparable financial guarantees to the Big Four, no other bowl game would be able to climb higher up the proverbial mountain.

But the Fiesta had an innovative solution that gave it even more flexibility, the first significant corporate sponsorship of a bowl game. By 1986, it wasn't just the Fiesta Bowl, after all, but the Sunkist Fiesta Bowl, and bowl officials were able to use extra money from their new corporate sponsor to remain competitive with the Gator and Citrus Bowls.[30]

Skinner would later say, "If it wasn't for Sunkist, Miami/Penn State [...] would have never happened."[31]

And that matchup was a rousing success, on every level. The game date was tweaked again for the benefit of TV, moving it to January 2 so the Fiesta Bowl had everything all to themselves. The move worked. The game was ratings gold; NBC claimed it was viewed in more households than any college football game in history, roughly 21.9 million homes[32]. NBC even managed to get an interview with President Reagan at halftime.[33] The bowl also presented fat checks to both participating schools, and hotels, restaurants, and bars across the greater Phoenix area.

And hey, the actual football game was pretty good as well. The Hurricanes dominated the game in total yardage, outgaining Penn State 445 to 162, but turned the ball over an astonishing seven times, including five interceptions from Hurricane quarterback Vinnie Testaverde. Penn State essentially only had one sustained drive of the entire game, but it was enough to spring the monumental upset. Penn State won, 14-10, on an improbable goal line stand at the end of the game, securing an undisputed national championship.

The game proved to be exceptionally important for several reasons. Any sense of invulnerability among the most established bowl games vanished, as the Fiesta Bowl, despite being younger, could now claim just as powerful of an audience. And after hosting the de facto national title game, it could also boast prestige.

Whenever college football would formalize distinctions between bowl games, be it the Bowl Alliance system, the BCS, or the College Football Playoff, the Fiesta Bowl would be formally designated as a "major" bowl, and would host additional championship games, along with some of the most memorable bowl games in college football history. Personally, I'm partial to the 2003 National Championship Game, when Ohio State upset Miami in double overtime, a game that should be noted for its impeccable officiating, despite howls to the contrary from South Beach.

The Fiesta Bowl's rapid assent could have stopped at a bunch of different places. For one, organizers got a bit lucky that the bowl started right as Arizona State entered their most dominant run in school history. Organizers themselves admitted that selling tickets to an upstart bowl was made dramatically easier by the fact they could expect to host the hometown team several times, after all. Had a different WAC team managed to win the title in a few of those early years, like say, New Mexico in 1971, or Utah in 1973, the game may not have been able to sustain the same level of momentum, allowing it to become very competitive with guarantees needed to lure quality non-WAC teams to the desert.

But what about the 1975 game that put the Fiesta Bowl on the map?

The organizers were very fortunate to even get their premier matchup, Arizona State and Nebraska, which led to the bowl's ascendency. For starters, Arizona State didn't lock up a bid until the very last week of the season, after they beat a 9-2 Arizona team, 24-21. That 1975 Arizona squad was one of the best Wildcat teams in years, but they had also lost to an average New Mexico team earlier in the season, and struggled more in WAC play than the Sun Devils. Their SRS rating was a full four points below Arizona State's that year, and S&P+ had Arizona State four spots higher (20th for the Sun Devils, 24th for Arizona)[34] and it seems clear that had they managed to beat the Sun Devils and grab a Fiesta Bowl bid, they'd be a worse opponent. For the Fiesta Bowl's sake, it's a good thing the local Sun Devils ended up winning the day.

Their opponent was hardly assured either. Nebraska, of course, initially declined the Fiesta Bowl invite[35], as they figured they'd get a trip to the Sugar Bowl if they didn't win the Big Eight. Instead, that bid went to Penn State at the last minute[36] (Penn State lost to Alabama in the Sugar Bowl that year, 13-6). By most measures, Penn State wasn't as good as Nebraska was that season. Their offense averaged a good 10 points less a game, and Penn State's schedule wasn't quite as impressive as Nebraska's. The Nittany Lions had also lost to an average NC State squad that year, and struggled with teams like Temple. They entered bowl season 8th in the AP Poll, while Nebraska was 6th.

Had Arizona State knocked off Penn State instead of Nebraska, the win would have still carried national cachet, if maybe not quite as much, but given Penn State's stout defense (it was statistically just as good as Nebraska's) and size, Penn State very easily could have beaten either Arizona squad that season, which would have robbed the WAC, and subsequently, the Fiesta Bowl, of critical praise, momentum, and attention.

The Fiesta's assault on New Year's Day was an important commercial legacy for the business of college football, but it wasn't the only one. While fans today live in a world where rights fees from TV deals continue to rocket upwards and upwards, that wasn't always the case. Immediately following the deregulation of the NCAA television rights monopoly in the early 1980s, rights deals across football actually fell dramatically, as the supply of televised games dramatically spiked.[37]

This impact spilled over to bowl games as well, leading to a major financial crunch of organizers, especially as they were forced to continue to compete in their ability to give high guarantees to assure the participation of football teams people actually cared about. Without the ability to negotiate for higher TV rates, and with limited ability to raise ticket prices, bowls needed to figure out a way to improve revenue.

The Fiesta Bowl was the first to figure out a consumer friendly way to do that, by bringing in a title sponsor. Soon, the ability to land a corporate sponsorship was paramount to the success of the bowl. If a game couldn't find a buyer, they typically went under, even if the game had been played for decades, like the Bluebonnet Bowl in Houston. Sometimes this led to some comical bowl names. (The Blockbuster Bowl? The BattleFrog Fiesta Bowl?) Sometimes it usurped actual history and tradition, like when the Sun Bowl had to actually change its name to the John Hancock Bowl in order to stay financially afloat[38]. But compared with rising ticket prices or eliminating games entirely, simply slapping a brand in front of the name of a game wasn't so bad.

If the Fiesta Bowl hadn't figured out a way to bring in a sponsor, another bowl probably would have figured it out a few years later. But the Fiesta was the first, setting the marketplace, and paving the way for the stability and long-term viability of many postseason games.

The biggest legacy, aside from some amazing football games, was the democratizing impact of the game. College football's postseason was loath to evolve in any way for decades, to the detriment of players and fans. The Fiesta Bowl showed that just because a game enjoyed favored status back in the 1950s doesn't mean that it should get to enjoy it forever. It showed that a game having the flexibility to invite fun teams without being hewn to conference obligations is actually pretty fun. And the sudden ascendancy of the game— the thrilling upset over Nebraska, and the 1985 showdown between Miami and Penn State—helped pave the way for tiny, incremental steps towards a more equitable postseason system, like the Bowl Alliance, the predecessor to the BCS.

Somebody else would have figured out how to get a brand to slap their name in front of a postseason bowl game. But would somebody else have decided to take a head on run at the bowl establishment, and at the perfect time when the NCAA was too vulnerable to stop them? That's less clear.

The Fiesta Bowl probably got a bit lucky that everything worked out exactly the way that it did, but college football fans should be grateful, especially Arizona State fans. Those games helped give them a golden ticket to a power conference. And for everybody else, it moved a stubborn system a little bit closer to a playoff, and a little bit closer to a slightly more democratic game.

What if LaVell Edwards left BYU?

_____

As of 2017, there are 129 teams competing in FBS, the highest level of college football, as Coastal Carolina jumped from FCS to the Sun Belt. Almost all of those teams can point to some great football accomplishment or moment, but when it comes to the highest recognition in the sport, the power conferences dominate everything.

Let's take the Heisman Trophy, for example. Since 1950, only five players who weren't playing on a power conference team took home the award. Four of those happened before 1965: Princeton's Dick Kazmaier in 1951, Pete Dawkins at Army in 1958, Joe Bellino at Navy in 1960, and Roger Staubach of Navy in 1962. In recent years, the elite programs of the sport, like Ohio State, USC, and Alabama have even further consolidated the award.

The national title picture is even more starkly slanted in favor of the biggest programs. Since Army claimed the AP national title in 1945, only one program outside of a power conference has won a national title. In the era of the BCS and the College Football Playoff, the chances of an outsider somehow winning are even smaller, as a team would not only need to go undefeated, but would need mass chaos with the rest of the country, and to get lucky with their non-conference scheduling. If the College Football Playoff remains at only four teams, there's a good chance it will never happen again.

But one team managed to win both of those, along with a slew of other national awards, despite being locked out of the power conference system and having a coach who probably shouldn't have been hired in the first place. In fact, it might have been the most unlikely mini-dynasty in college football history.

That school is Brigham Young University, led by LaVell Edwards in 1984.

Prior to Edwards, the football history at BYU was not kind. In the early days of college football, while the Midwest and Northeast served as the nerve center for the sport, the Cougars were producing forgetting seasons in the Rocky Mountain Conference, losing to teams like Northern Colorado, Wyoming, and Denver. Even when the Cougars occasionally had a great season, like an 8-1 finish in 1932, their poor schedules and relative isolation in the mountains prevented them from earning any national acclaim. This continued even as BYU jumped to the Mountain States Athletic Conference, and then the Skyline Conference in 1948.

Given what kind of school BYU was, it would make sense that they'd struggle in football.

First, BYU's Provo, Utah location didn't do them any favors. Utah isn't a very big state now, but it was even smaller in the formative years of college football, hitting a million residents in 1966. The Cougars shared the state with the University of Utah, their rival just to the north that absolutely dominated them (the two squads played nearly every year, and prior to 1965, the Cougars had won exactly twice in 40 years), as well as Utah State, a program that boasted some strong teams in the late 40s and early 1960s. LaVell Edwards himself admitted that even smaller rival Utah State appeared to be a superior program to BYU when he was being recruited, leading him to ultimately pick the Aggies[1]. If the Cougars were to focus their recruiting locally, they would often find themselves as the third-best program in a small state. Plus, their relatively remote location would make playing intersectional games difficult and expensive, and generating enough media hype to make a run in the AP Poll would be even harder. Salt Lake City wasn't exactly a bustling media center in the 1950s, after all.

Plus, BYU might just be the most unique school competing in FBS. They're directly owned and operated by the Church of Jesus Christ of Latter-Day Saints, better known as the LDS Church, or simply, the Mormons. While in recent years the LDS Church has become a fast-growing, global church, back in 1960, it could only boast around 2 million members nationwide[2], most of which were heavily concentrated in Utah and the surrounding states. The number of potential athletes who would be interested in attending a Mormon university, where they would need to follow Mormon standards of behavior (no drinking, no premarital sex, etc.[3])—even if they weren't Mormon themselves—was also small.

Any school with a high number of LDS student-athletes would also need to wrestle with the roster attrition that came with players leaving to serve missions. Mormons are encouraged to spend two years providing service, teaching about Mormonism, and assisting local congregations in a different location. Missions are essentially 24-hour jobs, with no time for practicing football, little time for lifting weights, and no guarantee you'd be able to eat enough to maintain the physique needed to play football. Forget maintaining your gains. There wasn't a guarantee you wouldn't come home testing positive for tuberculosis.

For much of the pre-Edwards era, players who interrupted their BYU football careers to serve missions did not return to the roster, creating more holes for coaches to fill.[4] This was, in part, because coaches would encourage players to complete their eligibility before serving a mission, as their scholarships would not be guaranteed when they returned.

It's also worth noting that BYU had another significant recruiting restriction during most of this era. While not explicitly segregated like say, Alabama or Ole Miss, African-American students, let alone student-athletes, were nearly non-existent at BYU.[5] Early LDS teachings restricted African-Americans from full ecclesiastical responsibilities in the church, and as a consequence the heavily Mormon student body was nearly completely white. This policy would eventually become politically radioactive, as other colleges—like Stanford, San Jose State, and Wyoming—began to protest against BYU for their racial policies.[6] While the LDS church didn't formally change their racially restrictive doctrines until 1978, the protests may have helped put pressure on the football team, as the Cougars recruited their first black football player in 1970[7]and would soon become a more racially diverse squad.

If BYU was going to overcome the disadvantages of being a private, Mormon-run, essentially all white and academically selective institution in a small state, they would need superior administrative investment and support. But prior to the late 1960s, it didn't appear it was getting that either. In an autobiography, LaVell Edwards complained that he constantly had to battle rumors on the recruiting trail that the LDS church was planning on dropping BYU football, and that the coaching staff needed to sell administrators on what was needed to be successful. Staff size, recruiting budgets, facility quality, and virtually every other indicator of institutional investment lagged at BYU, not just behind national powers, but regional opponents as well.[8]

So yeah, BYU wasn't very good at football for a long time.

The hiring of Edwards, on paper, didn't appear likely to change any of that either. Edwards joining BYU's staff as an assistant coach in 1962 certainly didn't electrify the fanbase. He had spent the last eight years coaching Granite High School in Salt Lake City (where he also coached JV basketball, wrestling, and golf[9]), and never managed to record a winning season, let alone a playoff bid or anything of renown outside of Salt Lake.

In fact, the only reason Edwards was hired at all was because BYU head coach Hal Mitchell had come to the conclusion that the only way BYU was going to win anything was by doing something dramatically different. He decided to bring back the single wing offense, one that involves virtually no passing.[10] Edwards ran that offense as a player at Utah State, and also at Granite High School, but outside of Princeton, virtually nobody else in the country was using it. Edwards would later say he was "the only Mormon running the Single Wing" at the time.[11] Ironic, given that eventually, he would be famous for it, Edwards would tell a reporter that as a high school coach, "I never called for a forward pass unless it was absolutely necessary[12]"

Mitchell's thinking wasn't wrong, and BYU's offense enjoyed a bit of success, but not enough to turn the team's fortunes around. Mitchell left BYU after the 1963 season, along with the single wing, and the seeds for BYU's future offensive explosion were planted.

After years of futility trying to win using a running-oriented offensive scheme, only with inferior athletes, new BYU coach Tommy Hudspeth decided to take to the air. In 1965, paced by Virgil Carter, who threw for 1,789 yards and 20 touchdowns, the Cougars finished 6-4, good enough to win the WAC over Arizona State—BYU's first conference championship ever. It wasn't enough to qualify for a bowl game, but it was a major improvement.

Things got even better in 1966, as BYU finished 8-2, again behind Carter's arm, who picked up his second consecutive WAC Player of the

Year award. The Cougars finished behind Wyoming, who went 10-1 and knocked off Florida State in the Sun Bowl. But then Carter left for the NFL, and the Cougars didn't have a ready replacement. The program regressed a bit, and Hudspeth unexpectedly left to pursue other opportunities in 1971.[13] Hudspeth ended up as an assistant at UTEP, and quickly became the head coach, where he would face off against the Cougars. Suddenly, BYU needed a new coach.

There weren't many options for BYU to choose from, since the country wasn't awash in LDS coaches (BYU's coach had always been a Mormon, and it remains an unwritten rule), and the school wasn't going to plunk down the large amount of money needed to pry a big name away from somewhere else for what would likely be a rebuilding job, so Edwards was almost the pick by default. Later, he would candidly admit that he expected to be fired, since hey, everybody else was too.[14]

Right away, the Cougars looked to try something different. Edwards hired Tennessee quarterback legend Dewey "Swamp Rat" Warren (that's not a typo, they used that name in the newspapers and everything, which, if you know anything about BYU, is even funnier) as their QB coach, after Edwards' initial hire, Ricks College head coach Ron Rydalch, decided to back out at the last minute.[15] Warren was only 27 when he accepted the job.[16]

Dewey is notable here not just for being exceptionally young, but also for being the first man with the nickname "Swamp Rat" to do something outside of coach in the South, become an ace banjo player, or become the Governor of Louisiana.

Dewey was not shy about what he wanted to do at BYU, telling the *Arizona Daily Star,* "We're going to throw the football and I don't care who knows it. Get this straight right now. I'm not one of those wishbone guys. I'm going to find some guys who can throw it and some guys who can catch it and we're going to throw the football. We may not complete a lot, but we're going to scare the devil out of somebody. There ain't going to be no wishbone around here."[17] And there wasn't.

Of course, transitioning to an Air Rat offense (nobody called it this, but they should have) after BYU's previous run-heavy scheme wasn't something that could be easily done in one season, especially since Dewey arrived after spring practice in Edwards' first season. BYU's fastest player, Golden Richards, was ruled academically ineligible for Edwards' first campaign, and would end up at Hawaii instead.[18] It was actually BYU's running back, Peter Van Valkenburg, who carried the offensive load, rushing for 1,386 yards, leading the country that season. BYU finished 7-4, beat Utah, and finished second in the WAC, only behind Frank Kush's juggernaut at Arizona State.

Perhaps the biggest adjustments at BYU were coming behind the scenes though, rather than on the field. Edwards successfully convinced BYU's administration to make an increased financial and structural investment in the program, expanding their coaching staff from six (smaller than Utah and Utah State's), to eight, and excusing assistants from classroom teaching duties.[19]

Edwards also worked to change attitudes within the program, and greater BYU culture, about missionaries. While previous teams had discouraged returned LDS missionaries from returning to the program, or encouraged players to delay their missions until their eligibility completed, Edwards guaranteed scholarships for players who were serving, and welcomed them back. The idea that a hard-hitting, competitive football team was somehow incompatible with Mormonism began to be dispelled.

This was not a directive that Edwards, a devout Mormon himself, shied away from. Rather than looking to the restrictions or challenges that came from coaching at an LDS-affiliated university, Edwards decided to embrace them. He would even credit his time leading a student congregation while an assistant coach as beneficial to his head coaching.[20]

It took one more season to fully transition offensive schemes, as the Cougars limped to a 4-5 season in 1973, Edwards' only losing campaign in Provo. But once the Cougars adjusted to life without "Fleet Pete", and had more time to teach their offensive system to their own personnel, and expose it to potential recruits, BYU's fortunes began to turn around. And for Edwards' sake, probably not a moment too soon.

Fans, and even some administrators, could be forgiven for being a little skeptical of the schematic changes, since BYU lost their first three games of the 1974 season, including a 34-7 blowout at the hands of a not-very-good Iowa State team. They then tied an equally poor Colorado State squad, 34-34, after the Cougars fumbled the ball on a kneel-down, allowing the Rams to tie the game in the closing seconds.[21] A 0-3-1 start of the season threatened to extinguish whatever goodwill Edwards had earned. But instead of folding, a few seniors held a team meeting, the players rallied, and BYU rallied to win their next seven games, including a sweep of the Arizona schools, and a blowout win over Utah.

BYU quarterback Gary Sheide, who probably would have been playing professional baseball instead if injuries hadn't derailed his career and sent him to junior college[22], finished in the top four nationally in pass attempts, completions, completion percentage, and total yardage, and lead the entire country in passing touchdowns, with 23. The Cougars were rewarded with their first bowl invitation, the Fiesta Bowl, which they lost to Oklahoma State, 16-6, a game they might have been able to win at Sheide not gotten hurt.

After one more rebuilding year—a 6-5 campaign in 1975—the dynasty was on, thanks in part to one more inspired hire. The first two quarterback coaches of the Edwards era didn't last very long. Swamp Rat left for Kansas State after two seasons, and was replaced by Dwain Painter, who left after the 1975 season to take the QB job at UCLA. BYU had established itself as a launching pad for young offensive minds, but still struggled a bit to find the right fit for their next passing game coordinator.

Thanks to a recommendation from Bill Walsh, Edwards reached out to Doug Scovil, who had been the quarterbacks coach for the San Francisco 49ers. Scovil turned down BYU's initial offer of $19,000 (about $86,000 in today's money), as he looked for more money[23]. But by the time spring practice rolled around, Scovil still hadn't found a position, and was so entranced by what BYU was doing, schematically, that he took the job anyway after visiting the team. The offense must have really energized him to make up for what probably wasn't always the easiest cultural fit. Later, after he took the head coaching job at San Diego State, Scovil would say "they're really nice people in Provo. They just throw lousy parties"[24]

Scovil tweaked the system that Painter and Swamp Rat had established, one that now further utilized the running backs and tight ends in the passing game, and provided the blueprint for what BYU would run in the coming decades, even as the coaches continued to change[25]. And those coming decades would be dramatically successful.

BYU would qualify for bowl games in 19 of the next 20 seasons, and the one year they didn't, 1977, it wasn't because they weren't good enough. BYU finished 9-2 on the year, even finishing in the AP Poll, and would have been invited to play in the Fiesta Bowl, but the Cougars turned it down, since it was played on a Sunday.[26]

BYU also finished in the AP Poll 13 times, including twice in the top five, and won fewer than eight games exactly twice. They grabbed a stranglehold over the WAC, and after decades of domination by Utah, to the point where it could scarcely be considered a rivalry, beat the Utes 15 out of 20 times.

Of course, the biggest accomplishment during this era? The 1984 national championship.

That championship is perhaps the most controversial of the pre-BCS era, and is probably worth a quick tangent to both examine how a non-power team managed to actually win a title, and to put this achievement in a bit of context.

Some fans, particularly those in say, Seattle, or Salt Lake City, howl that BYU shouldn't have been considered for the title because of their weak schedule. Unlike the MAC or the Big West, the WAC was part of the College Football Alliance (CFA), and so could technically be considered a major conference, but only by a technicality. Nobody would confuse New Mexico, Air Force and Colorado State with even average teams in the SEC, Southwest or Big Ten.

Today host Bryant Gumble famously asked, "who did they play, Bo Diddley Tech?",[27] and after Oklahoma head coach Barry Switzer disparaged the Cougar's schedule on multiple occasions, irate fans voted to name a sewage treatment plant in Midvale, Utah, after him.[28] As passive-aggressive trolling moves go, this one was awfully strong.

Those accusations didn't come out of thin air. By the time the dust had settled, BYU's 1984 schedule certainly didn't look very good. Their four non-conference games included a 3-8 Pitt team, a 5-6 Baylor squad, a 6-5 Tulsa team, and finally Utah State, who finished 1-10 in one of the worst conferences in the country, the now defunct Pacific Coast Athletic Association. All of this along with a conference schedule in the WAC that wasn't going to impress anybody.

None of this, of course, was BYU's fault. Pitt opened the season as the preseason #3 team, and Baylor had won seven games the year before. The school basically had to play Utah State, and getting a bigger name than Tulsa was probably logistically impossible. The fact that the rest of the WAC struggled (only three teams finished with winning records, and nobody else won more than eight games) was also outside BYU's control.

The Cougars probably could have silenced a few of their critics if they just crushed the teams on their schedule, but they didn't. They beat a crummy Wyoming team by just three points. They beat Hawaii by just five, along with Air Force. And they were probably fortunate to beat Pitt to open the season as well, as they needed a furious 11 point 4th quarter comeback.

But, if winning all of your games, even against inferior competition, was easy, more teams would be doing it, and in 1984, nobody else could. All of the other best power conference teams lost winnable games, like a 9-1-1 Oklahoma team dropping a game to a below .500 Kansas team, or South Carolina, who, after reaching the #2 spot, just ahead of BYU, promptly lost to a four-win Navy team. Florida, who might have actually been the best team in the country on a per-play basis, was ineligible for the postseason[29]. If Twitter had existed for the 1984 season, it would have been absolutely insufferable.

So BYU, buoyed after beating Pitt, methodically climbed up the rankings as everybody ahead of them lost, and then lost again for good measure. By the end of the year, even if you were convinced BYU was overrated, there wasn't really a practical alternative as a national champion. Washington, the one fanbase who is probably still the most upset over BYU's title, ducked a chance to play BYU in a bowl game, and their own resume doesn't look dramatically superior to BYU's when given a closer look.

Even Edwards would admit 1984 probably wasn't BYU's best team. Advanced metrics, like S&P+, would agree.[30] The 1985 squad had a superior defense, and the Cougars would have better quarterbacks and better offenses during his run, but when you're consistently a very good team, you give yourselves more chances to catch all the proverbial breaks. If anything, the 1984 national title wasn't just the result of every possible break going BYU's way, but also a testament to the stability and continuous success that Edwards had established. If BYU wasn't a regular bowl team before 1984, they don't win a national title in 1984, undefeated or not.

Of all of the unlikely aspects to BYU's dominating run, perhaps the most unlikely was the sheer longevity behind Edwards' tenure. Typically, exceptionally successful head coaches like Edwards don't stay in one place forever, especially if that one place isn't a destination job. BYU never paid like Ohio State or Notre Dame, never recruited like Ohio State or Notre Dame, and never played in an elite conference like Ohio State or... er, Alabama.

Edwards had multiple opportunities to leave, but he never did. Three specific opportunities jump out that could have changed the course of multiple programs.

The first happened in 1976, as the Cougars traveled to Orlando for the Tangerine Bowl, a game they would lose to Oklahoma State, 49-21. The BYU dynasty hadn't really taken off yet, as BYU had yet to finish in the AP Poll, win a bowl game, and their 9-3 mark represented the best in school history at that point. But one school had taken note of what BYU had accomplished, and decided Edwards was their man: Miami.

The Hurricanes had enjoyed some success in the 1950s, but the years since had been mostly unkind to the program. There were some whispers on campus that maybe the school would be best served getting out of the football business entirely.[31] After all, a school with selective enrollment, smaller alumni base, and large percentage of international students didn't appear to be the most likely landing spot for a football dynasty.

The administration decided to make one last heavy investment, and tried to grab Edwards with a five-year, $75,000 a year package[32] (and, as one Florida columnist would later note, that goes a long way "with no overhead from Jack Daniel's and Marlboros"[33]). Edwards made $28,000 that season in Provo, and he only had a one-year deal. School policy prohibited him from signing a longer contract.[34]

But Edwards wasn't comfortable with the pressures of having the program's future rest in his grasp, and, according to his autobiography, liked Provo better, so he stuck around (although BYU did give him a raise)[35]. This ended up working out just fine for everybody. Miami would hire Lou Saban instead, who gave the program enough success and stability to get them to

Howard Schnellenberger, whose personality type and ties to the area probably made him uniquely qualified to rebuild the program. Edwards apparently agreed, later saying, "I would have gone down there and just quietly worked hard and wound up quitting or getting fired."[36]

Without any ties to the area, and with a more low-key personality, it seems reasonable to think that Edwards wouldn't have the same kind of success in Miami in 1976 than he would in Provo. Had he left then, not only does BYU almost certainly not win the 1984 title (or any of the other huge awards that came after), but Miami potentially doesn't hire Schnellenberger, which could have jeopardized their entire run in the 1980s and 'The U' ethos that permeates their program today. It would be an entirely different football program. Maybe it wouldn't be in the ACC. Maybe it wouldn't even exist. Certainly, one of the chapters in this book wouldn't exist.

Newspaper reports tied Edwards to a few other college openings, including Missouri[37]. In his autobiography, Edwards also mentions Minnesota heavily trying to recruit him during the 1980s. Newspaper reports would indicate this was in 1983[38], as the Gophers tried to replace Joe Salem, who just finished 1-10, and gave up 84 points to Nebraska and 69 to Ohio State.

According to Edwards, officials from Minnesota flew out to Provo on a jet "just to talk", and tried hard to talk Edwards into making the switch, an experience that caused Edwards to decide to not talk to other colleges about possible openings[39].

There's a reasonable argument to make in 1983 that BYU was actually a better job than Minnesota. Certainly the Cougars had been more successful. From 1972-1983, the Gophers won more than six games just once, and had only been invited to one bowl game, which they lost. While Minnesota would have been able to pay more money, and there wouldn't be an honor code to deal with, or LDS mission attrition, they'd also have to play in the rugged Big Ten, against Ohio State and Michigan, which is a step up from say, New Mexico. Also, while it's cold in Provo, Minnesota plays on Hoth. It's not for everybody.

The Cougars won the national title the next year, and if Edwards left, it seems reasonable to think one of those razor-close games goes in another direction, and Washington wins the 1984 title instead.

Would the Gophers have rebounded? There wasn't really a great QB on the roster during that time, and while the coach the Gophers eventually hired (Lou Holtz) got the Gophers to a bowl game before quickly leaving for Notre Dame, Minnesota hasn't really been a consistent winner in the Big Ten since the 1960s. Edwards has experience developing talent in places that are tough to win, and it's easy to imagine him improving Minnesota—perhaps to the levels that Purdue enjoyed during the Joe Tiller era, another pass-happy coach from the West—but it's hard to see him enjoying the same success he had at BYU.

Of course, college teams weren't the only teams trying to hire Edwards. Perhaps the closest Edwards ever actually came to leaving Provo was for the NFL, when the Detroit Lions heavily pursued him.

The Lions reached out to Edwards in 1984, right after BYU won the national title, and Edwards said he was happy to listen. In his autobiography, Edwards admitted that the only job he'd leave BYU for would be the NFL, since he was curious as to how well his passing concepts would work at the highest level of football, and after coaching in high school and in college, saw the NFL as a natural stepping stone in his coaching career[40]. And shoot, if you could build a powerhouse and win a dang national title in Provo, why couldn't you win with the Lions?

Edwards was very interested, but the timing wasn't ideal. Edwards had to coach the East-West game in San Francisco. Then he went to Nashville for a coaching convention, and postponed a flight to Detroit so he could collect a Coach of the Year award, meet the President, etc. Another trip was postponed so he could finish a huge recruiting weekend in Provo. [41] It was those constant delays that reminded Edwards that well, if you can't step away from college stuff to go meet with the NFL, when are you going to do it? After initially accepting the job, he turned Detroit down[42], and the Lions hired Darryl Rodgers instead.

Did Edwards regret that? No. Things didn't turn out so well for Rodgers, and probably wouldn't have for Edwards either. Lions running back Billy Sims quickly suffered a knee injury and never completely returned to form, and as Edwards would tell later tell the *Deseret News*, "They never had a quarterback." Without the offensive talent needed, the Lions struggled, and eventually fired Rodgers. Edwards admitted, "I don't think I would have had any more success than he did." He's probably right.

But what about the Cougars? Had Edwards departed in 1984, finding a replacement might have been tricky. Dick Felt, a special teams coach and Edwards confidant, could have been tapped to try and keep as much continuity as possible. BYU's quarterbacks coach at the time, Mike Holmgren, would soon leave for the 49ers and would have a celebrated career as a professional coach. He would have made a compelling fit, but he isn't LDS, and it's unlikely the school would have hired a coach of a different faith.

Norm Chow was on the staff then too, but he didn't even become QBs coach until 1986. He'd have a long and productive career ahead of him as a QB coach and offensive coordinator (and a less than productive stint as the future head coach of Hawaii), but he'd almost certainly be too green to be considered an Edwards replacement. Other famous members of the Edwards coaching tree, like current Utah head coach Kyle Whittingham, or Kansas City Chiefs head coach Andy Reid, were also too junior to be hypothetically considered for an opening in 1984.

I suspect BYU would pick between Felt, Utah State athletic director and former BYU offensive line coach Dave Kragthorpe, or San Diego State tight ends coach and former BYU tight end and GA Brian Billick.

Billick, of course, would go on to have the most successful professional career, leaving SDSU in 1985 to turn around Utah State's offense, and then later to the NFL, where he would eventually win a Super Bowl as the head coach of the Baltimore Ravens. Would he be ready to take over a success college program without ever having been a college coordinator before? That might have been a tall order.

Kragthorpe had been a head coach before taking the Utah State AD position, he had some modest success at Idaho State, and would shortly leave to become Oregon State's head coach, trying to take a similar, pass-happy approach to the Pac-12. It didn't work well, as the Beavers failed to record a winning season, and left the program after 1990. My guess is that he'd be the most likely candidate to take over, and while he'd probably do better than he did in Corvallis, a step back from what the team was able to achieve post-1984 seems probable.

Edwards finally retired in 2000. While the Cougars never did compete for another national title, he did manage to come relatively close in 1996, guiding the Cougars to the first 14 win season in college football history, and a #5 finish in the AP Poll.

Other than the national title, and the entire warehouse full of individual national awards, conference trophies, and other assorted honors, the Edwards era has two other important legacies.

One is his massive coaching tree. Edwards never claimed to be a schematic savant. In fact, even though he's most well known for BYU's prolific passing, Edwards was a defensive assistant coach first, and is quick to credit the program's offensive prowess to his assistants.[43] More than perhaps anything else, Edwards was successful because of his ability to hire and develop assistants, especially at a difficult job. As a result, his coaching tree is vast, touching every level of football. For the NFL, Brian Billick, Andy Reid, and Mike Holmgren all coached under Edwards, and longtime NFL offensive coordinator Norm Chow did as well. Billick and Holmgren won Super Bowls, and Reid, dubious clock management skills aside, is one of the winningest coaches of his era.

All of these men worked for Edwards while relatively junior in their careers. If the Edwards era never gets off the ground, do they find their way into the NFL and still have the same level of success? It's hard to see how that happens for Chow, who was at BYU for over 20 years and has Edwards' concepts all over his offensive DNA. If nothing else, it's fair to say that the Edwards coaching room was one of the great launching pads for NFL offensive innovation.

But it wasn't just the coaching staff. Many of Edwards' players would become excellent coaches. Former BYU quarterback Steve Sarkisian would later become the coach at Washington, USC, and worked as an OC under Nick Saban at Alabama. BYU linebacker Kyle Whittingham would turn down the chance to become the coach after Edwards multiple times, and would become a dynamite coach at the University of Utah.[44] BYU fullback Kalani Sitake, recruited near the end of Edwards' career, is now the current head coach at BYU, after successful defensive coordinator stops at Utah and

Oregon State. BYU's current athletic director is a former Cougar defensive back, Tom Holmoe. And this isn't even a complete list.

It's quite a remarkable coaching tree, especially for a guy coaching a private school in the mountains that wasn't writing big checks. But you didn't have to live in Provo for a few years in order to soak up what Edwards was doing. His influence extended into the entire coaching community, because football nerds everywhere loved BYU's offenses.

One game that helped truly expand BYU's influence? One of the greatest college football games ever, the 1980 Holiday Bowl.

The differences in philosophy between the two teams could not have been more stark. BYU was throwing the ball more than anybody in the country, leading the country in total offense, while SMU was piloted by two elite running backs, Eric Dickerson and Craig James, nicknamed "the Pony Express." Those looking to this game as a referendum on BYU's ability to beat good teams with it's newfangled, pass-heavy offense would not have looked kindly on the Cougars, at least to start. BYU was completely unable to bottle up SMU's rushing attack, as James and Dickerson combined to rush for over 330 yards. With just four minutes left in the game, SMU had built a commanding 45-25 lead. BYU had never won a bowl game before, and it certainly didn't look like they'd be able to this year.

But instead, BYU pulled off perhaps the greatest comeback in college football, nay, in sports history. Paced by quarterback Jim McMahon, BYU threw a touchdown pass, recovered an onside kick, and promptly threw another, trimming the deficit to 45-39. The Cougars then improbably blocked a punt, giving them one last chance to win the game. As time expired, McMahon launched a Hail Mary to tight end Clay Brown, who hauled in the ball in traffic for the winning score. BYU somehow won, 46-45.

This paragraph doesn't do the game justice. Go take a break and look up the video on YouTube. It's amazing.

Not only did BYU manage to come back against a powerful team in very little time, but they did it completely by throwing the football. The Cougars actually rushed for negative yardage, but McMahon's 446 passing yards carried the day.

Watching that game, completely transfixed, was a young UTEP assistant coach named Hal Mumme, who would become BYU's most influential fan, and who would help change college football completely[45]. While with the Miners, Mumme would use some of BYU's tactics against them, helping spring one of the biggest upsets in college football history, when his woeful UTEP squad beat BYU in 1985. Mumme would eventually become friendly with Edwards and many other BYU staffers, as he tried to pick their brains about how specific plays worked, and how they were able to engineer one of the very few pass-heavy attacks in the country.[46]

In an interview with SB Nation, Humme essentially summarized the appeal the Cougars had nationwide, saying, "I had a guy tell me one time when we first started that he never turned off a BYU game. He had no connection to BYU or even the state of Utah, but if BYU was playing on TV he was going to watch the game. That always kind of struck a chord with me."[47]

It certainly did, changing the way college football was played for decades. Like Edwards, Mumme found himself in increasingly difficult jobs where conventional football strategy wouldn't be effective, due to the inability to recruit the same size and skill. Like Edwards, Humme decided to take to the air, repeatedly, creating an offense called the "Air Raid", which focused on mastering a few specific plays, spreading out offensive linemen, and throwing the dang ball all the time, often on short routes. Mumme admitted that he and his staff looked to Edwards as a major inspiration for their offenses, and that some of their most successful plays were nearly lifted wholesale from the BYU playbook.[48]

The Air Raid, and assorted principles, spread like wildfire across college football. A particularly famous Mumme disciple was Mike Leach, a BYU graduate himself who watched the Cougars during the Edwards era. Leach would coach with Mumme at Kentucky, and then would serve as an offensive coordinator at Oklahoma, before becoming a highly successful head coach at Texas Tech, and later, Washington State, famous for throwing the ball more than virtually any other coach in college football. Others, like Dana Holgorsen, found ways to tweak the system to incorporate more of a rushing attack.

Today, there are dozens of college football programs running some varia-tion of the Air Raid. Almost everybody in the Big 12 Conference uses it, in large part because of its massive popularity among Texas high school pro-grams. Washington State runs it in the Pac-12, and other schools, like Cal, borrow Air Raid principles. Other tweaks are run at Texas A&M in the SEC, Purdue in the Big Ten, and elsewhere. It has completely dominated high school football in the state of Texas, and is run at prep levels all over the coun-try as well. It is perhaps the most significant offensive development over the last twenty years.

Without Edwards, it's entirely possible there is no Hal Mumme, no Air Raid, no weird, drunk Pac-12 football at 1 AM where both teams combined for 124 passing attempts in a game. It's possible the schematic direction of an entire conference shifts, and underdog programs find themselves without another major tool at their disposal.

Looking back on things now, it also doesn't seem like a stretch that BYU football might not even exist today without Edwards. If Edwards never gets the BYU job, or left before his system could really go into effect by the early 1980s, it's possible, maybe even probable, that nobody else would be able to build a regular winner in the mountains. Without a massive fanbase, years of success, and a trophy case full of awards, BYU would struggle to be secure their lucrative football contract with ESPN, allowing them to function as an independent.

As the school struggles to figure out how it fits in with a national sports landscape, as a school that doesn't play on Sundays, with a strict student code of conduct that prohibits premarital sex, homosexual relationships, *and* beards, it isn't a leap to see how university leaders might just decide not to bother, like they did with the athletics programs at BYU-Idaho and BYU-Hawaii, which have both been canceled. Now, BYU's athletic success, not to mention their expensive infrastructure investments, makes dropping sports very hard to imagine, no matter how many times Utah fans on Twitter say it'll happen.

All in all, the Edwards legacy is truly impressive to behold. He may have built the most unlikely college football dynasty in history, taking a private school in the middle of nowhere with serious recruiting restrictions into a mid-major powerhouse that earned national awards and eventually, a national championship. His ability to hire and develop assistant coaches led to one of the most impressive coaching trees of the 20th century, and his offensive innovations were tweaked and studied by the most innovative minds in college football, changing the offensive philosophy of nearly an entire conference, and helping inspire offenses as disparate as Ohio State's, West Virginia's, and Oklahoma's.

That's to say nothing of BYU's influence on professional football, where Edwards alumni infiltrated offensive staffs and eventually won a Super Bowl. If you root for a team that employs a modern spread offense, on some level, you probably have LaVell Edwards to thank.

And to think that the entire operation could have fallen apart at multiple stages. BYU could have decided to hire a coach with a more distinguished background. Even a very successful local high school coach, after all, might have looked more impressive on paper than Edwards, a former high school coach who never had a winning record, and a defensive assistant on mostly bad BYU teams.

Edwards could have struck out on his early offensive coordinator hires, like Swamp Rat, preventing his pass-heavy attack from ever getting started. His 1974 squad could have failed to rebound after a disastrous 0-3-1 start, essentially ending his coaching career before it started. He could have left for Miami, or Minnesota, or Detroit, places where he'd probably be less successful than he was in the mountains. Given all of BYU's challenges, Edwards had virtually no margin of error. But he didn't need one. And he built a power.

You don't have to be a BYU fan, or a Mormon, or have any attachment to Utah to appreciate this era, and for what it's done for college football, providing a blueprint for underdogs to succeed, and the foundation for some of the most fun offenses of the 20th and 21st century. For all of our sakes, it's a good thing Edwards got the breaks that he did.

What if Howard Schnellenberger stayed at Miami?

I WAS BORN IN 1987, so I missed a lot of the important Miami dynasties. My first real emotional connection to the program came from the 2002 season.

The 2002 Miami Hurricanes were impossibly talented. They had won the national title the year before, and even though many left the roster for the NFL, they were still completely stacked with professional caliber talent. They had future NFL stars Willis McGahee and Frank Gore at running back, Andre Johnson to bully defensive backs at wideout, the electric and controversial Kellen Winslow Jr. at tight end, and an impossibly talented defense with future All-Pros Jonathan Vilma and Sean Taylor. They opened the season atop the polls, and after demolishing #6 Florida 41-16 in the second week of the season, they looked like they were going to stay there. The regular season felt like a coronation.

They were also exactly the sort of team I was conditioned to hate by my culturally conservative upbringing. They wore garish orange and green uniforms, devoid of the staid tradition I had learned to revere as an Ohio State fan. They scored lots of points, which, as a fan of a Jim Tressel coached team, felt alien. They were loud, proud, and had an attitude. Everybody where I lived was absolutely convinced they didn't play the game the right way, whatever that was.

They made the perfect foil in the championship game against my Ohio State Buckeyes, who rode their excellent freshman running back Maurice Clarett, a dynamite defense, and a ton of luck to the championship game. Their head coach, Jim Tressel, dressed like Mr. Rogers and was the literal antithesis of all things Miami. For a Mormon kid in rural Ohio, the 2002 championship game wasn't just a chance for my favorite team to win an elusive national title, it was practically a game between good and evil.

Now, was that fair? Of course not. I am aware that Jim Tressel eventually would have to resign in disgrace, after committing the heinous crime of rigging a raffle and lying about some football players getting free tattoos[1]. I'm aware that most of the Miami players were not, in fact, bad guys. I know this entire narrative is stupid. I'm just saying how I felt as an impressionable teenager.

That game ended up being the apex of the Miami dynasty. Ohio State won in a thrilling, double-overtime game. (Thanks to a completely correct pass interference penalty, I might add.) Miami sent roughly a gazillion players to the NFL, and started to slide out of the top five and into the top ten, then the top fifteen, and soon, out of the AP Top 25 entirely, battling with Nevada in bowl games in Idaho.

The Hurricanes have yet to recapture the glory they enjoyed from the 1980s to the 2000s. They've been passed by their local rivals, Florida and Florida State, both in recruiting rankings and recent success, and they've struggled to reestablish a presence in college football's elite. Miami has changed conferences, changed coaches, changed uniforms, even tried to change identities since that loss in the championship game.

Now, they're one of the most interesting programs in college football. On one hand, they're still in Miami-Dade County, the county with perhaps the highest concentration of elite high school talent in the country. By simply signing kids in a 30-mile radius from their campus, the Hurricanes would have a talented enough roster to compete for national titles. And even though those glory years were over a decade ago, Miami still has a championship history and some cultural cachet. And they're still right by the dang beach.

But they're also still a smaller private school that plays in an NFL stadium far from campus, often in front of crowds that might be more appropriate for a Mountain West game than for a team that fancies itself a national power. They're a school with a rich history that's playing road games against schools like Appalachian State and Arkansas State. They're a school that nearly canceled their football program entirely. But they are also one of the most important and influential dynasties in all of college football, one that said it was okay to have confidence, to have swagger, *to be the bad guy.*

Even if Miami never truly returns to their glory days, it's hard to overstate the influence of the program on college football as a whole. And those glory years were launched by an unlikely coach. Howard Schnellenberger was one of the greatest program builders in the history of the sport, and one who may have left at the possible height of his powers for an absolutely crazy reason.

Miami saw some success before Schnellenberger, but the early history of the program wouldn't have blown anybody away. Miami won the 1945 Orange Bowl, beating Holy Cross on a walk-off pick six to win 13-6. They became a consistently winning program under Andy Gustafson during and made four bowl appearances from 1948 to 1963. Miami won games a variety of different ways as well, from an innovative rushing attack under Gustafson's "drive series" attack[2], to one of the more passing friendly systems featuring Georgia Mira.

Unfortunately for the Hurricanes, the pre-Schnellenberger era also exemplified what made the Miami job difficult. For one, the athletic program struggled with funds. From the very beginning of the team back in 1925, when boosters wanted to hire Red Grange as head coach, only to be vetoed by the administration because his proposed $7,500 salary would have been too expensive, to Miami's inferior campus facilities, to Charlie Tate, Gustafson's successor, resigning in part because he was tired of "fighting the money battles"[3], the Hurricanes never enjoyed the financial stability that some of their peer institutions enjoyed.

Those financial problems led to inferior facilities and general program instability that came at the worst possible time. From 1970 to 1976, Miami had five different head coaches, with no bowl trips and only one winning record. Just a few miles up the road, Don Shula had turned the Miami Dolphins into an absolute juggernaut, culminating in their legendary undefeated season in 1972. With an exciting and dominating professional team, and with the whole Miami nightlife and beach scene to compete with, the Hurricane football program was dangerously close to a death spiral.

Why did Miami struggle with money? For one, South Florida may be a well-populated and developed region now, but that wasn't always the case. Miami was also relatively small for a private school, and one that drew heavily not just from Northeasterners, but also international students, particularly those from Latin America. That meant you had an alumni base that wasn't necessarily committed to sticking around South Florida and wasn't as invested in football, robbing the school of a deep donor base that they would need to grow.

In 1975, the situation neared a breaking point. UM trustees were informed that the school lost a whopping $3.5 million the year before. Since football was bleeding money and didn't appear close to turning things around soon, it was suggested that the school drop the sport, just like they had with basketball a few years earlier.[4]

The program might have been disbanded completely had a regent named Dr. John Green, who had served as an athletics board member at Georgia, not stepped in and pushed for the school to go for broke and try this football business one last time, only correctly.[5] Green pushed for the school to fire head coach Carl Selmer and name a high-profile replacement. The school reached out to tons of coaches, from Lavell Edwards at BYU, to Hayden Fry at Iowa, to Jackie Sherril (then at Washington State), to others with NFL ties[6]. Nobody would bite, which wasn't surprising. Miami's instability wasn't a secret, and the next coach knew that if things didn't go well, not only could he be fired, but the whole dang program could be shut down. That's a lot of pressure.

Green and Miami thought they had their man in Bill Dooley, the head coach at North Carolina, and brother of Vince Dooley, the highly successful head coach at Georgia. But when Dooley got to the airport in Chapel Hill to fly to his introductory press conference, he changed his mind. Miami had to cancel the presser and head back to the drawing board after another embarrassing failure.

The Hurricanes were able to secure their man the next time around, and hired former NFL head coach Lou Saban, who had accepted a job as athletic director at Cincinnati only 19 days before[7] (he quit without an explanation, a move that would not have played very well in the Twitter era). The school had to get creative to raise the funds needed for his contract and for the resources he'd need to rebuild the program, trying everything from a $1,500-per-plate roast of Ohio State head coach Woody Hayes to accepting a $250,000 guarantee to play Notre Dame in Japan[8]. The Irish destroyed them, but the check still cashed.

Saban didn't win a lot of games for the Hurricanes at Miami, but he helped lay a very important foundation, thanks to some excellent recruiting. His staff was able to land Lester Williams, one of the top defensive recruits in the country, as well as future NFL Hall of Fame QB Jim Kelly, who picked Miami over hometown Penn State because Joe Paterno wanted him to play linebacker instead of quarterback. Using a sales pitch that relied on his NFL experience and development ability, along with Miami's natural splendor, talent began to stockpile in Coral Gables at a level the school hadn't seen in decades.

But the entire operation almost fell apart before it could truly begin thanks to what would also become a recurring theme with Miami over the years—off the field troubles.

In the spring of 1978, three Miami football players threw a young man into an on-campus lake. As pranks go, things certainly could have been worse. Saban interpreted the event as something innocent, telling a newspaper reporter, "The whole thing sounds like a nice fiasco to me. Getting thrown in a lake? Sounds like fun to me."[9]

But Saban, who had just come back from a recruiting trip, didn't know the whole story before a reporter asked him about it. The players hadn't just dumped a random student into a lake; they targeted an employee at a campus gathering place for Jewish students, who was wearing a yarmulke. Suddenly, Saban looked anti-Semitic at a school with one of the most diverse populations in the South. No matter how much he apologized, it would have been very difficult for him to recover.[10]

And he didn't. After two seasons, where he compiled a combined 9-13 record, Saban resigned and took a job at Army. His players at Miami were not happy about it.[11]

Suddenly, Miami had to replace yet another football coach, while the sport's skeptics again pushed for the school to drop it altogether, or at least, compete at the D1-AA level, where it would be cheaper and out of the shadows of major powers like Florida and Alabama. If Miami had any aspirations of just the simple survival of their football program, let alone sustained success, they absolutely needed to nail their next hire.

Fortunately, they did. They hired Howard Schnellenberger.

Schnellenberger's background looked perfect for a rebuilding program. He was a former All-American end at Kentucky. He had learned from one of the most successful head coaches ever, Bear Bryant, where he was an assistant coach at Alabama and had recruited a quarterback prospect of some renown named Joe Namath. And he had extensive coaching experience in the NFL, both as an assistant coach and even, briefly, as a head coach of the Baltimore Colts. He checked every box.

But Schnellenberger was more than just an impressive resume. He was a commanding presence, buoyed by his supreme confidence, thick mustache, omnipresent pipe, and dapper dress. He always wore a sports jacket, even during the hottest Miami days. Sure, he sounded like a football coach, but he also looked like Colonel Mustard. He'd want to talk to you about pro-style offensive schemes, but he looked like a man really wanted to talk to you about British Imperialism. College football hasn't had another figure quite like him.

Immediately, Schnellenberger went to work molding Miami in his image. After spending time working in the NFL, he sought to bring a pro-style, timing-based passing attack to the college ranks[12]. Even in the late 1970s, the passing game wasn't nationally prominent in college football. While a few teams, like BYU under LaVell Edwards and San Jose State under Jack Elway, were slinging the ball around, most teams were still running out of the Wishbone, Power I, or other rushing-focused attacks. Only seven quarterbacks in 1979 completed at least 60% of their passes, and only 15 threw for at least 2,000 yards. If a team wanted to make the passing game an integral part of their offense, it would be risky, but it was clear that defenses weren't adequately prepared for it.

That wasn't easy to do. Passing-focused offenses required not just a good quarterback, but extensive coaching, practice reps, and resources. Miami might have had a great head coach, but they were sorely lacking in the resources department. The locker room and practice fields were so bad that coaches would deliberately skip them on recruiting visits. Their recruiting budget was so small that coaches would have to make calls to kids from off-campus pay phones, since they couldn't afford to do it from their offices. The film room for the coaches was a converted shower stall[13]. The weight room didn't have air conditioning. It probably smelled wonderful.

But Schnellenberger found a way to make it work. He brought in Earl Morrall, the QB of the undefeated 1972 Miami Dolphins and a part-time quarterback coach of the club, to help tutor the Hurricane's QBs[14]. That extra instruction was critical to helping Jim Kelly develop.

The other major immediate change with the Hurricanes program was with recruiting. South Florida was a major hub for high school talent, perhaps the most talent-rich area in the country, even in the late 1970s. But the Hurricanes traditional struggled to keep the best players from going to other programs in the state or to Big Ten programs like Michigan and Ohio State.

In order to combat that, Schnellenberger created "the state of Miami", the Hurricanes' new recruiting focus. In addition to the actual city of Miami, Schnellenberger's "state of Miami" extended to Tampa, Palm Beach, Fort Lauderdale, and essentially anything south of Orlando. Schnellenberger would have no qualms attending a media event in say, Tampa, and loudly proclaiming it to be part of the State of Miami[15]. Schnellenberger knew that the area had a bevy of fast players, from defensive backs to linebackers to wideouts, who could make a difference in their new schemes, and securing them was Miami's best path towards greatness.

The University of Miami might have had the reputation for being "Suntan U" during those days, but Schnellenberger's training camps were nothing close to a day at the beach. He modeled his program after the brutal training camps he experienced at Kentucky as a player, and under Bear Bryant at Alabama as an assistant coach. Offseason training was long, water breaks were few, and the player rulebook—which governed who could visit their dorms, when they could go out, and more—was extensive. Many players couldn't handle the rigor, and dropped out, just like they did at Alabama, Kentucky, and others.

But the ones who stayed saw there was a method behind the madness, and the Hurricanes quickly improved.

Miami won their first game in the Schnellenberger era, 24-12 over Louisville, in front of 40,000+ fans, more than double what Miami typically brought to the Orange Bowl. They weren't just there to see their mustached coach launch a new era of Hurricane football. Miami brought that many fans because local Burger Kings were giving away Hurricane tickets[16]. Whether inspired by football or fast food, the gambit worked. Soon, Miami wouldn't need to resort to gimmicks to put butts in the seats.

The Hurricanes finished 5-6 during that 1979 season, an up and down campaign with highs (a win over nationally ranked Penn State on the road, a game Schnellenberger would say "marks the arrival of the program to where we had hoped it was going.'[17]), and lows (a 40-15 crushing by Notre Dame in Japan, and a loss to FCS Florida A&M). But the seeds of a successful program, paced by South Florida speed, a stingy defense, and the quarterbacking of Jim Kelly, had been planted.

They would finish 9-3 their next season, beating Florida and Florida State (and, for good measure, Florida A&M), and knocking off Virginia Tech in the Peach Bowl. They ranked 18th in the final AP Poll. They'd do even better the next season, finishing 9-2, despite playing the second toughest schedule in the country. Jim Kelly cracked the national top 15 in passing yards, Miami beat top ranked Penn State, andand the team finished 8th in the final AP Poll after beating top ranked Penn State. After more than a decade in the proverbial wilderness, Miami was back, not just in the eyes of South Florida recruits, but thanks to ambitious national schedules facilitated by their independent status, in the eyes of the television watching national public.

After a step back in 1982, thanks to an injury to Jim Kelly (Miami's main QB that season? Future Georgia Bulldogs and later Miami Hurricanes head coach Mark Richt. I guess you could say Mark Richt lost control of Miami's QB depth chart), Miami reloaded, and looked to take another step forward in it's quest for a national title in Schnellenberger's fifth season. Restocking Miami with talent and putting them in position to compete for major bowls was a major accomplishment, but it might not have been Schnellenberger's biggest achievement. That was making the Hurricanes cool.

It wasn't because Miami had superior facilities. They still played at the Orange Bowl, which wasn't on campus. Their weight room, training facilities, practice fields and more still lagged far behind their peers. But Schnellenberger brought two things that the program lacked. First, he projected an unflappable sense of confidence, one that couldn't help but rub off on his players. His unique sense of discipline was also a perfect fit. Scnellenberger might have borrowed Bear Bryant's intensity, his grueling practice regimens, and his attention to detail, but different from other coaches about conformity. If a player was disciplined enough to sweat out murderous practices in South Florida heat, a high five or a celebration during the game wasn't going to make Schnellenberger lose any sleep. Players realized that they'd have the freedom to be themselves at Miami, helping make the program even more attractive to locals.

The Hurricanes had momentum and restocked talent. Even without Jim Kelly in 1983, they looked like they were ready to make a run at some bigger goals. But the season started off with a disaster, as Florida manhandled the Hurricanes 28-3 at the Swamp, knocking new quarterback Bernie Kosar around. If Miami wanted to make a run at a national title then, they would need not only perfection, but a fair amount of luck.

Behind the improving quarterback play of Kosar, Miami mowed down the rest of what would prove to be one of the most difficult schedules in the country that season. They dominated Notre Dame, 20-0, in what was rapidly becoming a heated rivalry. They smashed a Mississippi State team that had flummoxed them over the previous seasons, 31-7. They beat a nationally ranked West Virginia squad by 17, and beat #6 Florida State by the thinnest of margins, 17-16, securing their birth in the Orange Bowl and a shot at a national title.

But it was just an outside shot. Miami didn't enter the game as the nation's top ranked team and weren't even in the top three. That top distinction went to Nebraska, who rolled into the Orange Bowl undefeated, and based on the lopsided scores on their schedule (they beat #4 Penn State 44-6 to open the year, and scored more than 50 points a whopping seven times, including 84 against Minnesota), had a claim as one of the most dominant teams in modern college football history.

For Miami to win a national title, not only would they need to slow down a Nebraska offense that was averaging over 50 points a game and sported a Heisman-winning running back, but they'd also need everything else to break just right. Georgia would need to upset #2 ranked Texas in the Cotton Bowl, and it wouldn't hurt for #4 Illinois to somehow lose in the Rose Bowl, where they'd face an unranked UCLA squad. Vegas didn't think highly of Miami's chances. They entered the Orange Bowl as an 11-point underdog.

But the Hurricanes caught the breaks they needed. Illinois was crushed by UCLA, 45-9, and Texas lost a squeaker, 10-0, to the Bulldogs. Miami realized right before the game started that if they managed to spring the upset, they'd be national champions.

Nebraska had a massive side and strength advantage, but the Cornhuskers hadn't seen a passing attack like Miami's during the season. Kosar was able to effectively pick apart the Cornhusker secondary, while Miami's defense used confusing fronts to keep Nebraska's mammoth offensive line off-balance.[18] This led to a dramatic back-and-forth game, with the Hurricanes nursing a slim 31-24 lead with under two minutes to go. Cornhuskers quarterback Turner Gill marched Nebraska down the field, and set up what appeared to be the game-tying touchdown on a 4th and 8 on a pitch to running back Jeff Smith.

But rather than kick the extra point and preserve a tie, which still would have led to a Nebraska national title, the Cornhuskers opted to go for two. Hurricane Kenny Calhoun broke up a pass at the goal line, preserving the dramatic 31-30 win. The Miami Hurricanes, unranked in the preseason poll, and blown out in their first game of the season, had just beaten one of the best college football teams ever. They were national champions.

The Hurricanes looked to be on the precipice of a dynasty. Kosar was only a redshirt freshman. A talented recruiting class was coming in, and with Schnellenberger, just named the national coach of the year, at the helm, it looked like the Hurricanes should be competing for national titles over the next several years.

And then a funny thing happened. Schnellenberger left.

He didn't leave for the NFL, where he had previously coached. He didn't leave for another college job, even though newspaper reports indicated he could have gone back to his alma mater, Kentucky.[19] Instead, he left for a $3 million offer to head up the Spirit of Miami, a relocated Washington Federals squad in the fledgling United States Football League, a startup that sought to chip away at the NFL by competing in the spring. Schnellenberger wouldn't just coach the team, but also serve as general manager.[20]

Nobody at Miami expected Schnellenberger to leave, but perhaps they should have. The two sides occasionally clashed over administrative issues or institutional commitment (Schnellenberger wanted an on-campus stadium and a bigger budget, neither of which was forthcoming), and a national title only made those struggles worse.

The school's president, Tad Foote, celebrated the victory by only giving the football program 40% of the $1.8 million it earned from winning the Orange Bowl. The remaining 60% went to the school's general operating budget, Foote didn't stop there, unceremoniously removing an $800,000 subsidy and essentially rewarding a championship program with a budget cut. Since Miami relied on television broadcast money to balance the budget, it was imperative that the Hurricanes continued to be successful enough to justify multiple TV spots.[21] There was no margin for error.

Schnellenberger would tell the *Miami Herald*, "I simply do not think the overall priorities for college athletics here are high enough for me to continue to work with them."[22]

After having to fight those battles right after the battling the Nebraska offense, it's easy to see how near total control over a squad could be appealing. Only the timing couldn't have been worse.

Schnellenberger never coached a snap in the USFL. In late August 1984, the league's owners decided to shift USFL schedule to the fall, rather than the spring. Realizing that he'd have absolutely no shot at building interest if he had to directly compete with the Miami Dolphins, Spirit of Miami owner Woody Weiser backed out of the deal.[23] The franchise was then purchased by Donald Dizney, who was a part-owner of a USFL franchise in Tampa Bay.

Dizney had a very different vision for the team. For one thing, he wanted them in Orlando instead of Miami. And instead of Schnellenberger, he wanted Lee Corso[24], a Florida State grad who coached at Indiana and Louisville and whose true claim to fame would be his beloved crazy grandpa role on ESPN's *College GameDay*.

Schnellenberger had walked away from a championship college football team, and now suddenly found himself without a job. Let's pause for a second and remember that this did not happen in the 1930s, when a football could decide to walk away from coaching because he could make more money running a rubber factory or something. This was the 1980s, and acknowledge the absurdity of this—a championship coach leaving for a spot in a fly-by-night minor league. If say, Bob Stoops left Oklahoma after the 2000 season to go coach in the XFL or something, we'd probably still be talking about it. This is absolutely nuts.

Schnellenberger didn't coach anywhere for the 1984 season, a year he would later refer to as his "redshirt" year.[25] Fortunately for Schnellenberger, there was another rebuilding project waiting for him soon though, his hometown Louisville Cardinals.

Louisville basketball may enjoy a long history of success, but the same couldn't be said about their football team, a relative latecomer to big time football, having spent their early years toiling in the SIAA, facing teams like Morehead State and Centre. After popular and successful head coach Lee Corso left after four seasons to take over at Indiana in 1972, the program quickly fell back into irrelevance. Louisville didn't have a football conference affiliation after 1974, leaving the Missouri Valley Conference, and spent much of that early independence era facing off against former MVC teams, lesser regarded Southern independent programs like Memphis, MAC programs, and others bottom of the barrel in D1-A, schedules that outside of the occasional game against a Florida State or Miami, weren't likely to build much interest.

Because of that, Louisville faced a similar situation to Miami. Their football program wasn't just losing games; it was bleeding fan interest and money. They didn't have their own football stadium, instead sharing a rundown park with a minor league baseball team, requiring the football team to schedule practice around the baseball team's needs. The Cardinal athletic department conducted a study to determine if the entire operation would have been a better fit in D1-AA, allowing the school to truly double down on basketball. In the end, the school decided to give big time football one last shot to succeed, and hired Schnellenberger.

Everybody laughed when Schnellenberger boldly proclaimed that Louisville was "on a crash course with a national championship. The only variable is time" during his opening press conference. After all, in 1985, Louisville wasn't even on a crash course to the Freedom Bowl. And his early teams didn't do much to change anyone's mind. In his first season, Louisville was one of the worst teams in the country, finishing 2-9, losing to Eastern

Kentucky. They gave up 39 points a game, worst in the country, and did not beat a single D1-A team. Schnellenberger would say the squad was "two years behind" what he found at Miami when he started.[26]

Like Miami, Louisville had infrastructure problems that made recruiting difficult. Cardinal assistant Bill Trout recounted a story of how right before a major recruiting weekend, a bunch of cows walked over from the nearby state fairgrounds and took a dump near the walkway to the football building. Hardly the red carpet treatment needed to lure fickle high schoolers. Trout left coaching after that season to get into farming.

"Tomatoes don't need to pass the SAT," he told the *Los Angeles Times*.

In fact, the next few years weren't much of an improvement either. The Cardinals went 3-8 in 1986 and 3-7-1 in 1987. The only D1-A teams they managed to beat were Tulane (who also stunk) and Akron. Nowadays, many coaches, even at smaller programs, would have been fired for those kinds of results. But Louisville wisely stayed the course, trusting that Schnellenberger still had a little Miami Magic left in him. Or maybe they didn't have a choice. After all, it's not like other great candidates were beating down the door to coach the Cardinals.

The rebuilding process worked. After those three years of struggles, Louisville started to turn things around. In 1988, the Cardinals rebounded in a big way, vaulting to a 8-3 record (their most wins in 15 years), although they failed to secure a bowl invite. They boasted another winning record in 1989, before truly exploding, vaulting to a 10-1-1 record in 1990.

Their defense was exceptionally stingy, only allowing more than 20 points only one time, although that number was aided by a weak schedule. Louisville didn't actually beat a single team with a winning record in the regular season. But given where the program was over the last decade, even beating a bunch of bad teams would have been an impressive feat.

The Cardinals looked to be on course to face North Carolina State in the All-American Bowl, a perfectly fine prize for an independent program without much of a tradition, but political turmoil would open up a shot at a bigger prize.

Because the state of Arizona voted not to recognize Martin Luther King Day as a holiday, many bigger programs decided against accepting a spot in the Fiesta Bowl. But Louisville, who would have been desperate for a big-time TV slot and a major bowl purse (a $2.5 million dollar payday), accepted the bid[27]. The Fiesta Bowl made a donation to Louisville's minority scholarship, and the Cardinals flew to Arizona to face Alabama.

Louisville crushed a down Alabama squad, 35-7, blocking a punt for a touchdown, and returning an interception for another. They finished 11th in the AP Poll, easily their best in program history, and won their first bowl game. It wasn't quite the national championship that Schnellenberger hoped for (he repeatedly said the goal was to win a national title at Louisville), but it was still a major accomplishment. Louisville football now had a signature win and could begin to build fans and community support.

That was the high water mark at Louisville for Schnellenberger. The Cardinals would upgrade their schedules significantly over the next few years, with opponents like Ohio State, Florida State and Tennessee replacing previous cannon fodder, and elite success was hard to sustain. After two losing seasons, Louisville went 9-3, finished 24th in the final AP Poll, and knocked off Michigan State in the Liberty Bowl.

But the school's decision to leave their independent status to join the newly created Conference USA angered Schnellenberger, as he believed the Cardinals wouldn't be able to compete for a national title without regular access to power competition.[28] (He was right, for what it's worth.) After the 1994 campaign, Schnellenberger left Louisville.

From here, the magic wears off the Schnellenberger story a bit, as things turn sour and then downright weird. Schnellenberger left for Oklahoma, where he coached only a single disastrous 5-5-1 campaign and managed to alienate nearly single member of the donor community thanks to his lack of respect for Sooner tradition and history.

He left the sport for a few years, then resurfaced at an unlikely place. In 2001, Schnellenberger took the reigns at Florida Atlantic, a school just starting a football program. Schnellenberger shepherded the program through a transition from D1-AA to D1-A (now FBS), building a donor base, football infrastructure, and identity. By 2007, the school qualified for a bowl game (the "youngest" FBS football program to do so, at the time), and made a second in 2008, winning both games. He retired in 2011.

FAU has yet to make a bowl game since Schnellenberger retired. In fact, the only thing the school has been known for since he left was an ill-fated attempt to allow its new, on-campus stadium to be sponsored by a for-profit prison company, (the internet mockingly referred to the proposal as "Owlcatraz"[29]), and for hiring Lane Kiffin in 2016.

Still, the Schnellenberger legacy is immense. It is not hyperbolic to credit him as the father of three different college football programs. He turned Miami, Louisville and FAU into bowl caliber (or better) squads after all three faced fan apathy, institutional neglect, and resource drains. He's a national champion. And his deep, gravely voice, as low as Barry White, and his outlandish goals and predictions, nearly always backed up on the field, as part of college football lore of the 1980s, and beyond.

But his legacy also feels incomplete. For all of his success, Schnellenberger only made bowls in back-to-back seasons just once, at Florida Atlantic in 2007 and 2008. He never really sustained the success he built at Miami or Louisville, and never got started at Oklahoma. We know he was one of the greatest, if not the greatest, program builder in college football history. But could he have built a dynasty? Could he have become one of the true greats of the sport?

What if he never left Miami?

Schnellenberger's peers were not shy in their predictions. Former Miami offensive line coach Art Kehoe said that, "if Schnellenbeger had stayed at Maimi, he'd be the greatest coach in the history of football, bar none. He'd have ten titles, and he'd be more legendary than Bear Bryant."[30]

Larry Coker, a former national title winning coach at Miami himself, asked, "Who knows how many national titles Coach Schnellenberger would have won if he'd stayed? His success would have been off the charts."[31] And Bill Trout, a former Miami assistant who would follow Schnellenberger to Louisville, also claimed he could have won five national titles had he stuck around in Coral Gables.[32]

Bruce Feldman of FOX Sports, who covered Miami and wrote "'Cane Mutiny", agreed, telling me "I don't know about ten titles, just because that is nearly impossible during that era of college football, but given who he had coming into the program, multiple titles were a very realistic possibility. If he'd stayed another five years, I'd have been surprised if he didn't win at least one more national title at UM."

In 2001, with the benefit of hindsight, even Schnellenberger understood that leaving the dynasty he had brewing for the USFL was a mistake. He would later tell *The Oklahoman* that, "Yeah, it was a horse-[expletive] decision."[33]

It's not like Miami cratered without it's dapper-dressed, pipe-smoking headman. Ten days after Schnellenberger left, the school hired Jimmy Johnson away from Oklahoma State. After a small step backwards in his first season (the Canes finished 8-5), Miami stormed back to national title contention. They finished in the AP Top Ten in 1985, finished second in 1986, and won the national title with a perfect 12-0 record in 1987. From 1987 through 2005, outside of one 5-6 campaign after the school was hammered with NCAA sanctions, Miami finished in the AP Top 25 every season.

But the identity of the program shifted in the post-Schnellenberger era. Hurricane teams weren't strangers to self-expression or dramatic flair during the early 1980s. How could they be, with their coach wearing a suit on the sidelines, even when it was over 90 degrees outside? But that edge grew even more under Johnson, and then careened a bit out of control under Johnson's successor, Dennis Erickson.

Johnson, who had a degree in psychology, had a more accessible personality than Schnellenberger and knew exactly what buttons to push to keep his team engaged without going over the edge with excessive penalties or off the field concerns.

Building a program is different from sustaining one. Schnellenberger proved he's one of the greatest program builders in modern college football history, knowing how to push administrators, donors, and players. But even with the elite talent that Miami had stockpiled, knowing how to fight off complacency and ego is a different skill, and one that would be required to win multiple national titles. I'm not sure if Schnellenberger had those skills, since they were never really demonstrated during his tenure, but multiple Miami titles (perhaps in 1984 or 1986) seems like a fair bet.

Louisville arguably benefited even more from Schnellenberger. At a time when the school realized they'd need to make an investment in a real coach if they were ever going to succeed at a high level, a coach that not only won a national title but was also a Louisville native just happened to hit the market.

"Schnellenberger raised the floor for Louisville football," Mark Ennis, a writer for popular Louisville blog Card Chronicle and a local radio host, told me. "He helped show success was possible."

Thanks to Schnellenberger, both from his success on the field and his infectious personality, Louisville was able to raise enough money to build their own stadium and move out of their crummy baseball field. There's no way that Louisville would have been able to hire a coach with anywhere near the credentials as Schnellenberger had he decided to stay at Miami instead.

Would the program be in FCS right now without him? Ennis doesn't think so. "There's no way Louisville would be in the ACC at this point without Howard. I think they'd be a peer of Memphis, or Southern Mississippi, or maybe East Carolina, without him."

I agree. A Louisville continued to grow as a city, and as the university transitioned away from being just a commuter school, somebody was eventually going to be able to help consolidate corporate and donor interest enough to build a program. But without that jumpstart, it's hard to see how it happens in time for the school to be a power conference option.

Without Schnellenberger, Miami doesn't become a national title–winning NFL factory, and Louisville is churning out respectable seasons in the American Athletic Conference and hoping to beat Cincinnati and Memphis. Without a football team, most of America would think Florida Atlantic is a bank rather than a university. That's quite a legacy.

Those closest to him think Miami could have won multiple, maybe even ten, national titles had he stuck around. Even if compliancy, institutional politics, and just plain bad luck set in, Miami's talent and momentum were strong enough that they'd almost certainly win at least one more title had the area's favorite pipe smoker remained on the sidelines.

The moral of the story? Urban Meyer, if, by some chance, you're reading this book, and you get an opportunity coach in say, the Arena League, or the XFL Part II—you should pass. You'll never know what you might be leaving behind if you say yes.

And if you *do* say yes... well, triple check that contract.

What if the Metro Conference became the first superconference?

———

OF ALL OF THE MEDIA narratives that have dominated college football over the past decade, perhaps none has attracted more interest than conference realignment. After the ACC raided the Big East in 2003, those conversations increasingly shifted towards the inevitability of so-called superconferences, 16-team behemoths built up to dominate television revenue, and eventually, as the building blocks towards a new playoff system.

As of 2017, that hasn't exactly been what's happened. Many conferences expanded to 14, but no major conference has taken the plunge to 16 yet, and no playoff bid has been explicitly tied to winning a major conference. There hasn't seemed to be much momentum in that direction either, outside of off-season thinkpieces and message board chatter.

Could we get there by the mid 2020s? Maybe, maybe not. But the hand-wringing over superconferences isn't new. In fact, like virtually everything worth worrying about in college football, it's happened before.

We actually had a real, 16-team superconference in 1996, after the Western Athletic Conference (WAC) expanded by adding Rice, TCU, SMU, San Jose State, UNLV and Tulsa. Despite what WAC officials hoped, schedul-ing difficulties and the sheer geographic sprawl of the dang thing (it spanned from Louisiana to Hawaii), led to many of their biggest brands spinning off to form the Mountain West Conference (MWC) in 1999.[1]

But before the WAC spanned a third of the globe, before the ACC stretched from Miami to Louisville to Boston, and before the 14-team Big Ten reached from Nebraska to New Jersey, we nearly had a superconference that would have redefined college sports. Let's call this the Raycom Superconference, an idea that, if executed, would have almost certainly changed the makeup of multiple power conferences, national titles, and could have elevated programs that later found themselves on the periphery of big time football.

This story also starts with basketball. Specifically, Metro Conference basketball. Founded in 1975, the Metro Conference consisted of Louisville, Cincinnati, Memphis (or Memphis State, as it was known at the time), Saint Louis, Georgia Tech and Tulane. Other major programs, like Virginia Tech and Florida State, would join shortly thereafter.

Heading into the 1990s, the Metro faced a bit of an identity crisis. Unlike many other conferences, the Metro didn't exactly have a closely defined geographic identity, stretching from the southern tip of the Midwest to New Orleans and northern Florida. It also didn't have a defined institutional identity, as it combined large, urban commuter schools like Cincinnati with AAU research powerhouses like Tulane. In the mid 1980s, it wasn't even particularly Metro, as urban schools like Saint Louis and Georgia Tech defected, to be replaced with Southern Miss and South Carolina. There are a lot of words you can use to describe Hattiesburg, Mississippi, after all, but metropolitan isn't one of them.

But perhaps most importantly, the Metro didn't sponsor football. It wasn't because their schools didn't play football. In fact, by the 1990s, every school did, but at varying degrees of aptitude. Florida State, by the late 80s, was already a burgeoning national power. Louisville and Tulane... well, they got plenty of fresh air and exercise. Each institution played as an independent, where they were free to pursue scheduling and revenue arrangements, as they saw fit.

That might have been just fine in the mid 1970s, but by the early 1990s, that arrangement was becoming more and more tenuous. As potential television revenue grew and bowl opportunities became even more tied to big-name conferences, the sustainability of football independence was getting harder and harder.

Simply deciding to unite the eight Metro schools in a football conference wasn't practical. Florida State, who went 32-4, with three top three AP finishes from 1987-1989, would have never agreed to locking themselves into sharing revenue and playing annual games against Louisville, Tulane, Southern Miss and Cincinnati—at least, not without getting something major in return. If the Metro wanted to survive, it would need to try something different.

Raycom, a Southern television network that already regularly broadcasted college sports, had an idea to do something dramatically out of the box, something that would have shaken up college sports irreversibly. If the Metro needed to expand to survive, why not expand... by a lot? Why not create a true superconference?

In January 1990, athletic directors from the Metro Conference asked representatives from Raycom to produce a report that proposed creating a "major, 16-team Super Conference", which would encompass over "35-45 percent of the nation's television households". [2] While the proposed makeup of the league took on a few different forms, the final 16-team proposal included Boston College, Rutgers, Temple, Syracuse, West Virginia, Pittsburgh, Cincinnati, Louisville, Miami, South Carolina, Virginia Tech, East Carolina, Memphis State, Florida State, Tulane, and Southern Mississippi. All of these teams were currently independent in football (Raycom didn't propose poaching anybody) and had expressed varying degrees of interest in joining a conference.

The proposed conference would remain a 12-team league for basketball and other sports, so Boston College, Syracuse and Pittsburgh could retain their Big East affiliation, and East Carolina could remain in the Colonial Athletic Association. After all, Big East basketball was a big deal, and ECU wouldn't have really been competitive in other sports. Raycom proposed dividing the basketball league into two divisions, to save on travel costs. [3]

Unlike a more traditional North/South or East/West split like other large conferences would later employ, Raycom proposed something even more revolutionary. The 16 teams would be split up into four groups of four. Each division would include two groups, and every other year the divisional groupings would change, so every school could get a chance to play every other school on a more regular basis.

The suggested groupings in the proposal were [4]:

Group 1: Boston College, Rutgers, Temple, Syracuse
Group 2: Miami, South Carolina, Virginia Tech, East Carolina

Group 3: Memphis State, Florida State, Tulane, Southern Mississippi
Group 4: West Virginia, Pitt, Cincinnati, Louisville.

This sounds more complicated than it actually is, in practice. Let's say the Metro put Groups 1 and 2 in Division A, and 3 and 4 in division B. That would mean Boston College's seven league games would be against Rutgers, Temple, Syracuse, Miami, South Carolina, Virginia Tech and East Carolina. In two years, the Metro would shift the divisions to be 1 and 3, 2 and 4, so Boston College would play Florida State, Tulane, Memphis, and Southern Miss in addition to their own group.

Basically, it would mean that every school would get annual games with a few others in geographic proximity, but the divisions might not be geographically balanced. You could, hypothetically, get a Miami vs. Florida State Metro championship game for some years. Or a Temple vs. Pitt one. At least one newspaper report indicated that the divisions could be redrawn as often as every two years, though.[5]

That wasn't the only proposed conference breakdown. Later reports would investigate multiple other ideas, like breaking the conference into a two divisions, with all of the strong teams in one division. A more traditional North-South division was examined, along with a 16-team, no-division title that simply protected a few rivalry games a season.[6] But the final proposed called for the four-grouped system above.

The Raycom proposals offered something for everybody. For the independent programs with less leverage, like Rutgers, East Carolina and Temple, it provided stability, the scale to go after multiple bowl opportunities, and the chance to get occasional home games against major programs like Florida State.

For the smaller Metro programs, the Raycom Superconference offered some basic revenue sharing, something the old Metro didn't have. In an interview with Central New Jersey's *Courier-News*, Metro conference commissioner Ralph McFillen said "We're going to be a revenue-sharing conference, but it's going to be designed in such a way that would not be a financial 'hit' to those that generate large sums."[7] In the Raycom proposal, member institutions would retain 90 percent of their "major athletic revenue", while allocating 10 percent for revenue sharing. A later newspaper report would describe the arrangement as "almost tailor-made for Miami."[8]

According to one projection based on likely 1991-1992 earnings, that would have meant a major program like Florida State or Miami would have taken in over $6 million in gross revenue, while a Rutgers or Tulane would make around $600,000.[9] Of course, as the Metro improved their TV bargaining position, or as the conference earned more bowl revenue, the "floor" projections could have easily grown. The Orange Bowl was reportedly very interested in hosting the Metro champion, for example, and the Fiesta Bowl, Citrus Bowl and Sunshine Bowl were reportedly also interested in hosting Metro teams, each with healthy payouts.[10] One report projected as many as seven Metro teams could earn bowl bids, and eve in the early 1990s, when bowls weren't as numerous, that doesn't seem far-fetched.

This is important, because three programs in the Metro—Cincinnati, Memphis State and Louisville—were reportedly losing money[11], while others, like Florida State, were raking in big bucks. Such a split might have been low enough to not scare away a Florida State, while still providing at least some cushion for Rutgers or other have-nots in the conference.

More importantly, those revenues would have gone up for everybody, perhaps dramatically. As college football prepared to fully grasp a post-College Football Alliance TV contract world, the Raycom Superconference would suddenly have a substantial television footprint. Per the report, the superconference would have had a presence in 43% of total US television households, dwarfing the Big Ten and the Big East, the previous market leaders with 19% each. Plus, the conference would be able to hold a conference championship game, one that could have easily produced millions of dollars in revenue.

As the rest of college football would later learn in the 2000s, you don't even need to be a good football program to pitch TV market access. Using an argument similar to what they would later use to help convince the Big Ten, Rutgers associate athletic director Kevin MacConnell told the *Asbury Park Press*, "We have the market, the academics and athletic programs that are clean and legitimate. We have untapped potential. We were on television eight times in New York last year and finished 2-7-2. To get that is pretty darn good."[12] This is essentially the only time you'll find somebody mention

"Rutgers football" and "pretty darn good" in the same story until the mid 2000s.

This entire proposal wasn't just the fever dream of an overdramatic message board commenter. Raycom officials produced numerous reports, tracking everything from projected attendance, to academic selectivity, to amount of financial aid given by each school[13]. It was taken seriously enough by Metro administrators, as well as several independent programs, to warrant multiple meetings. The Raycom proposal indicated West Virginia had a high degree of interest (as did newspaper reports[14]), as did Temple and Rutgers, especially as the possibility of an Eastern Seaboard conference looked more and more remote once Penn State joined the Big Ten.

Not everybody was thrilled with the idea. One Louisville columnist criticized the plan, calling for Louisville to instead align with DePaul, who was looking to start an urban, Midwestern-focused conference oriented towards basketball, Louisville's primary sport. "Rather than improve a mediocre league, better that U of L look at something with the potential to be special, something with rivalries, winning traditions, important TV markets and a genuine passion for dribbling," wrote Rick Bozich for the *Louisville Courier-Journal*.[15]

Ultimately, it wouldn't be Louisville basketball, or Temple, or Rutgers that would decide the fate and viability of the Raycom Superconference. As the Greenwood (SC) *Index-Journal* wrote, "It has become clear that Florida State, Miami, and South Carolina-in that order, are foundation blocks the new Metro must have to make the plan work. The three schools have received official letters of inquiry from the Southeastern Conference and are also interested in Atlantic Coast Conference membership."[16] All three schools were quick to remind the press that they had options, and were non-committal, although interested, in the new alignment[17].

Raycom president Ken Haines told me that "almost everybody was on board with the plan, even programs like Florida State and South Carolina." Indeed, Florida State athletic director Bob Goin was quoted saying "I think it sounds like a great concept. It's a very clever setup, something would definitely benefit us."[18] The two programs expressing the most reservations, according to Haines, were Syracuse, who wanted more time to study the proposal, and Miami, who sought a more prestigious academic arrangement.

Ultimately, despite the eye-popping TV numbers and possibilities, the Raycom Superconference was an idea too far ahead of its time. Enough administrators just couldn't pull the trigger on essentially creating a new TV-focused entity out of nowhere. Florida State decided to join the ACC, South Carolina went to the SEC, and Miami left for the Big East, which started a football conference, taking their basketball-playing independents with them.

Without a heavy television anchor, the Metro died on the vine, disbanding shortly thereafter. The smaller programs became the backbone to what would eventually become Conference USA.

But what if it hadn't? What if this crazy plan was actually put into action?

First, let's try to get an idea for what kind of football conference this actually would have provided. The first possible year of Raycom Superconference play was 1991, so let's take a look at the S&P+ numbers for possible teams[19]. They were, in order:

Miami: #2 (12-0)
Florida State: #3 (11-2)
Syracuse: #18 (10-2)
East Carolina: #24 (11-1)
Virginia Tech: #41 (5-6)
Boston College: #43 (4-7)
West Virginia: #47 (6-5)
Pittsburgh: #50 (6-5)
South Carolina: #51 (3-6-2)
Memphis: #61 (5-6)
Cincinnati: #73 (4-7)
Rutgers: #76 (6-5)
Southern Miss: #78 (4-7)
Temple: #92 (2-9)
Louisville: #97 (2-9)
Tulane: #98 (1-10)

The Hurricanes would finish that season as the AP Poll champions (the Washington Huskies would win the Coaches Poll), and Florida State finished

4th in the final AP and Coaches Poll. Having two teams finish the in top five would be a significant achievement for any conference. But after Syracuse (who lost to Florida State 46-14 earlier that season), and the best East Carolina season in decades, the depth fell off relatively quickly. Those trends would remain in 1992, whereafter Florida State, Miami, and Syracuse, the rest of the conference would fall somewhere between slightly above average and dreadful.

The real 1991 Florida State team crushed BYU (ranked #19) and Michigan (#3), and barely lost to Florida (#5) in the last week of the regular season. With an obligation of seven Raycom Superconference games, would FSU be able to squeeze all of those powerful non-conference games in? We'd have to hope so, because using the hypothetical Florida State schedule provided in the Raycom presentation, the Seminoles wouldn't play Miami, Syracuse or East Carolina in the regular season. Their top ranked opponent in S&P+ would be West Virginia, who they'd get at home, at #47. Meh.

If the schedule was set up so Florida State and Miami wouldn't play for four years, outside of a conference championship game, does the college fan even benefit? Does the conference? Do the schools? In the early years of the league, that wouldn't be clear.

More balance would probably come later, though. Over the course of the early to mid 90s, Syracuse, West Virginia, Boston College and Pitt all took turns producing teams that played at Top 25 levels. By 1993, Frank Beamer had turned Virginia Tech from a forgettable also-ran into a regular Top 25 threat. If there wouldn't be much of a foil for the Florida schools at first, by the middle of the 1990s, there would at least be stiffer competition.

Plus, it probably isn't fair to look at the performances of the middle tier of the Metro in a vacuum. After all, a Raycom Superconference would undoubtedly increase their stature, their access to television money, and their ability to make strategic investments within their program. Rutgers, Temple and Tulane were dreadful during a lot of the mid 90s, but membership in the new premier television conference might have helped provide resources to keep things from bottoming out quite as badly. Plus, with a little extra scratch, Steve Logan's ECU teams from the mid 90s, or Jeff Bower's Southern Mississippi teams from the late 90s, could have been even stronger.

Essentially, in the proposed configuration the new conference would have likely given the world a better version of Big East football, one with two national title contending programs, in Miami and Florida State, with Virginia Tech becoming a factor by the late 1990s. Was it the best conference in the country? No. Would there have been some putrid games on TV because of it? Temple, Rutgers, and Tulane were in the conference, so yes, some of it would have been completely unwatchable. But would it have been a solid league, capable of sending a few teams to compete for national titles or major bowls? Sure.

"There were some great teams there. It could have been a really solid league," added Haines.

Of course, such a huge alignment shift would have had implications beyond just the Metro. It would have touched a good half-dozen other conferences as well.

For starters, the Big East does not sponsor football in this scenario. After all, every single Big East program with an FBS football team in 1990 would be playing in the new superconference. As TV revenue grew, and became an even more integral part of the athletic department operations, as it did throughout the 1990s and 2000s, it seems reasonable to think there would be increased pressure on Boston College, Syracuse and Pitt to park all of their sports in the Raycom, to help build on what would have been a very unbalanced hoops league. Certainly basketball-focused schools like Louisville would have pushed for this option.

In real life, the Big East basketball schools ended up having a painful divorce in 2012. In a world with the Raycom, that divorce probably happens much sooner, with the final result looking similar, a ten team, private school, basketball focused Big East.

An interesting question then, would be what happens to Connecticut. UConn, a capable FCS program began to investigate a possible move to FBS back in 1990, eventually deciding to make the jump in 1997[20], and to the Big East conference in the early 2000s. Without an immediate conference home, that jump probably doesn't happen. Perhaps the Raycom would decide to kick out struggling Temple, just like the Big East eventually did[21], thus opening up a spot for the Huskies. Maybe the ACC would have brought in UConn. But it seems most likely that, not seeing an obvious landing spot, the Huskies would remain in FCS football.

Perhaps the biggest loser of this arrangement would have been the ACC. While the ACC was technically considered a major conference (it was a member of the College Football Alliance, after all), and even won a national title in 1981 thanks to Clemson, it certainly wasn't considered as strong as the ACC in the 90s and 2000s, and would have been a step below the SEC, Big Eight, and other major leagues.

While Clemson was a regularly strong team, and programs like Maryland and North Carolina would occasionally make appearances in the final AP Top 20, it didn't have the depth, start power, or major bowl agreements that their other leagues did. There was no automatic tie to a major bowl game, like the Big Ten enjoyed with the Rose Bowl, or the SEC had with the Sugar. The top teams in the ACC would routinely end up in the Gator or Citrus Bowl instead. Landing Florida State helped change the league's perception as a "basketball league", and moved it further into major college football. The ACC's bowl lineup changed for the better nearly immediately after it locked down Florida State. [22]

Without Florida State, the ACC's expansion options in the early 90s looks very slim. Other schools that were reported as possible ACC targets, like Cincinnati, Louisville, West Virginia, and Virginia Tech, along with Miami, would have also been snapped up by the Metro. Unless the ACC would have been able to swipe another team from an existing league, or take a flyer on Connecticut, who would have been a huge geographic outlier, a Raycom Superconference would have forced the ACC to remain at eight teams.

One potentially interesting thought experiment would be what happened if the league somehow followed North Carolina basketball coach Dean Smith's advice. When asked who he thought the ACC should add, he suggested Vanderbilt, one of the stronger basketball schools within the SEC.[23] Nashville isn't on the Atlantic Coast (a fact that wasn't unnoticed by Smith, who mentioned that "they wouldn't qualify, but Maine would") but it isn't that far from many other conference schools and would have allowed the league to double-down on it's identity as a basketball conference. Plus, Vanderbilt, as an academically selective private school with a middling football tradition, might have been more at home, academically and culturally, in the ACC. Officials at both the SEC and Vandy[24] were quick to pour water on Smith's suggestion, though.[25]

It's a fun thought, and the Commodores may have been a more legitimate target if the ACC had lost a program (like say, Clemson, or Georgia Tech) and needed to expand just to get to eight, but there's little evidence that Vanderbilt was seriously considering bolting, just speculation fueled by Smith's comments, and Vanderbilt AD Paul Hoolahan's ties to North Carolina. And given the SEC's superior financial position, television exposure, and their historical ties to teams like Tennessee, prying the Commodores away would have been awfully tricky, even if it might have made more basketball sense.

The SEC would also need to find a new team, as expanding specifically to get to 12, and thus, to be the first league to hold a lucrative conference championship game. In real life, the league added Arkansas and South Carolina, but the Gamecocks become a part of the new superconference in our scenario. The Gamecocks weren't the SEC's top choice for expansion, or even in their top three. Published reports indicated that the league's brass were targeting Florida State, Miami, Arkansas, Texas and Texas A&M[26]. Texas, the big fish in the SWC, wasn't just potentially interested in the SEC, but also the Pac-12 and the Big Ten, a better academic fit for the Longhorns, even if it would be a geographic stretch[27]. But a higher power kept the Longhorns, and other Texas institutions from leaving, at least at the moment.

No, not God. State legislators.

The Texas schools were essentially blocked when the legislature threaten to withhold state funding if either Texas school decided to leave the SWC, a bold move, given that there was no formal invitation.[28] Important figures in Texas politics had a vested interest in the SWC continuing to exist, after all. Rob Junell, a former Texas Tech football player and chairman of the Texas House Appropriations Committee, along with several other high-powered alumni from Baylor, engineered the political pushback, trying to get the SEC to take Baylor and Texas Tech along with the Longhorns and Aggies. And if they couldn't secure a big time football future for their alma maters, then nobody in Texas would have left.[29]

State Senator David Sibley, one of the influential Baylor grads, would later tell *Sports Illustrated* that if the SEC interest came just two years earlier, which was certainly possible, TCU and Houston alumni would have been in similar positions to shift the entire conversation.[30] Disappointed Rice fans should have pushed harder for their graduates to occupy important positions in Texas politics.

In real life, the political maneuvering held, and no Texas schools defected to the SEC. It was only after striking out on everybody else that the SEC, like a high schooler in Charleston with too many Cs, decided to settle for South Carolina.

Prior to 1990, some SEC administrators would have preferred the conference add either Tulane or Georgia Tech, founding members of the conference who left in the 1960s. Adding either would have helped solidify the league's standing in important southern cities, and also would have improved the SEC's academic prestige, which had taken a public pounding. But by 1990, neither program would have added much in the way of new TV eyeballs. From an athletic standpoint, the most attractive option for the SEC would probably have been Georgia Tech, assuming university leaders in Atlanta found a way to smooth over hurt feelings at Mississippi and Mississippi State, along with Alabama.

The calculus behind the superconference seems sound, and such a grouping would have helped Raycom establish a very strong television presence. But the grouping of schools also seems mismatched, without a geographical identity, spanning from Northeastern schools, to Florida, to the Deep South. The size of the schools, their athletic budgets, their football success, and virtually every other marker also differed wildly, from national championship contenders, to some of the worst programs in D1.

Without really robust revenue sharing, I'm not sure how such disparities could continue without internal pressures within the league. Would Florida State or Miami want to be required to play schools like Tulane, Rutgers or Temple every season? The Seminoles and Hurricanes scheduled lots of Metro teams already during the 1980s, and the games were seldom competitive. If forced scheduling, especially in their pod system, prevented them from getting the marquee games they'd need to compete for national titles or major bowls, there'd be some serious tension, especially the new TV deal exasperated already stark revenue gaps between Florida State and, say, Rutgers.

There's also the question of how other sports would work. Some programs, like Louisville and Memphis, were emphatically basketball schools, making more money, and enjoying more fan support, from hoops. Pitt, Syracuse, and Boston College parked their basketball teams in the popular, and lucrative Big East conference. Others, like Tulane and Miami, didn't even have basketball teams, at least for a little while, just a few years earlier.

You can paper over significant geographical and philosophical differences if everybody is making money hand over fist, like the Big Ten is able to do. But if that isn't the case, or gets threatened, it's easy to see where lots of internal tension could start, just like it did with the Big East.

I suspect that after a few years, other conferences, like the SEC, ACC, or others, would make plays to try and convince teams to leave the Raycom arrangement, offering them slightly less expansive TV coverage in exchange for better schedules, better travel, and eventually, more money. Perhaps Florida State would join Arkansas (or Miami) in the SEC, building a dynamite power. Others, like Louisville, Pitt and Boston College, may head to the ACC, like they eventually did in real life.

I asked Keith Dunnavant about this, and he agreed, saying that while the superconference could have worked for a while, "eventually, the same market forces that hit the Big East would hit the Metro."

The only way conferences have managed to patch together true historical haves and have-nots is with robust and complete revenue sharing, like the Big Ten and SEC. When conferences allow a larger member to dominate resources, like the modern Big 12 has done with Texas, and the modern Mountain West has done with Boise State, you create tension, and ultimately, hurt competitiveness. That world wasn't so clear in 1990, but given the schools involved, it's likely it would have become clear by say, 2001.

The entire proposal is a fascinating idea. Would other major conferences jump to make dramatic moves just to keep pace? Could it have pushed the timeline for conference-specific television channels forward? Certainly Raycom could have helped the Metro produce their version of the wildly successful

Big Ten Network years before the Big Ten and Fox managed to make it work in the mid 2000s, if they wanted to. Could it have beaten the SEC to producing lucrative, and important, conference championship games? Could it have given the Southwest a few more years before it's dramatic implosion?

"Had the conference actually formed, the changes everywhere would have been significant," added Haines.

It's harder to see it lasting for the long haul. But credit athletic administrators and folks at Raycom for thinking outside the box. They saw the way the world was going, but they were just a little bit ahead of their time.

What if West Virginia beat Pitt in 2007?

———

THERE HAVE BEEN A LOT of weird seasons in college football history. The WWII seasons produced some pretty strange results. Unlikely champions were crowned in 1981, 1984 and 1990. But the weirdest one? It's gotta be 2007.

2007 wasn't just a weird season because of who ended up the national champion (a two-loss LSU team, the only time that's happened in the modern era), but for the sheer unpredictability from week to week. A comprehensive account would require its own book, but a few of the weirder things that happened are worth mentioning right up front.

On September 1, the Michigan Wolverines, ranked 5th in the preseason AP Poll, hosted FCS Appalachian State in what was supposed to be a tune-up game before higher profile matchups with Oregon and Notre Dame. As one of the very first games ever on the newly launched Big Ten Network, which wasn't on a lot of carriers yet, many Big Ten fans didn't get to watch it live. They missed a classic, as the Mountaineers blocked a field goal to upset Michigan, 34-32. It was only the second time a ranked team lost to an FCS opponent. Michigan dropped out of the rankings the next week, everybody decided they needed the Big Ten Network in their lives[1], and Appalachian State t-shirts suddenly became almost as popular in Columbus as Buckeye ones. I was an undergrad at Ohio State when this happened. It was one of the highlights of my college experience.

Then, on October 6, the 1-3 Stanford Cardinal visited the mighty USC Trojans. USC entered the game with a 35-game home winning streak and were massive 41-point favorites. Stanford lost to USC by 42 points the year before, and to make matters worse, they had to go with their backup QB, who had thrown exactly three passes to date. It didn't matter. USC threw four interceptions and lost, 24-23. It was the biggest upset, as far as point spread goes, in college football history.

On November 3, Navy beat Notre Dame. Notre Dame had beaten Navy 43 years in a row. That's pretty important! The following week, Navy won a football game over North Texas 72-64. That wasn't particularly important or anything. But a football team scored 72 points and actually needed just about all of them, which is bananas.

Perhaps even more surprising than the upsets were the teams consistently winning. Rutgers, the school that invented college football and then spent most of the next 150 years totally sucking at it, somehow became good and upset a top five team. To make things even crazier, that top five team was South Florida, which didn't even have a football team a decade earlier. Other perennial doormats like Kansas, Wake Forest, UConn and Hawaii were excellent, and historical power programs like Miami (FL) and Nebraska missed bowls. Missouri finished in the top five. This is not typical.

As if that weren't enough, upsets ravaged everybody—especially those at the top. The #2 team in the nation lost a whopping seven times during the season. An unranked team knocked off a top five squad 13 times over the course of the season. Teams like Vanderbilt, Maryland, Kentucky and Kansas knocked off top ten squads and played important roles in the season. Illinois beat *two* top five teams (Wisconsin and Ohio State). This unprecedented high number of upsets, spurred by injuries, recruiting mistakes from major powers, and just plain weird luck, threw the BCS selection process into chaos. Amid the wreckage, one non-blue blood team sat in prime position to make a championship game near the end of the season: West Virginia.

It's not like West Virginia being in championship contention that season came completely out of left field. Sure, the Mountaineers lacked the elite recruiting of programs like USC, LSU, Michigan or Texas, but like all those teams, they were in the top five of the preseason AP Poll (WVU was 3rd, and even got a single first place vote). They boasted one of the most terrifying and unique backfields of anybody in the country, with quarterback Pat White and a pair of stud running backs in junior Steve Slaton and freshman Noel Devine.

Under head coach Rich Rodriguez, the Mountaineers unleashed a spread-to-run attack, forcing defenses to account for the speedy White as a passing and running threat on nearly every play, while also getting opportunities for Slaton and Devine to attack defenses in space. This approach isn't uncommon in 2016, with offenses everywhere from Ohio State to Kansas State to Clemson borrowing some principles. But in 2007, it was revolutionary. Defenses everywhere were struggling to contain this explosive Mountaineer running game.

In the first game of the season, against Western Michigan, WVU scored 62 points and rushed for seven yards per carry. They crushed in-state rival Marshall and regional rival Maryland over the next two weeks, and then blew out a decent East Carolina team by 41 points, holding the Pirates to under 200 yards of offense. It wasn't a murderer's row of a schedule, but West Virginia passed every test they faced.

In fact, the only test they failed was against South Florida the next week, a game where Pat White was injured and had to miss the second half, and where the Mountaineers turned the ball over six times. But thanks to the slew of other upsets, WVU didn't fall too far in the polls. Solid wins over a ranked Rutgers squad (31-3), Cincinnati (28-23) and then a commanding win over UConn to clinch a Big East title (66-21) put the Mountaineers in contention for a major bowl game.

And thanks to a cascade of upsets, those bowl prospects kept looking better and better. Oregon QB Dennis Dixon blew out his ACL, and the Ducks plummeted out of the top five. Kansas dropped out of the undefeated ranks after losing their rivalry game to Missouri. LSU fell in triple overtime for the second time of the season. By the time all the dust had settled, all West Virginia had to do was win their last game of the season. With a win, they'd earn the #2 BCS ranking, and the right to play Ohio State in the national title game.

That last game? Against archrival Pitt. It was the 100th meeting between West Virginia and Pitt. The two schools sit just 75 miles or so from each other, battle each other for recruits, and share no love lost for each other.

Even with the run of upsets during the season, and with emotions certain to be running high for the game, few were expecting this to be much of a game. For starters, Pitt entered the game with a 4-7 record, a second-to-last place in the Big East, and no shot at a bowl game. The Panthers were better than their record (they finished 49th in S&P+, well ahead of many bowl teams, and boasted a top 15 defense[2]) and had NFL talent on their roster, but a woeful passing game and penchant for self-destruction in close games had ruined their season. Against an offense as explosive as the Mountaineers, the Panthers would be ill-equipped to make up even a very modest deficit. Plus, the game was in Morgantown, where the Mountaineers enjoy a powerful home field advantage. West Virginia was a 28-point favorite.

Perhaps only one person saw this coming. Before the game, while talking with reporters, Big East commissioner Mike Tranghese reminded reporters that this wasn't a regular football season. This was 2007. "USC lost to Stanford at home. [...] I believe anything can happen."[3]

I'm going to go ahead and spoil the ending for you here, in case the chapter heading and this thick foreshadowing didn't do it for you. Pitt won, 13-9.

It was a profoundly weird game. West Virginia's dynamic rushing attack was completely grounded, barely eking out 100 yards as a team. They had previously averaged over 300 per game. In fact, Pitt running back LeSean McCoy outrushed the entire West Virginia team by himself, going for 148 yards. The Mountaineers lost three fumbles, including one on the opening kickoff in the second half that set up Pitt's only touchdown. And star quarterback Pat White dislocated his thumb and missed almost all of the second half.

White returned for the last two drives, bandaged up, and got the Mountaineers deep into Pitt territory, only for both drives to stall out. The sleek, fast, dynamic Mountaineers got dragged into a rock fight instead of their planned track meet, and they came up just short.

Mountaineer head coach Rich Rodriguez was dumbfounded, pausing multiple times during his press conference after the game, while the audible celebration of Pitt players carried on in the background. "The whole thing was a nightmare," he told reporters.[4]

With the loss, West Virginia plummeted out of national title contention, forced instead to settle for a Fiesta Bowl berth against Oklahoma, a game they would win. A 10-2 season and a major bowl bid is nothing to sneeze at, but the Mountaineers blew perhaps their best chance yet at an elusive national title.

But this was about more than just West Virginia missing a chance at holding a big trophy because their rival ruined their season. That's unfortunate, but not unprecedented in college football. What is remarkable is how the full aftermath of this game changed the trajectory of like, five other major college programs. Maybe even more.

First, let's look at the actual championship game. By this point, Ohio State had improbably locked up the #1 spot in the BCS rankings, even though they themselves had been upset by Illinois in their second to last game of the season. They boasted the best defense in the country via S&P+, but their offense was much less elite (22nd[5]), and many commentators, even some in Columbus, suspected Ohio State's lofty ranking had more to do with the fact that nobody else in the country could stay ranked more than two weeks before an anvil fell on their head, rather than their own elite performance.

For the last several decades, no team with more than one loss was seriously considered a national title contender. But with West Virginia losing to Pitt, suddenly, there weren't other credible one-loss teams to match up against Ohio State. Kansas only had one loss, but they didn't even win their division, let alone conference. Hawaii was undefeated, but they played a gazillion time zones away from anybody who voted in the AP Poll and beat mostly terrible teams in the WAC. That was the list. Everybody else had two losses.

So LSU, the SEC champion whose two losses both came in double overtime (against decent Kentucky and Arkansas teams), earned the championship spot. The Tigers were still an excellent team and a bad matchup for the Buckeyes. While there has been some revisionist history about how this game actually went—helped in large part by the fact that the Buckeyes got the doors blown off of them by Florida in the previous year's national title game—it's true that LSU's speed all over the field was superior to Ohio State's. The Buckeyes didn't have the offensive personnel to climb back from an early hole, and the Tigers won the title, 38-24.

If WVU beats Pitt, LSU can't win the title that year because they'd be stuck in the Sugar Bowl. Assuming Pat White was healthy, this is a much better matchup. Ohio State's defense would have been better than anything WVU faced during the season, but WVU's skill position talent was just as fast as the LSU players that gave them so much trouble. S&P+ actually ranked West Virginia as the best team in the country in 2007 (Ohio State was 4th), and as much as it pains me to admit this, the Mountaineers would probably have been slight favorites in this game.

(If you're in Columbus, please don't show anybody at the school that paragraph. I don't want my degree taken away.)

So either Ohio State wins the national title here, erasing the prevailing narrative that the Big Ten was too big and slow to compete in nationally elite games, and profoundly changing Jim Tressel's legacy at Ohio State. Or West Virginia breaks free, finally wins a national title, and brings a moment of glory to the beleaguered Big East conference, which had already suffered defections from power programs like Miami and Virginia Tech, and whose long-term future was in question.

But that's just the football game. It also changed some major coaching decisions.

Two weeks after West Virginia's loss to Pitt, but before the bowl game, head coach Rich Rodriguez accepted the head coaching job at Michigan. This would turn out to be a disastrous decision for Rodriguez. The Wolverines had run a more pro-style offense for decades, and they didn't have the personnel or the institutional buy-in to make the transition to Rodriguez's spread offense effectively. There were also cultural clashes, as Rodriguez alienated boosters with his lack of proper respect for Michigan traditions. Plus, Michigan culture is more than a bit stiff and arrogant, and—I promise I'm saying this out of love and not as a pejorative—Rodriguez is kind of a redneck. It wasn't going to work, and he was fired after three disastrous seasons.

But if the Mountaineers had won? They would be playing for a national championship! Would a hypercompetitive guy like Rodriguez leave his team for a bigger payday when they were on the cusp of winning it all? That seems pretty hard to believe, and it seems equally hard to believe that Michigan, who had other potential targets, would have been willing to wait until January to make a hiring decision. WVU boosters had already demonstrated a willingness to pay to keep Rodriguez around (they raised the money to keep him from bolting to Alabama earlier[6]), and with a title on the line, they likely would have found a way to keep him for at least one more season.

Michigan's other major targets included LSU head coach (and Michigan graduate) Les Miles and Rutgers head coach Greg Schiano, who would then leave to coach Tampa Bay in the NFL. Either would have been vastly better cultural fits for Michigan's fanbase and program, and both would have almost certainly been better than Rodriguez. Still, both coaches would have been unlikely to deliver a championship, given how badly Miles would struggle to develop quarterbacks after 2007, and if Schiano's flameout with the Tampa Bay Buccaneers demonstrated what kind of coach he was at that time.

So now we're looking at a different 2007 national champion, a different coach at Michigan, and maybe different coaches at LSU or the Tampa Bay Buccaneers. But there's yet another angle to consider here. A recruiting angle.

West Virginia, along with virtually everybody else in the country, was hot on the trail to sign Terrelle Pryor, a five-star quarterback out of Jeannette, Pennsylvania, and the top ranked recruit in the country, according to Rivals.[7] But he wasn't just any awesome quarterback; he was one that would have been an absolute perfect fit for Rich Rodriguez's spread offense.

Pryor was six-foot-six and skilled enough to earn D1 offers to play basketball as well as football. He also brought elite speed and elusiveness. He had the size and strength to fight through tackles, but was fast enough to break through the open field. He was the next evolution of Pat White, and in an offense that would be specifically built around his skill set, rather than forcing him to be something he wasn't—a dropback, pocket passer—he could have been absolutely devastating at West Virginia.

Pryor apparently agreed, and had WVU as one of his five finalists, with many analysts thinking that the Mountaineers were actually the favorite. Coming off a national title, a coach who has best positioned to take advantage of his gifts, and Pryor's familiarity with the campus, it seems reasonable to think that, had WVU won, they would have secured his commitment.

But after Rodriguez left West Virginia, Pryor eliminated the Mountaineers from contention and added Michigan instead.[8] After an especially long recruiting process, he made a somewhat surprising choice: Ohio State.

Pryor ended up becoming the most polarizing Buckeye in my lifetime. Maybe ever.

On the field, it's hard to quibble with the results, even though his skillset was an awkward fit with Jim Tressel's offense. Ohio State hadn't utilized mobile quarterbacks very much in their scheme over the last several years, leading to occasional "square peg, round hole"–type moments. Still, Pryor earned Big Ten Freshman of the Year honors in 2008 and led the Buckeyes to an 8-1 record as a starter, also splitting time with Todd Boeckman.

Pryor followed up a promising freshman campaign with an even better sophomore season, now with the QB job unquestionably his. The Buckeyes finished 11-2, winning another Big Ten title and the Rose Bowl over Oregon, 26-17. Pryor was named MVP of the Rose Bowl, after an efficient performance that denied lightning-fast Oregon the football.

The 2010 season was even stronger with Pryor at the helm. Ohio State went 12-1[9], finished in the AP Top 5, and perhaps most importantly to Buckeye fans, finally beat an SEC team in a Bowl game. They knocked off a talented Arkansas squad, 31-26, in the Sugar Bowl, ending a streak of nine consecutive bowl losses to the conference.

Pryor's pocket presence would never be confused for the elite in the sport, and because of Ohio State's scheme, personnel, and coaching, he wasn't going to be a 70% passer. But he did toss 57 touchdown passes in his three-year career, ran for 17 more, and accumulated over 8,000 yards of total offense as a quarterback. Plus, Ohio State won a share of the Big Ten title in all three years, and Pryor never lost to Michigan. Sure, the Buckeyes never won a title during his era, but by any statistical measure, he'd go down as one of the very best quarterbacks in Ohio State history.

There's a pretty big elephant in the room here, though. You'll notice that Pryor only played three seasons. It wasn't because he decided to skip his senior year to go after a top ten NFL Draft selection or anything. Pryor also just happened to be the face of a massive scandal that would bring down head coach Jim Tressel and strip the program to its foundation.

Pryor, along with four other Ohio State players, traded Buckeye memorabilia (like championship rings) for tattoos and money, an arrangement that violated NCAA bylaws and should have rendered him ineligible in 2010. Ohio State coach Jim Tressel was informed of this arrangement via an email but declined to inform his superiors at Ohio State, a crime worse than the actual tattoo scandal in the eyes of the NCAA. By the time the dust had settled, Tressel was forced to resign, Pryor left Ohio State for the NFL supplemental draft, and four key players were suspended for five games for the 2011 season. The suddenly shorthanded Buckeyes went 6-7 the next season, losing the Gator Bowl.

But, that sudden collapse paved the way for Ohio State to then hire Urban Meyer, who built an even more powerful Buckeye dynasty.

Even now, you can find Buckeye fans whose opinion of the Pryor years run the entire gamut from "one of the best ever" to "I wish he had never enrolled." He did nothing but win and rolled up impressive stats, but it was hard to shake the feeling that he didn't quite live up to his massive potential. He should have been loved for dominating Michigan, but he was never quite embraced by even Buckeye fans during his tenure. He was the face of one of the more embarrassing scandals in Ohio State history and led to the firing of a legendary coach. But that sudden collapse paved the way for Ohio State to hire Urban Meyer.

I can't help but think he would have had an easier ride at West Virginia. There would be no awkward schematic fit. He'd have a more sympathetic fanbase, one that was less predisposed to take star recruits for granted and may have been more willing to overlook his flaws. And his schedule would have been way weaker. Paired with a running back like a Noel Devine, and facing off against late 2000s UConn, Syracuse and Louisville? Pryor could have won a dang Heisman Trophy.

A potential national title, then a Heisman a few years later, would have been especially huge for West Virginia, given where the program was in the late 2000s. 2007 was probably the high water mark for the beleaguered Big East Conference, which had recently lost Miami, Virginia Tech and Boston College to the ACC. Rutgers, UConn, South Florida and Cincinnati all had strong seasons, but the depth didn't quite hold, and the conference lacked a truly elite program. But if Rodriguez had stuck around for a few years, West Virginia is likely a perennially top-ten squad, changing the narrative around the league, and perhaps boosting not only recruiting for West Virginia, but for other conference programs as well.

Would this have saved the Big East? Probably not. No matter how many football games West Virginia won, it wasn't going to make Morgantown a major television market or make the league more attractive for Syracuse and Pitt, who would be the next programs to leave. But it would put WVU in a dramatically better position for the next cycle of conference realignment. If WVU is rolling at the peak of their powers, could they overcome their TV market and academic research deficiencies to earn an ACC invite, instead of joining the dysfunctional and awkwardly fitting Big 12? Or failing that, would they have been able to build up their infrastructure to better compete at a high level in the Big 12, or in a post–Rich Rod world? It's possible.

In a year of improbable upsets, perhaps none was a far reaching as the 100th Backyard Brawl. It completely swung the 2007 national title game and easily could have determined the coaching fate for Michigan and West Virginia, and maybe LSU or Rutgers too. It could have prevented the messy post–Rich Rod power struggle at West Virginia, which ended with Bill Stewart surprisingly getting the head coaching job after the Mountaineers upset Oklahoma. It may mean that future WVU head coach Dana Holgorsen never heads to Morgantown either. Maybe he ends up coaching Kansas? Iowa State? As a full-time Red Bull spokesman?

It also held the long-term future of Ohio State in its hands. If Pryor never comes to Columbus, that probably means no massive tattoo scandal. Which means no Urban Meyer. And that means no Ezekiel Elliott blowing past Alabama in the 2014 College Football Playoff (because Elliott would presumably be playing for Missouri). Ohio State would likely have at home in 2014 after losing in the Capital One Bowl or something under Jim Tressel. Urban Meyer would either still be on TV or coaching at Notre Dame. The Facebook comments at Land-Grant Holy Land would be much angrier. There would be no "Actually, The Spot was good" memes on Twitter.

That's not a world I'd prefer to live in, personally. So thanks, Pitt. LSU and Ohio State fans are in your debt.

What if UAB hired Jimbo Fisher?

IT TAKES A LOT OF hard work and luck to start a successful, big-time college football program.

It's one thing if you started your program in 1900. Many of the examples in this book have shown that a program started way back when could flail around for decades, only to eventually nail a hire and find its way towards consistent respectability. Or, you know, cheat. (Kansas State, Oregon, and Wisconsin immediately jump to mind as examples. You can probably think of others.) But starting a college football program from scratch today is a different operation altogether. You need to work much harder to build a fanbase, when a community has had generations to support other programs. Finding a conference home, especially one that doesn't require program-killing travel, becomes more complicated. On all levels, the margin for error becomes much smaller.

That isn't to say that it's impossible. South Florida launched an FBS program in 2000, and climbed all the way to #2 in the AP Poll by 2007. Florida Atlantic University didn't play a football game until 2001, and went on to win bowl games in 2007 and 2008. Others like Marshall and Boise State found high level football success relatively quickly after promotions from lower divisions of football.

But for many other programs, especially those starting from scratch, the road to FBS success is perilous. The line between "Motor City Bowl" and "losing to UMass in front of 11,000 fans" is a fine one.

A program looking to start a high-level college football team likely needs an advantageous location. The odds of a big-time football program being successful in a place like, say, Vermont or Alaska would be very long, given their low local population centers, lack of proximity to potential recruits and talent, and lower local appetite for college football. Also, bear attacks.

The perfect place for a college football expansion team would probably be a medium-sized city in a college football hotbed state. It would also help to not directly compete with a massive, established program, or popular professional team. And if that school had a large enrollment and some record of athletic success in other sports, well, even better.

Based on that description, the University of Alabama at Birmingham had just about everything going for them when they established a program in 1991. After five solid years playing at the NCAA Division III level, the Blazers joined the FBS in 1996.

But the story of UAB shows that advantageous geography isn't the only requirement for a potentially successful football program. It also needs institutional buy-in and support, and in that department, UAB was doomed from the start. Power struggles with the Alabama Board of Regents prevented UAB from ever securing adequate facilities and financial support, and discussions about killing the entire program were common almost from the beginning.

The Blazers nearly overcame these institutional roadblocks, however. The team's success and ambitions set up a massive power struggle in the mid 2000s that not only determined the future trajectory of UAB football (including its eventual dismantlement), but the direction of two different major college football powers, and maybe even multiple national championships.

But we're getting ahead of ourselves a little bit here. It probably helps to start at the beginning, and like all good college football stories set in the Deep South, this one starts... with basketball.

No, really.

When UAB decided to launch their D1 athletics program in 1978, they started off with a bang. The Blazers convinced UCLA's men's basketball head coach Gene Bartow to head to Birmingham to coach their team as well as serve as athletic director. A coach as successful as Bartow, who had come close to NCAA championships at both Memphis and UCLA, jumping ship to an expansion program was a bit unusual, even in the late 1970s. Bartow would later write that he "left UCLA for one major reason: (UAB) offered me three times what I was earning." [1] He also specifically denied he was leaving to escape the mob, which hey, is always a great sign for your flagship athletics hire.

The Blazers saw nearly immediate success under Bartow. They made the NIT in only their second season (back when that was a bigger deal), and then made the NCAA Tournament the very next year. That kicked off a run where UAB made the NCAA Tournament each of the next seven seasons, including a run to the Elite Eight, where they knocked off basketball blueblood programs like Virginia and Bobby Knight's Indiana. In a short amount of time, UAB men's basketball transformed from a university administrator's pipe dream to a peer of Alabama, the heavyweight of the state. Things were looking pretty good for the Blazers.

Any statewide goodwill that UAB might have picked up during their underdog run was short-lived. In 1991, Bartow wrote a letter to the NCAA that alleged that Alabama was running afoul of NCAA regulations, using testimony from his players that transferred from Alabama as proof. According to the *Los Angeles Times*, who obtained the letter, Bartow wrote[2]:

"I have had four ex-Alabama players. In each case, they have described rules violations (involving) them and other players there. Not once did an NCAA person investigate them to ask any questions about what went on at Alabama. [...] If an investigator would just ask two questions of six or eight former players who have dropped out of that program, I think you would get some interesting answers. [...] I really believe somebody would blow the whistle on them."

Bartow didn't just accuse the flagship institution in the state of cheating at basketball. He insinuated that said cheating came from the single most important person in Alabama athletics history—former Alabama head football coach Paul "Bear" Bryant, who also served as Alabama's athletic director until 1982.

Again, from the *LA Times*:

"'You think of the Charley Pell situation at Florida, the Jackie Sherrill situation at Texas A&M and the Danny Ford situation at Clemson, and now we have the Auburn situation,' he wrote, referring to several highly publicized NCAA infractions cases. 'All [of the coaches involved] were trained by Coach Paul [Bear] Bryant at Alabama. David, cheating in recruiting has been a way of life here in this state. [...] I do think that when Coach Bryant died, Ray Perkins [Bryant's successor] tried to clean up the Alabama program. When Ray left and Bill Curry came in, I think [Curry] ran a pretty honest program in football, and I think [current coach] Gene Stallings is probably trying hard to keep it clean.'"

To call out Bear Bryant in the state of Alabama would be almost as controversial as launching a smear campaign against Jesus. Even if those allegations were true, trying to snitch on the Tide would be political suicide. And one person who took especially strong umbrage to those remarks was Bear's son, Paul Bryant Jr.

Bryant Jr. would become an especially prominent member of the Alabama Board of Regents, and made no secret of his contempt for UAB athletics, and eventually, UAB football.

"Gene Bartow, out of his mouth, told me on many, many occasions that the aim of the board of trustees was to kill UAB football in the last 8-10 years," said Jimmy Filler, UAB's biggest booster and the creator of the UAB Football Foundation, to CBS Sports.[3]

UAB football certainly struggled to replicate the success of UAB basketball. Instead of spending big to lure in an established name from another successful program like they did with Bartow, UAB hired Watson Brown. Brown had spent the last four seasons as an offensive coordinator at Oklahoma and Mississippi State. Prior to those stints, he was the head coach at Vanderbilt for five years, where he amassed a whopping 10-45 record. He had also been the head coach at Rice for two years, and for a single season at Cincinnati. And while all three of those jobs were certainly difficult, in eight seasons as a D1-A head coach, Brown had never even won five games in a season, let alone made a bowl game.

Brown kept UAB reasonably competitive, but the program never experienced anything close to a breakthrough. From 1996 to 2003, UAB never won fewer than four games, but they also never won more than seven and failed

Matt Brown

to qualify for a bowl game. Attendance was low, and the administration was getting nervous.

But in 2004, things started to break the Blazers' way. UAB went 7-4, averaging 31 points a game, good for finishing in the top 25 in the country in scoring offense. They beat Mississippi State and clobbered Baylor. Their reward? A trip to the Hawaii Bowl. They lost that game against Hawaii 59-40, but they finished the season with a sense that maybe, just maybe, the program had finally turned the corner.

That enthusiasm was short-lived. The Blazers would finish 5-6 in 2005, and 3-9 in 2006. Brown resigned after the 2006 season to accept the head coaching position at D1-AA Tennessee Tech.[4] After 2006, UAB found themselves looking for a new coach, somebody to help build not just a winning program, but some sense of fan and institutional support as well.

Alabama, and even Birmingham specifically, is full of talented high school football players, but even in 2006, UAB would have been considered a very hard job. For starters, the Blazers played in the cavernous Legion Field instead of an on-campus stadium. The aged, former home of the Iron Bowl between Alabama and Auburn sat over 70,000 fans, an impossibly high number for an middling Conference USA team, and lacked amenities of modern stadiums. The board nixed plans for a smaller stadium that would have fit UAB's needs better. Even when the Blazers were well supported, the home-field atmosphere was lacking compared to their conference peers like Southern Miss and Louisiana Tech. The fact that the stadium was located in a less-than-desirable neighborhood in town didn't help matters.

Plus, UAB's academic standards were higher than many other teams in Conference USA, making recruiting more difficult. In fact, Alabama State Representative Jack Williams told me UAB was at least as tough to get into as a football player as programs like Northwestern and Rice, and the school wasn't budging on those standards. The program facilities, from a lack of a quality on-campus practice facility, to locker rooms, lagged behind other Conference USA programs. Add all of that to an administration that was less than supportive to UAB football, and the job as head coach did not seem especially appealing.

And yet, improbably, UAB's boosters managed to nearly convince a very good coach to take the job: LSU offensive coordinator Jimbo Fisher.

On paper, everything about this hire seemed perfect. Fisher had significant Alabama ties, having served on the coaching staffs at Auburn and Samford, which was just down the road from UAB. At LSU, Fisher had helped groom JaMarcus Russell into a top NFL draft pick and turned Josh Booty and Rohan Davey into highly successful college quarterbacks. After six years as a coordinator for the Tigers, Fisher found himself in demand.

UAB offered Fisher roughly $600,000, with $300,00 of that being covered specifically by athletic department boosters, to save the school's beleaguered budget. The school was ready to send a plane to pick him up and take him to an introductory press conference. [5]All they needed was for the Alabama trustees to sign off on the deal. It should have been a rubber stamp move. Who wouldn't approve of a school signing a national title winning coach at an affordable cost?

Well, Paul Bryant Jr, apparently. The Alabama board nixed the deal, under the flimsiest of motives—the need for fiscal responsibility.[6] In college football. In the South.

So why did Alabama *really* kill the Fisher contract? There are two possible reasons. One, of course, is that Fisher is a good coach. UAB hiring a good football coach would, naturally, increase the chances that they might become a good football team. That would make undermining, if not eventually killing UAB football more difficult for the board.

The other reason was even more cravenly self-interested. Alabama might have wanted him. The Blazers weren't the only football program in the state struggling, after all. The Crimson Tide had struggled to replicate the success the program enjoyed under Bear Bryant, Gene Stallings, and other greats. In 2006, Mike Shula went 6-6, leading to his departure, and the program's embarrassing loss in the Independence Bowl. The Tide hadn't finished in the AP Top 25 for two consecutive seasons since 1995 and 1996. For a program with its history and ludicrously high expectations, pretty good wasn't even close to good enough. Tide boosters had their sights set significantly higher.

Fisher wasn't an experienced enough candidate to be considered for the Alabama head coaching job in 2006, but Alabama boosters had already zeroed in on Miami Dolphins head coach Nick Saban, who hired Fisher at LSU. Being able to guarantee Fisher's availability as an offensive coordinator for Saban might make the Alabama job even more attractive to him, or so boosters thought. That, of course, would be a harder sell, if Fisher were the head coach at UAB.

If that was the plan, Alabama didn't execute it very well. Jimbo Fisher didn't end up working for Saban at Alabama. Instead, Fisher decided to take the offensive coordinator position at Florida State.

Things turned out pretty good for Fisher. Fisher took over the head coaching position at Florida State in 2010, and found success early, going 19-8 over his first two seasons, with two bowl wins. In 2013, he won a national title, and in 2014, the Seminoles went undefeated in the regular season, grabbing one of the spots in the first College Football Playoff. His program has recruited better than nearly any other program during the mid 2010s, and Florida State seems well equipped to compete at a high level for the foreseeable future.

When asked about the UAB contract in 2014, right before the Seminoles played for a national title, Fisher told AL.com "Somebody made a decision... It's funny in this business. You coulda went here. You coulda went there. Luckily, I'm glad they made that decision."[7]

Nick Saban also somehow managed to find a way to get over not getting Fisher as his offensive coordinator. After a slow first season, Saban built perhaps the most dominant dynasty in modern college football history. By his second season, Saban won double digit games every single year, won four national titles, made the playoffs both seasons, and dominated recruiting in a way unknown to the sport. Alabama turned out pretty okay.

And UAB? Well, UAB's consolation prize in the Jimbo Fisher sweepstakes wasn't great. The Blazers also struck out on retaining offensive coordinator Pat Sullivan[8], who would leave to become a successful head coach at cross-town Samford. Alabama State Rep. Jack Williams, a UAB booster and former proprietor of the UAB site on Rivals.com, also told me that Rick Neuheisel, who would go on to coach at UCLA, was also seriously considered.

The Blazers eventually settled on Neil Callaway, an offensive line coach at Georgia, which looked like an uninspired decision even at the time.[9] Callaway had never been a head coach before, and his hiring raised eyebrows among the national press.

If the Alabama regents hired Callaway, an Alabama grad himself and a relative to a member of the Alabama board, as some sort of sleeper agent to bring the Blazers down from the inside, well, that would be some impressive, Bond-villain level of diabolical scheming. And it would gotten the results they were looking for.

In 2007, Callaway's first season at UAB, the Blazers went 2-10, with one of those wins against Alcorn State. The Blazers were in the bottom 15 teams nationally in scoring offense (19.6 per game), and scoring defense (35.1), and lost every single game by at least two scores except one, an eight-point loss to Tulsa. Part of those struggles may have been due to roster attrition, as the Blazers trotted out less than 70 players on scholarship. UAB barely improved the next season, finishing 4-8.

Callaway coached at UAB for five seasons before getting fired, compiling a 18-42 record and presiding over some of the worst UAB teams in school history, which, despite that being a relatively short history, is saying something. He was coaching the offensive line at Western Kentucky the next season.

UAB's fortunes didn't improve. Their next hire, Garrick McGee, came to the program with some fanfare after his success at Arkansas[10], but didn't perform any better, going 5-19 over two years. McGee's tenure might be best remembered for his final game, a spectacular 62-27 drubbing by Southern Mississippi, a team that had lost its previous 23 games.

The losses were one thing; UAB fans were probably used to that. But the Alabama board continued to meddle in the football program, preventing any positive momentum from taking root. Despite efforts from the city of Birmingham and UAB boosters, the board tabled proposals for an on-campus stadium, a move that stifled recruiting and the program's ability to attract staff[11].

More importantly, the program was unable to construct adequate practice facilities, forcing the program to retreat and practice at D3 Birmingham Southern when it rained, since UAB's field would flood.[12]Plans to improve UAB's turf, even when it wouldn't have cost the school any money, were reportedly killed. [13]Other Conference USA programs would point to the lack of administrative support as proof that UAB might just cut the team altogether, further limiting recruiting. Building a program from scratch is hard anywhere, but trying to do it with one hand constantly tied behind your back is basically impossible.

At the end of the 2014 season, Alabama voted to shut down UAB football, citing a lack of fan support and a need for financial responsibility. The vote was justified in part by some highly dubious studies[14] indicating the program was bleeding money. Amid a national outcry, faculty protests, and Conference USA threatening to expel their basketball program and other successful sports[15], the university would eventually decide to restart the program in 2017. But any hope for UAB breaking a cycle of failure in the near future felt pretty dead.

But what if UAB actually *was* able to hire Jimbo Fisher? Would that have changed its fortunes?

Let's start with what this would mean for UAB first. Is it likely that Jimbo could have built the Blazers into a Conference USA powerhouse? Probably not, since even with a good coach, UAB still had major structural limitations. In the mid 2000s, UAB still lacked a quality practice facility, on-campus stadium, conference-standard locker room facilities, and, oh yeah, a university administration that actually wanted them to succeed. If a coach became too successful too quickly, they may be inviting a power struggle with Bryant and the board, and no matter how popular or successful a UAB football coach might have been around 2009, it's hard to imagine them winning a fight with a Bryant.

But that doesn't mean that UAB may not have improved. The Blazers were near the bottom of Conference USA when it came to recruiting, and given Fisher's ties to Louisiana and Alabama from previous coaching stops, getting the Blazers to at least a Conference USA average level seems probable. Even though Conference USA was more competitive in the mid 2000s than it is now, it isn't like East Carolina or Houston were regularly bringing blue-chip recruits that would bury a program like UAB.

The cupboard was not completely bare in Birmingham either. UAB's QB from 2007 to 2009 was Joe Webb, who was good enough to get drafted in the 6th round by the Minnesota Vikings, and even picked up a few starts on Sundays. Webb was never an especially efficient college QB, but under the tutelage of a QB whisperer like Fisher, it's likely Webb would have improved. In 2009, Webb finished with 21 TD passes to 8 INTs, on 59.8% passing, while rushing for another 1,427 yards. Webb might not have fit the exact mold of a successful Fisher QB, but If Webb bumped that up to say, 62% passing, or threw one or two fewer picks, the 2009 UAB team that went 5-7 could easily have made a bowl game.

UAB in 2007 was probably going to stink no matter what. But with Fisher, and some marginally improved recruiting, it isn't a stretch to imagine UAB finding ways to win at home against ECU (they lost 17-13) and against Memphis (they lost 33-30) to get to 6-6. In 2009, thanks to an even more improved Joe Webb, and a more balanced offensive unit, they could go 8-5, flipping close losses against SMU, Central Florida, and East Carolina, a game where they outgained the Pirates by nearly 200 yards.

Maybe that's enough to build UAB into something bigger. Maybe that's enough to force the administration to begin to support the program. But given Fisher's pedigree, even with his ties to Birmingham, expecting him to stay at UAB for the long term wouldn't have been realistic. Given the extenuating political circumstances at UAB, two bowls in two seasons would be enough to get Fisher in the conversation for a better job, before the Alabama board could bring the hammer down on the Blazers. USF, who needed to replace Jim Leavitt that year, could have been a possibility. Miami could have been another possibility, although how comfortable Fisher, a man who makes his country background no secret, would feel in South Beach is a good question. If nothing else, a coach with experience working with a dysfunctional environment would have been attractive to the Hurricanes, who were about to face years of NCAA uncertainty after another benefits scandal. And of course, Florida State would likely also be opening around this time, depending on Bowden's retirement and succession plans.

What if Fisher had taken the coordinator job at Alabama? The first year likely wouldn't have been appreciably different. Even though Fisher would clearly have been an upgrade as a QB coach and coordinator compared to Major Applewhite, who left after one season to return to Texas, the difference wouldn't be so large as to make up for the talent disadvantage and turn the team into a contender.

It's what happens in the future that becomes more interesting. Nick Saban replaced Applewhite with Fresno State's Jim McElwain. Alabama's quarterback play improved somewhat, but the real explosion came from the running game, as Glen Coffee exploded for 1,383 yards on nearly six yards a carry, and the Tide improved to 10-2, losing a close Sugar Bowl battle to Utah. In year three, Alabama won the national title, and the Alabama Dynasty was off and running.

Would Jimbo Fisher have brought a national title to Alabama sooner than that? Probably not, since beating eventual national champion Florida in 2008 would have been a tall order for anybody. But he certainly would have changed the trajectory of Jim McElwain's career.

McElwain parlayed his success at Alabama under the era's most prestigious and accomplished coach to a head coaching position at Colorado State, and then later, at Florida. Without getting a chance to shine at Alabama, it's possible McElwain never gets a head coaching position at all, let alone one as prestigious as Florida's. Perhaps, after a few years under Saban, those positions are eventually filled by Fisher. Florida, after all, would have also made a lot of sense.

Instead, Fisher ended up at Florida State. But what if he hadn't?

This might be the most interesting what-if trail to follow. Per *Florida Today*, other candidates Florida State was considering included Lawrence Dawsey, a former FSU assistant who was working with USF at the time, along with Valdosta State's Chris Hatcher[16], and George Henshaw, another former FSU assistant who was working with the New Orleans Saints at the time. None of those coaches ended up having a pedigree comparable with Jimbo Fisher.

Perhaps the most intriguing alternate candidate would have been Hatcher, who quickly built Valdosta State into a D2 powerhouse, recording a 76-12 record over seven seasons, including a D2 national title in 2004. A former quarterback himself, Hatcher's squads built impressive passing attacks, averaging over 34 points a game during his final 2006 campaign. He would have been a credible coordinator hire, and perhaps importantly, he would have come outside of the Florida State and Bowden coaching tree.

Instead of earning the FSU gig, Hatcher became the head coach at Georgia Southern. On paper, this made sense, given Hatcher's long success at the D2 level and ties to both Georgia and Florida. But his tenure never really got off the ground, and after an 18-15 mark over three seasons, he was fired. After a five-year stint at Murray State, Hatcher now coaches at Samford.

One wild card in this entire conversation, of course, is Bobby Bowden, who wasn't just Florida State's head coach but the patriarch of the entire program. Bowden had won over 300 games with the Seminoles and dragged it from an afterthought on the periphery of the sport to a national-title-contending behemoth.

But Bowden was getting old, and the fans were getting nervous. By 2006, Florida State was a far cry from the dominating teams of the late '90s. They finished 7-6, beating UCLA in the Emerald Bowl amidst multiple seasons of declining offensive production. Forcing a legend out is difficult and awkward, but Bowden, even in his late seventies, wasn't especially interested in leaving.

Hiring Fisher, who had played and coached for Bowden's son, Terry, helped make that transition much easier. After just one season, Florida State felt comfortable enough to make Fisher their "head coach in waiting", promising the job to him whenever Bowden decided to retire. That promise helped keep Fisher at Florida State, even after his hometown West Virginia Mountaineers reportedly showed some interest.[17]

Having a source of clarity with what happens next helped prevent an ugly, public battle over Bowden. But what if Florida State struggled more? The 2007 Florida State squad, Fisher's first as offensive coordinator, wasn't great, finishing with a 7-6 record and a loss to Kentucky in the Music City Bowl.

Let's say Hatcher is the OC instead, and Florida State's offense drags just a little more. If they lose to say, #21 ranked Alabama, and a road game at #2 Boston College, suddenly, Florida State is missing their first bowl game since 1981, and the heat intensifies on Bowden. Likely Bowden would have chosen to retire, after some strong suggestions from boosters, in 2008 or 2009.

There were a few interesting and plausible head-coaching candidates around that time. If Florida State wanted to go in a completely different direction from Bowden, they could have turned to West Virginia and grabbed Rich Rodriguez, who would accept the Michigan opening that season after the Wolverines swung and missed on a few candidates. Rodriguez would have been a dramatically better cultural fit at a school like Florida State instead of Michigan, but his wide-open spread offensive scheme might have been a bit controversial in Tallahasee, which had gotten used to the pro-style formations during the Bowden era.

If Florida State wanted a candidate a little more conventional, or if for whatever reason, they were outbid in this hypothetical by Michigan, they might have been tempted to turn to LSU's successful defensive coordinator, Bo Pelini, who also boasted years of NFL experience and took the Nebraska position that offseason.

There are two other intriguing options if FSU was coach shopping before 2010. If Florida State wanted to find a candidate off the Bowden tree, Tommy Bowden's former assistant, Dabo Swinney, might have been on the market. After Tommy resigned six games into the 2008 season, Swinney, who had been working as a recruiting coordinator and wideouts coach at Clemson, would go on to rebuild the Tigers into a powerhouse, making the NCAA championship game in 2015 and winning it in 2016.

But would Florida State have been able to pry Swinney away from the Tigers, the place where he had coached since 2003? And would Florida State have even wanted to, given that Swinney hadn't even been a coordinator yet? That might have been hard to swing, even if Florida State's pocket books were deeper.

Failing that, there was another big name on the coaching market around this time that Florida State probably would have been interested in. He was a former NFL head coach. He had experience as a strong recruiter as a collegiate assistant, working for one of the most successful programs of the era. He had a background as an offensive innovator, an area of the ball where Florida State was struggling. And perhaps most important, he projected an era of youth and energy, an Anti-Bowden, if you will.

I'm talking about Lane Kiffin. Tennessee hired him that season, but Florida State almost certainly would have been able to get him if they wanted.

Given how the Kiffin and Pelini eras ended, picturing them at a place like Florida State, with high expectations and a sometimes confrontational fanbase (c'mon, you've seen Florida State fans on Twitter), feels really funny. The odds that Pelini would end a difficult press conference by cursing out a reporter or random passerby seem pretty good, especially in an environment with a less forgiving local media than Nebraska. A Pelini era likely wouldn't have produced a national title, but it would have produced some pretty good defenses, and even better GIFs.

Late 2000s Kiffin still lacked the maturity and management skills to be an effective head coach. He flamed out of the Raiders, struggled at Tennessee, and eventually, was fired from USC at the airport after an embarrassing loss to Arizona State. He's rehabilitated his career as an assistant for Nick Saban, but it's hard to imagine how a hypothetical head coaching job at FSU in 2009 would have ended differently than his actual head coaching positions did.

Unless Florida State ends up with Dabo (unlikely), Florida State probably doesn't win the 2013 national title, and Jameis Winston doesn't win the Heisman Trophy. In fact, there's a decent chance Winston doesn't end up at Florida State at all, but at a runner-up in his recruitment, Stanford[18].

In fact, with a redshirt freshman Winston at the helm, it isn't hard to see the Cardinal upsetting either Auburn or Alabama as the 2013 champs. After all, Stanford finished 5th in BCS standings that year, winning the Rose Bowl, before getting upset by Michigan State. All three of Stanford's losses came by a score or less, and the Cardinal failed to break 30 points in any of them. With a big, strong-armed QB, Stanford instead flips their games against Utah and USC to get to the title game, and then upsets Auburn to earn their first national title since 1940. Florida State fans rage on the internet as their offense fails to rebound to the levels of the late 1990s, and boosters plan to ditch Pelini or Kiffin. Alabama's dynasty rolls on, and UAB fans try in vain to finally get an on-campus stadium built, providing Fisher's brief burst of success didn't embolden administrators to kill the program earlier.

So that's at least one national title, the existence of an FBS program, and fortunes of multiple programs, from Stanford to Alabama to Florida, that all hinged on some bitter, petty board members vetoing a contract because a former athletic director insulted a state icon more than a decade earlier.

Makes sense, right? Well, that's just college football.

Thanks Yous And Stuff

I REALIZE THAT NOBODY ACTUALLY turns to this page unless they're expecting their own name on it. The acknowledgements page is probably just another exercise in self-indulgence. But hey, this is *my* book, and you made it this far, so please permit me a tiny bit more self-indulgence. After all, even though my name is on the cover and all, I had an awful lot of help.

I know it's author code to list your spouse last on these things, but I'd be remiss if I didn't mention what an enormous help my wife Taylor was in the creation of this project. When Taylor and I were first dating, Land-Grant Holy Land didn't exist, and I was a boring, 9-to-5 human resources flunky. Sportswriting wasn't really on the agenda, and since Ohio State completely sucked that year, I wasn't even watching that much college football. She had no idea what was coming.

Right after we got married, I helped launch LGHL, wrote at nights for years, and eventually turned that into a full-time sportswriting career. Taylor didn't really sign up for everything that goes along with that, but she's been exceptionally supportive. She let us move from Chicago to Washington DC, right after she found out she was pregnant, so I could take a full-time job at SB Nation. She picked up other family responsibilities when I worked a gazillion hours during football season. She didn't roll her eyes when I explained that working really meant sitting on the couch and watching football until 2 AM. (Okay, maybe she rolled her eyes a little bit.)

And without her keen eye in noticing things that I take for granted, her willingness to help with our daughter when I needed to put my head down and write, and her emotional support when I was ready to throw my laptop out our window, none of this would have happened. There would no sports-writing career, no book, no nothing. I would be sitting in a cubicle some-where, sending invitations to strangers on LinkedIn. Basically, thank God for my wife.

I'd also want to thank my two late parents, Gary Brown and Regina Figueiredo. Neither of them were especially big into sports, but they were passionate about books, writing, and art. Both pushed me, supported me, and helped develop me into a writer, a mantle that my two sisters, Maya and Gabriella, also took up. I'd like to think my folks would be proud of me right now, even if this book accidentally sucks. I know my dad would be proud, even if he never read the book and only used it to kill spiders around the house. My mom has probably already found at least two typos that made it past copyediting and is silently judging me from beyond.

More practically, I owe a huge debt to many of my SB Nation friends and colleagues. I am truly blessed to work with so many smart, creative, and compassionate college football minds, and my work, thinking, and day-to-day life has been improved by them. In particular, I want to thank Bill Connelly, who was not only an enormously helpful guy to just bounce football ideas off of, but gave important practical writing and research advice as well. Bill has written two very good college football books. Go buy them. Go follow him on Twitter. You'll learn a ton. I certainly have.

I also want to single out my colleagues Luke Zimmermann, who hired me at SB Nation and ran LGHL with me, and Steven Godfrey, who took me aboard some reporting adventures even when I was fabulously underqualified and answered a lot of my stupid questions. This book would not have hap-pened if I didn't work with a team that was so passionate about the weirdness of this wonderful, and very stupid, sport. That collective SB Nation voice is a part of this text, and everything that I write. Everybody who has worked here with me has been a part of that.

Thanks to Ryan Connors, who ran Testudo Times, SB Nation's Maryland blog, and also worked as my research assistant. Ryan helped me track down a few books Maryland wouldn't let me check out, and was a valuable resource, especially for the Bear Bryant chapter. He has a bright future in journalism ahead of him.

Speaking of SB Nation, thanks so much to the readers at Land-Grant Holy Land, and all other SB Nation college blogs. It's been a pleasure writing for you, talking football with you, and learning from you. I wouldn't have written a book without your support. I love you all. The Spot was good. And don't let the last 80,000 words distract you from the fact that Notre Dame finished 4-8 in 2016.

I'm sure I'm forgetting many other people, but I'm very grateful to all of the people who lent their opinions, expertise and advise during this book. That includes folks like Bruce Feldman, Keith Dunnavant, Duff Tittle, Dr. Ron Smith, Mark Ennis, Ken Haines and JP Gooderman. Dave Revsine also graciously not only shared valuable insights on the early years of college football, but also the practical process of researching and writing a dang book. Without the generosity of these individuals, this book doesn't happen.

Thanks to my editor, Dan Crissman, who graciously saved me from myself and my multiple egregious violations of proper comma usage. This book is way better because of his help.

Thank you to Michelle Goldchain of Curbed, who took the headshot for this book.

Also, thanks to my childhood buddy Patrick Martyn, who read many drafts of this book, and helped check for clarity. He added some of the jokes too. When I've needed a sanity check, he's been there.

I would be remiss if I didn't thank the University of Maryland for allowing me to buy a community library card, which I used to read almost every single college football book in their stacks. Thanks to the Prince George County Library System, who also supplied a few research texts, and more importantly, a place for me to occasionally work in a toddler-free zone. Digital archives and officials at Tulane University, the University of Maryland, the University of Michigan, and Brigham Young University were also especially helpful.

A quick thanks to some invaluable tools in researching this book, Newspapers.com and Proquest, which allowed me to search the historical archives of newspapers. For my fellow writers, Newspapers.com is cheap, and I cannot recommend subscribing enough.

Finally, thanks to my daughter, Penelope. She's only two, so she wasn't much help as a copyeditor, and honestly, her suggestions weren't particularly useful. But when I was tired, and wanted nothing more than to close my laptop and all of my books, play NBA2K17, and go to sleep at 10:00 PM, she provided the motivation to actually finish this dang thing.

All of my work, after all, is for her.

ENDNOTES

WHAT IF MICHIGAN NEVER REJOINED THE BIG TEN?

1. Voltmer, Carl D. *A brief history of the Intercollegiate Conference of Faculty Representatives, with special consideration of athletic problems.* New York, 1935.

2. Watterson, John Sayle. *College football: history, spectacle, controversy.* Baltimore: Johns Hopkins University Press, 2006

3. Kryk, John. *Stagg vs. Yost: the birth of cutthroat football.* Lanham, MD: Rowman & Littlefield, 2015.

4. Edds, Kevin. "Football's Founding Fathers: Today's college game shaped by UVA." Virginia Magazine. Fall 2011. http://uvamagazine.org/articles/footballs_founding_fathers.

5. Watterson, John Sayle. *College football: history, spectacle, controversy.* Baltimore: Johns Hopkins University Press, 2006

6. Watterson, John Sayle. *College football: history, spectacle, controversy.* Baltimore: Johns Hopkins University Press, 2006

7. Watterson, John Sayle. *College football: history, spectacle, controversy.* Baltimore: Johns Hopkins University Press, 2006

8. Voltmer, Carl D. *A brief history of the Intercollegiate Conference of Faculty Representatives, with special consideration of athletic problems.* New York, 1935

9. Voltmer, Carl D. *A brief history of the Intercollegiate Conference of Faculty Representatives, with special consideration of athletic problems.* New York, 1935

10. Voltmer, Carl D. *A brief history of the Intercollegiate Conference of Faculty Representatives, with special consideration of athletic problems.* New York, 1935

11. Voltmer, Carl D. *A brief history of the Intercollegiate Conference of Faculty Representatives, with special consideration of athletic problems.* New York, 1935

12. Kryk, John. *Stagg vs. Yost: the birth of cutthroat football.* Lanham, MD: Rowman & Littlefield, 2015.

13. Wojnowski, Bob, John U. Bacon, and Angelique S. Chengelis. *A legacy of champions: the story of the men who built University of Michigan football.* Farmington Hills, MI.: CTC Productions & Sports, 1996.

14. Kryk, John. *Stagg vs. Yost: the birth of cutthroat football.* Lanham, MD: Rowman & Littlefield, 2015..

15. Kryk, John. *Stagg vs. Yost: the birth of cutthroat football.* Lanham, MD: Rowman & Littlefield, 2015.

16. Watterson, John Sayle. *College football: history, spectacle, controversy.* Baltimore: Johns Hopkins University Press, 2006

17. Wojnowski, Bob, John U. Bacon, and Angelique S. Chengelis. *A legacy of champions: the story of the men who built University of Michigan football.* Farmington Hills, MI.: CTC Productions & Sports, 1996.

18. Kryk, John. *Stagg vs. Yost: the birth of cutthroat football.* Lanham, MD: Rowman & Littlefield, 2015.

19. Wojnowski, Bob, John U. Bacon, and Angelique S. Chengelis. *A legacy of champions: the story of the men who built University of Michigan football.* Farmington Hills, MI.: CTC Productions & Sports, 1996.

20. "Yost Is Making Michigan Nervous By Not Signing." *Baltimore Sun*, December 10, 1911.

21. "Michigan Runs Up A Big Score." *Chicago Daily Tribune*, October 13, 1904.

22. Watterson, John Sayle. *College football: history, spectacle, controversy*. Baltimore: Johns Hopkins University Press, 2006

23. Watterson, John Sayle. *College football: history, spectacle, controversy*. Baltimore: Johns Hopkins University Press, 2006

24. Watterson, John Sayle. *College football: history, spectacle, controversy*. Baltimore: Johns Hopkins University Press, 2006

25. Watterson, John Sayle. *College football: history, spectacle, controversy*. Baltimore: Johns Hopkins University Press, 2006

26. "Yost & Michigan Leave the Western Conference (1906-08)." MVictors. com. March 15, 2010. http://mvictors.com/100th-anniversary-michigan-leaves-the-conference/.

27. Voltmer, Carl D. *A brief history of the Intercollegiate Conference of Faculty Representatives, with special consideration of athletic problems*. New York, 1935

28. Wojnowski, Bob, John U. Bacon, and Angelique S. Chengelis. *A legacy of champions: the story of the men who built University of Michigan football*. Farmington Hills, MI.: CTC Productions & Sports, 1996.

29. Lester, Robin. *Stagg's university: the rise, decline, and fall of big-time football at Chicago*. Urbana: University of Illinois Press, 1999.

30. Yost & Michigan Leave the Western Conference (1906-08)." MVictors. com. March 15, 2010. http://mvictors.com/100th-anniversary-michigan-leaves-the-conference/.

31. Revsine, Dave. *Opening kickoff: the tumultuous birth of a football nation.* Guilford, CT: Lyons Press, 2015.

32. Revsine, Dave. *Opening kickoff: the tumultuous birth of a football nation.* Guilford, CT: Lyons Press, 2015.

33. "Michigan-Minnesota: The Little Brown Jug Series." MGoBlue.com. http://www.mgoblue.com/sports/m-footbl/spec-rel/061709aaa.html.

34. Reed, Rachel. "The Origins of the Little Brown Jug." Bentley Historical Library. http://bentley.umich.edu/features/the-origins-of-the-little-brown-jug/.

35. Wojnowski, Bob, John U. Bacon, and Angelique S. Chengelis. *A legacy of champions: the story of the men who built University of Michigan football.* Farmington Hills, MI.: CTC Productions & Sports, 1996

36. Kryk, John. *Stagg vs. Yost: the birth of cutthroat football.* Lanham, MD: Rowman & Littlefield, 2015.

37. Wojnowski, Bob, John U. Bacon, and Angelique S. Chengelis. *A legacy of champions: the story of the men who built University of Michigan football.* Farmington Hills, MI.: CTC Productions & Sports, 1996

38. Emmerich, Michael. *100 things Michigan State fans should know & do before they die.* Chicago, IL: Triumph Books, 2013.

39. Thomas, Jeanna. "The history of Carmen Ohio." Land-Grant Holy Land. February 16, 2014. http://www.landgrantholyland.com/2014/2/16/5414320/the-history-of-carmen-ohio.

40. Kryk, John. *Natural enemies: the Notre Dame-Michigan football feud.* Kansas City: Andrews and McMeel, 1994.

41. Kryk, John. *Natural enemies: the Notre Dame-Michigan football feud.* Kansas City: Andrews and McMeel, 1994.

42. Kryk, John. *Natural enemies: the Notre Dame-Michigan football feud.* Kansas City: Andrews and McMeel, 1994.

43. Kryk, John. *Natural enemies: the Notre Dame-Michigan football feud.* Kansas City: Andrews and McMeel, 1994.

44. Kryk, John. *Natural enemies: the Notre Dame-Michigan football feud.* Kansas City: Andrews and McMeel, 1994.

45. Bacon, John U. "Column: When Ward, Ford Played Ball for UM." *The Ann Arbor Chronicle* RSS. February 24, 2012. http://annarborchronicle. com/2012/02/24/column-when-ward-ford-played-ball-for-um/index.html.

46. Wojnowski, Bob, John U. Bacon, and Angelique S. Chengelis. *A legacy of champions: the story of the men who built University of Michigan football.* Farmington Hills, MI.: CTC Productions & Sports, 1996

47. Young, David. *Arrogance and scheming in the Big Ten: Michigan State's quest for membership and Michigan's powerful opposition.* Holland, MI: DJY Pub., 2011.

48. "What if Michigan Never Returned to the Big Ten?" MVictors.com. February 15, 2017. http://mvictors.com/what-if-michigan-never-returned-to-the-big-ten/.

49. "Michigan Stadium -- Getting It Built University of Michigan Athletics." Bentley Library. http://bentley.umich.edu/athdept/stadium/stadtext/stadbild.htm.

50. Notre Dame finished 4-8 in 2016. People forget that.

51. Kryk, John. *Natural enemies: the Notre Dame-Michigan football feud*. Kansas City: Andrews and McMeel, 1994.

52. UP. "Irish Willing To Join Big Ten." *Detroit Free Press*, November 27, 1929.

53. Kryk, John. *Natural enemies: the Notre Dame-Michigan football feud*. Kansas City: Andrews and McMeel, 1994.

54. He was offsides, by the way.

.

WHAT IF CHICAGO STAYED IN THE BIG TEN?

1. Lester, Robin. *Stagg's university: the rise, decline, and fall of big-time football at Chicago*. Urbana: University of Illinois Press, 1999.

2. Lester, Robin. *Stagg's university: the rise, decline, and fall of big-time football at Chicago*. Urbana: University of Illinois Press, 1999.

3. Bernstein, Mark F. *Football: the Ivy League origins of an American obsession*. Philadelphia: University of Pennsylvania Press, 2001.

4. Lester, Robin. *Stagg's university: the rise, decline, and fall of big-time football at Chicago*. Urbana: University of Illinois Press, 1999

5. Bernstein, Mark F. *Football: the Ivy League origins of an American obsession*. Philadelphia: University of Pennsylvania Press, 2001

6. Lester, Robin. *Stagg's university: the rise, decline, and fall of big-time football at Chicago*. Urbana: University of Illinois Press, 1999.

7. Whalen, James. *Gridiron greats now gone: the heyday of 19 former consensus top-20 college football programs*. Jefferson: McFarland, 1992.

8. Watterson, John Sayle. *College football: history, spectacle, controversy*. Baltimore: Johns Hopkins University Press, 2006.

9. "Chicago legend passes on; Berwanger dies at age 88." *Chicago Chronicle*. July 11, 2002. http://chronicle.uchicago.edu/020711/obit-berwanger.shtml.

10. "Chicago legend passes on; Berwanger dies at age 88." *Chicago Chronicle*. July 11, 2002. http://chronicle.uchicago.edu/020711/obit-berwanger.shtml.

11. "Chicago legend passes on; Berwanger dies at age 88." *Chicago Chronicle*. July 11, 2002. http://chronicle.uchicago.edu/020711/obit-berwanger.shtml.

12. "Heisman Was Only Part Of The Deal." *Chicago Tribune*. September 5, 1999. http://articles.chicagotribune.com/1999-09-05/sports/9909050015_1_jay-ber-wanger-celebrity-obsessed-society-college-football.

13. Watterson, John Sayle. *College football: history, spectacle, controversy*. Baltimore: Johns Hopkins University Press, 2006.

14. AP. "Chicago, Pacific to Honor Stagg in 1938." *The Eugene Guard*, December 8, 1937.

15. Lester, Robin. *Stagg's university: the rise, decline, and fall of big-time football at Chicago*. Urbana: University of Illinois Press, 1999.

16. Bartlett, Charles. "Maroons Hold Michigan and Harmon, 85-0." *The Chicago Tribune*, October 22, 1939.

17. Watterson, John Sayle. *College football: history, spectacle, controversy*. Baltimore: Johns Hopkins University Press, 2006.

18. Lester, Robin. *Stagg's university: the rise, decline, and fall of big-time football at Chicago*. Urbana: University of Illinois Press, 1999

19. "Ninety Years of College Football Recruiting." Ninety Years of College Football Recruiting. February 6, 2014. http://mode.github.io/blog/2014-02-06-signing-day/index.html.

20. Association, Michigan State University Alumni. "How MSU Became A Member of the Big Ten Conference." MSU Alumni Association. http://alumni.msu.edu/magazine/article.cfm?id=2507.

21. Watterson, John Sayle. *College football: history, spectacle, controversy*. Baltimore: Johns Hopkins University Press, 2006.

22. "Ara Parseghian: 1956-1963 | Northwestern University Library." A History of Football at Northwestern: Ara Parseghian: 1956-1963 | Northwestern University Library. http://exhibits.library.northwestern.edu/archives/exhibits/football/7.html.

23. "Northwestern Daily Urges Quit Big Ten." *Chicago Tribune*, December 1, 1955.

24. AP. "Officials Deny ND Will Join Big Ten." *The News Palladium (Benton Harbor)*, October 14, 1969.

25. White, Gordon S. "Ivy League Considers Adding 2 Schools." *The New York Times*. January 9, 1982. http://www.nytimes.com/1982/01/10/sports/ivy-league-considers-adding-2-schools.html.

26. Cohen, Ben. "Northwestern, the Would-Be Ivy." *The Wall Street Journal*. October 4, 2013. https://www.wsj.com/articles/SB10001424052702304906704579113410766027876.

27. Bansch, John. "Getting Out Of the Big Ten Would Help Wildcats." *The Indianapolis Star*, November 22, 1989.

28. Tibbals, Loren. "Ara Tells How He'll Rebuild ND." *Akron Beacon Journal*, December 16, 1963.

WHAT IF MARYLAND KEPT BEAR BRYANT?

1. Jones, Wilbur D. *"Football! Navy! War!": how military "lend-lease" players saved the college game and helped win World War II*. Jefferson, NC: McFarland & Co., 2009.

2. Jones, Wilbur D. *"Football! Navy! War!": how military "lend-lease" players saved the college game and helped win World War II*. Jefferson, NC: McFarland & Co., 2009.

3. Herskowitz, Mickey. *The legend of Bear Bryant*. Austin, TX: Eakin Press, 1993.

4. Herskowitz, Mickey. *The legend of Bear Bryant*. Austin, TX: Eakin Press, 1993.

5. Attner, Paul. *The Terrapins: Maryland football*. Huntsville, Ala.: Strode, 1975.

6. Herskowitz, Mickey. *The legend of Bear Bryant*. Austin, TX: Eakin Press, 1993.

7. Attner, Paul. *The Terrapins: Maryland football*. Huntsville, Ala.: Strode, 1975.

8. Dunnavant, Keith. *Coach: the life of Paul "Bear" Bryant*. New York: St. Martin's Griffin, 2005.

9. Attner, Paul. *The Terrapins: Maryland football*. Huntsville, Ala.: Strode, 1975.

10. Attner, Paul. *The Terrapins: Maryland football*. Huntsville, Ala.: Strode, 1975.

11. Attner, Paul. *The Terrapins: Maryland football*. Huntsville, Ala.: Strode, 1975.

12. Dunnavant, Keith. *Coach: the life of Paul "Bear" Bryant*. New York: St. Martin's Griffin, 2005.

13. Attner, Paul. *The Terrapins: Maryland football*. Huntsville, Ala.: Strode, 1975.

14. "Coach Halts U of M 'Strike'" *The Baltimore Sun*, January 16, 1946.

15. Dunnavant, Keith. *Coach: the life of Paul "Bear" Bryant*. New York: St. Martin's Griffin, 2005.

16. Herskowitz, Mickey. *The legend of Bear Bryant*. Austin, TX: Eakin Press, 1993.

17. "Coach Halts U of M 'Strike'" *The Baltimore Sun*, January 16, 1946.

18. "Coach Halts U of M 'Strike'" *The Baltimore Sun*, January 16, 1946.

19. Attner, Paul. *The Terrapins: Maryland football*. Huntsville, Ala.: Strode, 1975.

20. Herskowitz, Mickey. *The legend of Bear Bryant*. Austin, TX: Eakin Press, 1993.

21. Attner, Paul. *The Terrapins: Maryland football*. Huntsville, Ala.: Strode, 1975.

22. AP. "Shaughnessy Denies Calling Team 'Bums'" *The Courier Journal*, November 29, 1946.

23. Attner, Paul. *The Terrapins: Maryland football*. Huntsville, Ala.: Strode, 1975.

24. Attner, Paul. *The Terrapins: Maryland football*. Huntsville, Ala.: Strode, 1975.

25. Attner, Paul. *The Terrapins: Maryland football*. Huntsville, Ala.: Strode, 1975.

26. Hernsom, Bob. "Tatum: OU's vain attraction They called the big guy Coach... among other things." NewsOK.com. August 21, 2001. http://newsok.com/article/2752360.

27. Attner, Paul. *The Terrapins: Maryland football*. Huntsville, Ala.: Strode, 1975.

28. Hernsom, Bob. "Tatum: OU's vain attraction They called the big guy Coach... among other things." NewsOK.com. August 21, 2001. http://newsok.com/article/2752360

29. Hernsom, Bob. "Tatum: OU's vain attraction They called the big guy Coach... among other things." NewsOK.com. August 21, 2001. http://newsok.com/ article/2752360

30. Hernsom, Bob. "Tatum: OU's vain attraction They called the big guy Coach... among other things." NewsOK.com. August 21, 2001. http://newsok.com/ article/2752360

31. Keith, Harold. *Forty-seven straight: the Wilkinson era at Oklahoma*. Norman: University of Oklahoma Press, 2003.

32. Keith, Harold. *Forty-seven straight: the Wilkinson era at Oklahoma*. Norman: University of Oklahoma Press, 2003.

WHAT IF TULANE AND GEORGIA TECH NEVER LEFT THE SEC?

1. AP. "Sewanee Grads Oppose Policy." *The Monroe News-Star*, January 26, 1938.

2. "Plunging from peak prestige." Plunging from peak prestige - Tulane GreenWave.com | Tulane Athletics. http://tulanegreenwave.com/sports/ 2016/6/13/genrel-102702aac-html.aspx.

3. Ghio, Barney. "Barney's Corner." *The Shreveport Times*, October 5, 1949.

4. "Plunging from peak prestige." Plunging from peak prestige - TulaneGreenWave. com | Tulane Athletics. http://tulanegreenwave.com/sports/2016/6/13/genrel- 102702aac-html.aspx.

5. Mohr, Clarence L., and Joseph E. Gordon. *Tulane: the emergence of a modern university, 1945-1980*. Baton Rouge: Louisiana State University Press, 2001.

6. Mohr, Clarence L., and Joseph E. Gordon. *Tulane: the emergence of a modern university, 1945-1980*. Baton Rouge: Louisiana State University Press, 2001.

7. Mohr, Clarence L., and Joseph E. Gordon. *Tulane: the emergence of a modern university, 1945-1980*. Baton Rouge: Louisiana State University Press, 2001.

8. Steinfort, Roy. "Tulane President Offers Grid De-Emphasis Plan." *The Shreveport Times*, November 29, 1951.

9. UP. "Battle Shapes Up In SEC Over De-Emphasis." *The Town Talk (Alexandria, LA)*, November 30, 1951.

10. "Plunging from peak prestige." Plunging from peak prestige - TulaneGreenWave. com | Tulane Athletics.

11. Steinfort, Roy. "Tulane President Offers Grid De-Emphasis Plan." *The Shreveport Times*, November 29, 1951.

12. Bois, Jon. "Georgia Tech 222, Cumberland 0." SBNation.com. October 7, 2016. http://www.sbnation.com/college-football/2016/10/7/13199052/georgia-tech-cumberland-college-222-0-game-history-records.

13. "William Alexander Bio." William Alexander Bio - RamblinWreck.com. http://www.ramblinwreck.com/sports/m-footbl/mtt/alexander_william00.html.

14. Curry, Bill Curry. "Always inspiring, always teaching, 'The Whistle' was one-of-a-kind." ESPN. September 30, 2008. http://www.espn.com/college-football/news/story?id=3618461.

15. Curry, Bill. "Always inspiring, always teaching, 'The Whistle' was one-of-a-kind." Always inspiring, always teaching, 'The Whistle' was one-of-a-kind. September 30, 2008. http://www.espn.com/college-football/news/story?id=3618461.

16. AP. "Dodd's 'Luck' Won Another Bowl Victory." *Ocala Star-Banner*, December 31, 1956.

17. AP. "Tech's Legendary Coach Dodd Dedicated To Players, Winning." *The Albany Herald*, June 22, 1988.

18. Sharnik, Morton. "A ROUGH DAY FOR THE BEAR." SI.com. November 26, 1962. https://www.si.com/vault/1962/11/26/592367/a-rough-day-for-the-bear.

19. Sharnik, Morton. "A ROUGH DAY FOR THE BEAR." SI.com. November 26, 1962. https://www.si.com/vault/1962/11/26/592367/a-rough-day-for-the-bear.

20. AP. "Tech Files Protest." *The Herald-Journal*, November 22, 1961.

21. AP. "Tech Tells Bama Off Officially." *St.Petersburg Times*, November 22, 1961.

22. Sims, Bob. "Southeastern Conference charter schools move on in different directions." AL.com. February 24, 2008. http://blog.al.com/bn/2008/02/southeastern_conference_charte.html.

23. "Fifty years ago, Georgia Tech left the SEC." *Atlanta Journal-Constitution*. January 25, 2014. http://www.myajc.com/sports/fifty-years-ago-georgia-tech-left-the-sec/07w1mrefY4QgzlmzzSXr9O/.

24. Walsh, Christopher J. *Where football is king: a history of the SEC*. Lanham, MD: Taylor Trade Pub., 2006.

25. "Fifty years ago, Georgia Tech left the SEC." *Atlanta Journal-Constitution*. January 25, 2014. http://www.myajc.com/sports/fifty-years-ago-georgia-tech-left-the-sec/07w1mrefY4QgzlmzzSXr9O/.

26. Parker, Don. "A LOW-PRESSURE ENGINEER." SI.com. October 21, 1957. https://www.si.com/vault/1957/10/21/605519/a-lowpressure-engineer.

27. Parker, Don. "A LOW-PRESSURE ENGINEER." SI.com. October 21, 1957. https://www.si.com/vault/1957/10/21/605519/a-lowpressure-engineer.

28. Sims, Bob. "Southeastern Conference charter schools move on in different directions." AL.com. February 24, 2008. http://blog.al.com/bn/2008/02/southeastern_conference_charte.html.

29. Walsh, Christopher J. *Where football is king: a history of the SEC*. Lanham, MD: Taylor Trade Pub., 2006.

30. Mohr, Clarence L., and Joseph E. Gordon. *Tulane: the emergence of a modern university, 1945-1980*. Baton Rouge: Louisiana State University Press, 2001.

31. "Plunging from peak prestige." Plunging from peak prestige - TulaneGreenWave. com | Tulane Athletics.

32. Magruder, Jack. "Ex-Coach Plays Easy Money With Tulane." *The Arizona Daily Star*, July 28, 1985.

33. "Plunging from peak prestige." Plunging from peak prestige - Tulane GreenWave.com | Tulane Athletics. October 24, 2002. http://tulanegreenwave. com/sports/2016/6/13/genrel-102702aac-html.aspx.

34. Walsh, Christopher J. *Where football is king: a history of the SEC*. Lanham, MD: Taylor Trade Pub., 2006.

35. Duncan, Jeff. "Super Bowl 2013 will leave Tulane football fans pondering the possibilities." NOLA.com. January 31, 2013. http://www.nola.com/superbowl/index.ssf/2013/01/super_bowl_2013_will_leave_tul.html#incart_river.

36. AP. "Tulane Wants Back in SEC." *The Daily News*, November 3, 1989.

37. Bibb, John. "Tulane Folly An Example for Vandy." *The Tennessean*, November 18, 1989.

38. Hurt, Cecil. "Ingram Likes Classroom Progress of Tide Football Players." *The Times Daily*, July 19, 1990.

39. AP. "Tulane May Join SWC In June." *Del Rio News Herald*, April 4, 1991.

40. Guillory, William. "Tulane among 12 finalists for Big 12 expansion, ESPN reports." NOLA.com. September 1, 2016. http://www.nola.com/tulane/index.ssf/2016/08/tulane_among_12_finalists_for.html.

41. Sugiura, Ken. "Looking back at Tech, Tulane's decision to leave SEC." *Atlanta Journal-Constitution*. September 5, 2014. http://www.myajc.com/sports/college/looking-back-tech-tulane-decision-leave-sec/lr37CxxIUKSY4G38mEO9zJ/.

42. Bibb, John. "Tulane Folly An Example for Vandy." *The Tennessean*, November 18, 1989.

43. Sugiura, Ken. "Looking back at Tech, Tulane's decision to leave SEC." *Atlanta Journal-Constitution*. September 5, 2014.

44. Berkow, Steve. "Some SEC schools received $40M-plus in 2016 fiscal year." *USA Today*. February 2, 2017. https://www.usatoday.com/story/sports/ncaaf/sec/2017/02/02/sec-tax-return-639-million-in-revenues-2016-fiscal-year/97400990/.

45. NCAA. *COLLEGE FOOTBALL PLAYOFF SUMMARY OF REVENUE DISTRIBUTION 2015-16*. PDF.

46. Connelly, Bill. "Celebrating the insanity of 1990." Football Study Hall. April 30, 2016. http://www.footballstudyhall.com/2016/4/30/11543646/1990-college-football-season-georgia-tech-colorado.

47. Sugiura, Ken. "Looking back at Tech, Tulane's decision to leave SEC." *Atlanta Journal-Constitution*. September 5, 2014. http://www.myajc.com/sports/college/looking-back-tech-tulane-decision-leave-sec/lr37CxxIUKSY4 G38mEO9zJ/.

48. Connelly, Bill. "1998 broke so many hearts." Football Study Hall. April 11, 2016.   http://www.footballstudyhall.com/2016/4/11/11405994/1998-college-football-tennessee-ohio-state-florida-state-kansas-state-ucla.

WHAT IF THE PCC BECAME THE AIRPLANE CONFERENCE?

1. Thelin, John R. *Games colleges play: scandal and reform in intercollegiate athletics*. Baltimore, MD: Johns Hopkins University Press, 1996.

2. "BOOSTERS MESS IT UP IN WASHINGTON." SI.com. February 20, 1956. https://www.si.com/vault/1956/02/20/604653/boosters-mess-it-up-in-washington.

3. Kemper, Kurt Edward. *College Football and American Culture in the Cold War Era*. Urbana, Illinois: University of Illinois Press, 2009.

4. Thelin, John R. *Games colleges play: scandal and reform in intercollegiate athletics*. Baltimore, MD: Johns Hopkins University Press, 1996.

5. Strite, Dick. "Pacific Coast Conference, After Shaky Start, Gained National Prominence Only To Die In Near Disgrace." *The Eugene Guard*. July 2, 1959.

6. "The Airplane Conference." *The Bend Bulletin*, July 2, 1958.

7. Smith, Ronald A. *Play-by-play: radio, television, and big-time college sport*. Baltimore, MD: Johns Hopkins University Press, 2001.

8.   Smith, Ronald A. *Play-by-play: radio, television, and big-time college sport*. Baltimore, MD: Johns Hopkins University Press, 2001

9.   Dunnavant, Keith. *The fifty-year seduction: how television manipulated college football, from the birth of the modern NCAA to the creation of the BCS*. New York: T. Dunne Books, 2004.

10. *The Eugene Guard*, January 10, 1962.

11. Abrams, Al. "Sidelights on Sports." *Pittsburgh Post-Gazette*, June 30, 1959.

12. "American Conference? Nation's Top Independents May Near Alignment This Week." *The Decatur Herald*, January 8, 1959.

13. UP, comp. "Eight Major College Teams May Form Nationwide Loop." *The Shreveport Times*, October 24, 1956.

14. Samuelsen, Rube. "Airplane Conference Gets Boost From Two Famous Sports Boosters ." *Ogden Standard-Examiner* . October 26, 1958.

15. Dyer, Braven. "Krause Favors Two-Point Ruling." *Los Angeles Times*, November 29, 1958.

16. "'Conference Quite Likely' Hamilton." *Pittsburgh Post-Gazette*, February 12, 1959.

17. Kemper, Kurt Edward. *College Football and American Culture in the Cold War Era*. Urbana, Illinois: University of Illinois Press, 2009

18. Samuelsen, Rube. "New Big Ten Pact Appears Certain." *Pasadena Independent Star-News*, June 11, 1961.

19. MacCambridge, Michael. *ESPN college football encyclopedia*. New York, NY: ESPN Books, 2005.

20. Kemper, Kurt Edward. *College Football and American Culture in the Cold War Era*. Urbana, Illinois: University of Illinois Press, 2009

21. Kemper, Kurt Edward. *College Football and American Culture in the Cold War Era*. Urbana, Illinois: University of Illinois Press, 2009

22. McLeod, George. "Harris Leans to New Loop." October 12, 1961.

WHAT IF PENN WAS ALLOWED TO KEEP ITS TV DEAL?

1. Bernstein, Mark F. *Football: the Ivy League origins of an American obsession*. Philadelphia: University of Pennsylvania Press, 2001.

2. Dunnavant, Keith. *The fifty-year seduction: how television manipulated college football, from the birth of the modern NCAA to the creation of the BCS*. New York: T. Dunne Books, 2004.

3. Smith, Ronald A. *Play-by-play: radio, television, and big-time college sport*. Baltimore, MD: Johns Hopkins University Press, 2001.

4. Smith, Ronald A. *Play-by-play: radio, television, and big-time college sport*. Baltimore, MD: Johns Hopkins University Press, 2001.

5. Smith, Ronald A. *Play-by-play: radio, television, and big-time college sport*. Baltimore, MD: Johns Hopkins University Press, 2001.

6. Smith, Ronald A. *Play-by-play: radio, television, and big-time college sport*. Baltimore, MD: Johns Hopkins University Press, 2001.

7. Smith, Ronald A. *Play-by-play: radio, television, and big-time college sport*. Baltimore, MD: Johns Hopkins University Press, 2001.

8. Smith, Ronald A. *Play-by-play: radio, television, and big-time college sport.* Baltimore, MD: Johns Hopkins University Press, 2001.

9. Bernstein, Mark F. *Football: the Ivy League origins of an American obsession.* Philadelphia: University of Pennsylvania Press, 2001.

10. Bernstein, Mark F. *Football: the Ivy League origins of an American obsession.* Philadelphia: University of Pennsylvania Press, 2001.

11. Bernstein, Mark F. *Football: the Ivy League origins of an American obsession.* Philadelphia: University of Pennsylvania Press, 2001.

12. Smith, Ronald A. *Play-by-play: radio, television, and big-time college sport.* Baltimore, MD: Johns Hopkins University Press, 2001.

13. Bernstein, Mark F. *Football: the Ivy League origins of an American obsession.* Philadelphia: University of Pennsylvania Press, 2001.

14. Bernstein, Mark F. *Football: the Ivy League origins of an American obsession.* Philadelphia: University of Pennsylvania Press, 2001.

15. Smith, Ronald A. *Play-by-play: radio, television, and big-time college sport.* Baltimore, MD: Johns Hopkins University Press, 2001

16. Smith, Ronald A. *Play-by-play: radio, television, and big-time college sport.* Baltimore, MD: Johns Hopkins University Press, 2001

17. Smith, Ronald A. *Play-by-play: radio, television, and big-time college sport.* Baltimore, MD: Johns Hopkins University Press, 2001

18. Watterson, John Sayle. *College football: history, spectacle, controversy.* Baltimore: Johns Hopkins University Press, 2006.

19. Watterson, John Sayle. *College football: history, spectacle, controversy.* Baltimore: Johns Hopkins University Press, 2006.

20. Watterson, John Sayle. *College football: history, spectacle, controversy.* Baltimore: Johns Hopkins University Press, 2006.

21. Walsh, Christopher J. *Where football is king: a history of the SEC.* Lanham, MD: Taylor Trade Pub., 2006.

22. Dunnavant, Keith. *The fifty-year seduction: how television manipulated college football, from the birth of the modern NCAA to the creation of the BCS.* New York: T. Dunne Books, 2004.

23. Bernstein, Mark F. *Football: the Ivy League origins of an American obsession.* Philadelphia: University of Pennsylvania Press, 2001

24. Dunnavant, Keith. *The fifty-year seduction: how television manipulated college football, from the birth of the modern NCAA to the creation of the BCS.* New York: T. Dunne Books, 2004

25. Dunnavant, Keith. *The fifty-year seduction: how television manipulated college football, from the birth of the modern NCAA to the creation of the BCS.* New York: T. Dunne Books, 2004

26. Bernstein, Mark F. *Football: the Ivy League origins of an American obsession.* Philadelphia: University of Pennsylvania Press, 2001

27. Bernstein, Mark F. *Football: the Ivy League origins of an American obsession.* Philadelphia: University of Pennsylvania Press, 2001

28. Smith, Ronald A. *Play-by-play: radio, television, and big-time college sport.* Baltimore, MD: Johns Hopkins University Press, 2001.

29. Dunnavant, Keith. *The fifty-year seduction: how television manipulated college football, from the birth of the modern NCAA to the creation of the BCS.* New York: T. Dunne Books, 2004

30. Bernstein, Mark F. *Football: the Ivy League origins of an American obsession.* Philadelphia: University of Pennsylvania Press, 2001

31. Bernstein, Mark F. *Football: the Ivy League origins of an American obsession.* Philadelphia: University of Pennsylvania Press, 2001

32. Smith, Ronald A. *Play-by-play: radio, television, and big-time college sport.* Baltimore, MD: Johns Hopkins University Press, 2001

33. Smith, Ronald A. *Play-by-play: radio, television, and big-time college sport.* Baltimore, MD: Johns Hopkins University Press, 2001

34. Bernstein, Mark F. *Football: the Ivy League origins of an American obsession.* Philadelphia: University of Pennsylvania Press, 2001

35. Smith, Ronald A. *Play-by-play: radio, television, and big-time college sport.* Baltimore, MD: Johns Hopkins University Press, 2001

36. Smith, Ronald A. *Play-by-play: radio, television, and big-time college sport.* Baltimore, MD: Johns Hopkins University Press, 2001

WHAT IF NEBRASKA NEVER HIRED BOB DEVANEY?

1. ""Big Nine" to Stay." *The New York Times*, December 7, 1913.

2. Sherwood, James E. *Nebraska football: the coaches, the players, the experience.* Lincoln: University of Nebraska Press, 1987.

3. "Nebraska Sends Balloon Team Tumbling." *Chicago Daily Tribune*, November 10, 1918.

4. "Origin of the Cornhusker Nickname." Huskers.com. September 7, 2013. 2017. http://www.huskers.com/ViewArticle.dbml?ATCLID=2802.

5. Zimmerman, Paul. "Nebraska Named For Rose Bowl." *LA Times*, December 2, 1940.

6. Sherwood, James E. *Nebraska football: the coaches, the players, the experience.* Lincoln: University of Nebraska Press, 1987.

7. Sherwood, James E. *Nebraska football: the coaches, the players, the experience.* Lincoln: University of Nebraska Press, 1987.

8. Baker, George. "Biff Jones' Rebuff of Huey Long Cost Him Coaching Job At LSU." *The Washington Post*, September 8, 1963.

9. AP. "Nebraska Names Biff Jones To Succeed Bible as Coach ." *New York Times*, January 29, 1937.

10. Devaney, Bob. *Devaney.* Lincoln: Devaney, 1981.

11. "Biff Jones To Leave Nebraska for West Point." *Chicago Daily Tribune*, January 24, 1942.

12. "Biff Jones To Leave Nebraska for West Point." *Chicago Daily Tribune*, January 24, 1942.

13. Sherwood, James E. *Nebraska football: the coaches, the players, the experience.* Lincoln: University of Nebraska Press, 1987.

14. UPI. "Big Eight Prepares for Action." *Ames Daily Tribune*, November 2, 1960.

15. "Former Husker AD Dye dies at 97." JournalStar.com. April 13, 2012. http://journalstar.com/sports/huskers/former-husker-ad-dye-dies-at/article_ f2a2ead6-f00d-50df-b803-325999020523.html.

16. "Hank Foldberg Ponders Offer From Huskers." *Toledo Blade*, December 9, 1961.

17. McEwen, Tom. *The Gators: a story of Florida football*. Huntsville, Ala.: Strode Publishers, 1974.

18. Dutton, Bob. "Devaney's Time Has Passed But He Didn't Want to Go." NewsOK.com. January 12, 1993. http://newsok.com/article/2418137.

19. AP. "Ralston Eyes NU But Feels He's No. 2." *The Lincoln Star*, December 24, 1961.

20. UPI. "Dye Eyes 3, Choice Due Soon." *The Lincoln Star*, December 29, 1961.

21. AP. "Nagel Of Utah Candidate for Nebraska Post." *Miami Daily-News Record*, December 21, 1961.

22. Reports, From Staff. "From the archives: How Wyoming attempted to prevent Nebraska from hiring Bob Devaney." Omaha.com. December 12, 2016. http://www.omaha.com/huskers/blogs/bigred/from-the-archives-how-wyoming-attempted-to-prevent-nebraska-from/article_df4224a6-76a0-11e6-ace8-0f5bd096fae4.html.

23. Devaney, Bob. *Devaney*. Lincoln: Devaney, 1981.

24. Devaney, Bob. *Devaney*. Lincoln: Devaney, 1981.

25. Devaney, Bob. *Devaney*. Lincoln: Devaney, 1981.

26. AP. "Wyoming Delays Coach's Release." *The Baltimore Sun*, January 10, 1962.

27. Reports, From Staff. "From the archives: How Wyoming attempted to prevent Nebraska from hiring Bob Devaney." Omaha.com. Accessed April 06, 2017. http://www.omaha.com/huskers/blogs/bigred/from-the-archives-how-wyoming-attempted-to-prevent-nebraska-from/article_df4224a6-76a0-11e6-ace8-0f5bd096fae4.html.

28. UPI. "Wyoming Blasts Coach, Nebraska." *The Washington Post*, February 4, 1962.

29. Devaney, Bob. *Devaney*. Lincoln: Devaney, 1981.

30. Devaney, Bob. *Devaney*. Lincoln: Devaney, 1981.

31. Devaney, Bob. *Devaney*. Lincoln: Devaney, 1981.

32. LOONEY, DOUGLAS S. "Glory Days It wasn't until '62 that Husker history really began -- with the arrival of Bob Devaney." SI.com. January 17, 1995. https://www.si.com/vault/1995/01/17/8229913/glory-days-it-wasnt-until-62-that-husker-history-really-began--with-the-arrival-of-bob-devaney.

33. Devaney, Bob. *Devaney*. Lincoln: Devaney, 1981.

34. AP. "Nebraska Wins Gotham Bowl, 36-34." *Eugene Register-Guard*, December 16, 1962.

35. Dutton, Bob. "Devaney Leaves With Bad Taste." *Seattle Times*. February 7, 1993. http://community.seattletimes.nwsource.com/archive/?date=19930207&slug=1684142.

36. Dutton, Bob. "Devaney Leaves With Bad Taste." *Seattle Times*. February 7, 1993. http://community.seattletimes.nwsource.com/archive/?date=19930207&slug=1684142.

37. White, Gordon. "Blackman To Stay At Dartmouth." *The New York Times*, December 10, 1965.

38. Underwood, John. "The Desperate coach." SI.com. April 25, 1969. Accessed April 06, 2017. https://www.si.com/vault/1969/08/25/609897/the-desperate-coach.

WHAT IF ARIZONA STATE LOST THE 1975 FIESTA BOWL?

1. "1902 Rose Bowl University of Michigan Athletics." Bentley Library. October 13, 2013. http://bentley.umich.edu/athdept/football/bowls/1902rose.htm.

2. Reed, Billy. "Ben-Hur Played the Rose Bowl." SI.com. December 23, 1968. https://www.si.com/vault/1968/12/23/551873/benhur-played-the-rose-bowl.

3. "History." Rose Bowl Stadium. http://www.rosebowlstadium.com/about/history.

4. Scantlebury, Pete. "Florida football: Gators' first bowl game ended with coach's arrest in Cuba." SEC Country. December 26, 2016. https://www.seccountry.com/florida/the-1912-bacardi-bowl-floridas-fugitive-coach-in-cuba.

5. Wood, Michael T. "Bacardi Bowl: American Football and Cuba." Bacardi Bowl: American Football and Cuba. August 6, 2012. https://bacardibowl.blogspot.com/search?updated-max=2012-08-06T15%3A11%3A00-07%3A00&max-results=7&start=14&by-date=false.

6. Colston, Chris. *Tales from the Virginia Tech sidelines*. Champaign, IL: Sports Pub., 2003.

7. "Birth of a Bowl." Shover, Bill. Fiesta Bowl. https://fiestabowl.org/fiesta-bowl/birth-of-a-bowl/.

8. Morantempe, Malcom. "Upstart Fiesta Bowl Growing Into the Biggest Party of All: Fiesta Builds a Rich Tradition." *New York Times*, January 2, 1989.

9. Hoffer, Richard. "Bucking Tradition: By Taking Chances, Fiesta Bowl Brings In New Year With Success." *LA Times*, December 29, 1988.

10. Hoffer, Richard. "Bucking Tradition: By Taking Chances, Fiesta Bowl Brings In New Year With Success." *LA Times*, December 29, 1988.

11. Sherman, Ed. "Fiesta Bowl Brings Hardball to Football." *Chicago Tribune*, January 1, 1989.

12. Dunnavant, Keith. *The fifty-year seduction: how television manipulated college football, from the birth of the modern NCAA to the creation of the BCS*. New York: T. Dunne Books, 2004.

13. UPI. "Cornhuskers Not Chicken, Say Fiesta Bowl Officials." *Boston Globe*, November 21, 1975.

14. AP. "Fiesta Chicken 'Tasteless'" *Chicago Tribune*, November 21, 1975.

15. Dunnavant, Keith. *The fifty-year seduction: how television manipulated college football, from the birth of the modern NCAA to the creation of the BCS*. New York: T. Dunne Books, 2004.

16. Parker, Virgil. "ASU Rallies For Win, to face NU in the Fiesta." *Lincoln Evening Journal*, November 30, 1975.

17. AP. "Arizona State 'Shocking'" The Capital (Annapolis, Maryland), December 27, 1975.

18. AP. "Upset Win to Arizona State, Coach's Son Emerges As Hero." *Columbus Telegram*, December 27, 1975.

19. Dunnavant, Keith. *The fifty-year seduction: how television manipulated college football, from the birth of the modern NCAA to the creation of the BCS.* New York: T. Dunne Books, 2004.

20. Dunnavant, Keith. *The fifty-year seduction: how television manipulated college football, from the birth of the modern NCAA to the creation of the BCS.* New York: T. Dunne Books, 2004.

21. Dunnavant, Keith. *The fifty-year seduction: how television manipulated college football, from the birth of the modern NCAA to the creation of the BCS.* New York: T. Dunne Books, 2004.

22. Florence, Mal. "The Northwest: The Weak Link In the Pacific 8." *LA Times*, November 13, 1975.

23. "Pacific 8 Expansion a Solution?" *LA Times*, November 13, 1975.

24. Trombley, William. "Expansion of Pac 8--USC Power Play." *LA Times*, December 21, 1976.

25. Dunnavant, Keith. *The fifty-year seduction: how television manipulated college football, from the birth of the modern NCAA to the creation of the BCS.* New York: T. Dunne Books, 2004.

26. Dunnavant, Keith. *The fifty-year seduction: how television manipulated college football, from the birth of the modern NCAA to the creation of the BCS.* New York: T. Dunne Books, 2004.

27. Sherman, Ed. "Fiesta Bowl Brings Hardball to Football." *Chicago Tribune*, January 1, 1989.

28. Dunnavant, Keith. *The fifty-year seduction: how television manipulated college football, from the birth of the modern NCAA to the creation of the BCS.* New York: T. Dunne Books, 2004.

29. Goodwin, Michael. "BOWL WARS: STAKES GO UP." *The New York Times.* November 13, 1986. http://www.nytimes.com/1986/11/14/sports/bowl-wars-stakes-go-up.html.

30. White, Gordon S. "FIESTA BOWL, NBC SCORE NO. 1 COUP." *The New York Times.* November 16, 1986. http://www.nytimes.com/1986/11/17/sports/fiesta-bowl-nbc-score-no-1-coup.html..

31. Sherman, Ed. "Fiesta Bowl Brings Hardball to Football." *Chicago Tribune,* January 1, 1989.

32. "Fiesta Bowl Sets Record for TV." *The New York Times.* January 5, 1987. http://www.nytimes.com/1987/01/06/sports/fiesta-bowl-sets-record-for-tv.html.

33. Rosenberg, Howard. "Gipper Tries To Win One For Himself At Half Time." *Los Angeles Times.* January 05, 1987. http://articles.latimes.com/1987-01-05/entertainment/ca-2316_1_president-ronald-reagan.

34. Connelly, Bill. "1975 got funky in November." Football Study Hall. June 20, 2016. http://www.footballstudyhall.com/2016/6/20/11981482/1975-college-football-season-oklahoma-alabama-ohio-state-arizona-state.

35. UPI. "Nebraska Rejects Fiesta Bid." *Zanesville Times-Recorder,* November 18, 1975.

36. UPI. "Sugar Matchup Draws Fire." *Zanesville Times-Recorder,* November 18, 1975.

37. Dunnavant, Keith. *The fifty-year seduction: how television manipulated college football, from the birth of the modern NCAA to the creation of the BCS.* New York: T. Dunne Books, 2004.

38. "Sun About To Set On Bowl's Name." *Chicago Tribune,* March 9, 1989.

What if LaVell Edwards left BYU?

1.   Edwards, LaVell, and Lee Nelson. *Lavell Edwards: building a winning football tradition at Brigham Young University*. Provo, UT: Council Press, 1981.

2.   "The Church of Jesus Christ of Latter-day Saints membership history." Wikipedia. April 01, 2017. https://en.wikipedia.org/wiki/The_Church_of_Jesus_Christ_of_Latter-day_Saints_membership_history.

3.   "Honor Code." Home | Honor Code. https://honorcode.byu.edu/.

4.   MacCambridge, Michael. *ESPN college football encyclopedia*. New York, NY: ESPN Books, 2005.

5.   Smith, Darron T. *When race, religion, and sport collide: Black athletes at BYU and beyond*. Lanham, MD: Rowman & LIttlefield, 2016.

6.   Watterson, John Sayle. *College football: history, spectacle, controversy*. Baltimore: Johns Hopkins University Press, 2006.

7.   Drew, Jay. "BYU Football: Remembering the Black 14 Protest." The Salt Lake Tribune. November 6, 2009. http://archive.sltrib.com/story.php?ref=%2Fbyucougars%2Fci_13728556.

8.   Edwards, LaVell, and Lee Benson. *LaVell: airing it out*. Salt Lake City: Shadow Mountain, 1995.

9.   Edwards, LaVell, and Lee Benson. *LaVell: airing it out*. Salt Lake City: Shadow Mountain, 1995.

10.   Edwards, LaVell, and Lee Nelson. *Lavell Edwards: building a winning football tradition at Brigham Young University*. Provo, UT: Council Press, 1981.

11. 307 Edwards, LaVell. *The football coaching bible*. Champaign, IL: Human Kinetics, 2002.

12. 308 White, Maurey . "As His Team Takes The High Road, So Does LaVell Edwards ." *Des Moines Register*, December 25, 1991.

13. AP. "Replacement Sought For Tom Hudspeth." *Ogden Standard-Examiner*, January 24, 1972.

14. Edwards, LaVell, and Lee Nelson. *Lavell Edwards: building a winning football tradition at Brigham Young University*. Provo, UT: Council Press, 1981.

15. Edwards, LaVell, and Lee Nelson. *Lavell Edwards: building a winning football tradition at Brigham Young University*. Provo, UT: Council Press, 1981

16. "Warren Named To BYU Grid Staff." *Provo Daily Herald*, June 9, 1972.

17. Foust, Tom. "Utes Impressive." *Arizona Daily Star*, August 30, 1972.

18. Inouye, Ed. "Golden Richards Stars In Hawaii." *Provo Daily Herald*, October 22, 1972.

19. Edwards, LaVell, and Lee Nelson. *Lavell Edwards: building a winning football tradition at Brigham Young University*. Provo, UT: Council Press, 1981

20. Edwards, LaVell, and Lee Nelson. Lavell Edwards: building a winning football tradition at Brigham Young University. Provo, UT: Council Press, 1981

21. Edwards, LaVell, and Lee Nelson. *Lavell Edwards: building a winning football tradition at Brigham Young University*. Provo, UT: Council Press, 1981

22. Edwards, LaVell, and Lee Benson. *LaVell: airing it out*. Salt Lake City: Shadow Mountain, 1995.

23. Edwards, LaVell, and Lee Benson. *LaVell: airing it out*. Salt Lake City: Shadow Mountain, 1995.

24. 320 Distel, Dave. "Doug Scovil Isn't a Typical College Coach." *LA Times*, August 27, 1983.

25. Edwards, LaVell, and Lee Benson. *LaVell: airing it out*. Salt Lake City: Shadow Mountain, 1995

26. Call, Jeff. "Never on Sunday: BYU won't compete on the Sabbath Day, regardless of the consequences." DeseretNews.com. June 25, 2016. http://www.deseretnews.com/article/865656920/Never-on-Sunday-BYU-wont-compete-on-the-Sabbath-Day-regardless-of-the-consequences.html.

27. Devey, Andrew. "Top 5 BYU football quotes of all time." KSL.com. Accessed April 5, 2017. https://www.ksl.com/?sid=17059800.

28. Ubben, David. "BYU on the brain: Brigham Young football has special place in OU's psyche." NewsOK.com. Accessed April 05, 2017. http://newsok.com/article/3397415.

29. Connelly, Bill. "BYU winning in 1984 was fine." Football Study Hall. May 18, 2016. http://www.footballstudyhall.com/2016/5/18/11700220/1984-college-football-season-byu-washington-oklahoma-nebraska.

30. Connelly, Bill. "BYU winning in 1984 was fine." Football Study Hall. May 18, 2016. http://www.footballstudyhall.com/2016/5/18/11700220/1984-college-football-season-byu-washington-oklahoma-nebraska.

31. Feldman, Bruce. *'Cane mutiny: how the Miami Hurricanes overturned the football establishment*. New York, NY: New American Library, 2004

32. Guest, Larry. "Hurricanes Discuss Six-Figure Contract with BYU's Edwards." *Orlando Sentinel*, December 19, 1976.

33. Guest, Larry. "Forget Any Rumors, Edwards Staying Put." *Orlando Sentinel*, December 22, 1985.

34. Guest, Larry. "Hurricanes Discuss Six-Figure Contract with BYU's Edwards." *Orlando Sentinel*, December 19, 1976.

35. Edwards, LaVell, and Lee Benson. *LaVell: airing it out*. Salt Lake City: Shadow Mountain, 1995.

36. Guest, Larry. "Forget Any Rumors, Edwards Staying Put." *Orlando Sentinel*, December 22, 1985.

37. AP. "Mizzou Grid Applications." *The Chillicothe Constitution-Tribune*, December 5, 1977.

38. Soucheray, Joe. "It's No Contest, BYU Coach Passes Up Al 'U' Candidates." *Star Tribune*, December 4, 1983.

39. Edwards, LaVell, and Lee Benson. *LaVell: airing it out*. Salt Lake City: Shadow Mountain, 1995.

40. Edwards, LaVell, and Lee Benson. *LaVell: airing it out*. Salt Lake City: Shadow Mountain, 1995.

41. Edwards, LaVell, and Lee Benson. *LaVell: airing it out*. Salt Lake City: Shadow Mountain, 1995.

42. Call, Jeff. "Years after offer from Lions, Edwards coaching in Detroit BYU heads East to face Marshall in the Silverdome." DeseretNews.com. December 23, 1999. http://www.deseretnews.com/article/734542/Years-after-offer-from-Lions-Edwards-coaching-in-Detroit.html.

43. Edwards, LaVell, and Lee Nelson. *Lavell Edwards: building a winning football tradition at Brigham Young University*. Provo, UT: Council Press, 1981.

44. Benedict, Jeff, and Armen Keteyian. *The system: the glory and scandal of big-time college football*. New York: Doubleday, 2013.

45. Gwynne, S. C. *The perfect pass: American genius and the reinvention of football*. New York, NY: Scribner, 2016.

46. Gwynne, S. C. *The perfect pass: American genius and the reinvention of football*. New York, NY: Scribner, 2016.

47. Hall, Spencer. "An Interview With Hal Mumme, College Football's All-Time David." SBNation.com. June 26, 2012. http://www.sbnation.com/ncaa-football/2012/6/26/3118498/hal-mumme-interview.

48. Gwynne, S. C. *The perfect pass: American genius and the reinvention of football*. New York, NY: Scribner, 2016.

WHAT IF HOWARD SCHNELLENBERGER NEVER LEFT MIAMI?

1. Miss me with your Jim Tressel is a bad person takes, by the way. I don't care about rigged raffles. Tressel was awesome.

2. Hickman, Herman. "DRIVE AT MIAMI." SI.com. April 11, 1955. https://www.si.com/vault/1955/04/11/619946/drive-at-miami.

3. Hairston, Jack. "A Hall Of Famer Recalls The Highlights." *The Gainesville Sun*, April 19, 1988.

4. Feldman, Bruce. *'Cane mutiny: how the Miami Hurricanes overturned the football establishment*. New York, NY: New American Library, 2004.

5. Feldman, Bruce. *'Cane mutiny: how the Miami Hurricanes overturned the football establishment*. New York, NY: New American Library, 2004.

6.   Feldman, Bruce. *'Cane mutiny: how the Miami Hurricanes overturned the football establishment.* New York, NY: New American Library, 2004.

7.   AP. "Saban Steps Down as AD." *Tallahassee Democrat*, November 20, 1976.

8.   Feldman, Bruce. *'Cane mutiny: how the Miami Hurricanes overturned the football establishment.* New York, NY: New American Library, 2004.

9.   Feldman, Bruce. *'Cane mutiny: how the Miami Hurricanes overturned the football establishment.* New York, NY: New American Library, 2004.

10. Feldman, Bruce. *'Cane mutiny: how the Miami Hurricanes overturned the football establishment.* New York, NY: New American Library, 2004.

11. Tuite, James. "Saban: The Last Stop?" *New York Times*, January 6, 1979.

12. Feldman, Bruce. *'Cane mutiny: how the Miami Hurricanes overturned the football establishment.* New York, NY: New American Library, 2004.

13. Feldman, Bruce. *'Cane mutiny: how the Miami Hurricanes overturned the football establishment.* New York, NY: New American Library, 2004.

14. UPI. "Morrall Is Hired to Coach U. of Miami Quarterbacks." *New York Times*, February 20, 1979.

15. Liccicome, Bernie. "'State of Miami' Stretches Out To Tampa." *South Florida Sun-Sentinel*, July 21, 1983.

16. ESPN. 2009. http://www.espn.com/30for30/film?page=the-u.

17. White, Gordon. "MIAMI ENHANCES REPUTATION." *New York Times*, November 2, 1981.

18. Feldman, Bruce. *'Cane mutiny: how the Miami Hurricanes overturned the football establishment.* New York, NY: New American Library, 2004.

19. AP. "Schnellenberger visits Kentucky." *The Baltimore Sun*, December 3, 1981.

20. Liccicome, Bernie. "Schnellenberger 'escapes' to USFL." *The Chicago Tribune*, May 30, 1984.

21. Liccicome, Bernie. "Schnellenberger 'escapes' to USFL." *The Chicago Tribune*, May 30, 1984.

22. Asher, Mark, and David Dupree. "Schnellenberger Beckons Federals South." *The Washington Post*, May 24, 1984.

23. "Washington Federals Archives • Fun While It Lasted." Fun While It Lasted. http://www.funwhileitlasted.net/tag/washington-federals/.

24. "Orlando Renegades." USFL.info - Orlando Renegades. http://www.usfl.info/renegades/.

25. WOJCIECHOWSKI, GENE . "It's Fiesta Time for Schnellenberger : Louisville: Controversial bowl situation puts his rebuilt program in the spotlight." *Los Angeles Times*. November 30, 1990. http://articles.latimes.com/1990-11-30/sports/sp-5608_1_fiesta-bowl.

26. Natt, Ted. "Schnellenberger Seeks Miracle in Louisville." *Los Angeles Times*, August 20, 1989.

27. WOJCIECHOWSKI, GENE. "It's Fiesta Time for Schnellenberger : Louisville: Controversial bowl situation puts his rebuilt program in the spotlight." *Los Angeles Times*. November 30, 1990. http://articles.latimes.com/1990-11-30/sports/sp-5608_1_fiesta-bowl.

28. WOJCIECHOWSKI, GENE. "COLLEGE FOOTBALL '95 : Sooner Rather Than Later : Schnellenberger Starts Over With Oklahoma." *Los Angeles Times.* August 28, 1995. http://articles.latimes.com/1995-08-28/sports/sp-39728_1_oklahoma-football.

29. Sherman, Rodger. "Owlcatraz no more: FAU declines stadium deal." SBNation.com. April 2, 2013. http://www.sbnation.com/college-football/2013/4/2/4017440/fau-stadium-geo-group-prison-company.

30. Feldman, Bruce. *'Cane mutiny: how the Miami Hurricanes overturned the football establishment.* New York, NY: New American Library, 2004.

31. Bianchi, Mike. "Pipe Dream." *Orlando Sentinel.* August 16, 2001. http://articles.orlandosentinel.com/2001-08-16/sports/0108160254_1_boca-raton-slippery-rock-schnellenberger.

32. WOJCIECHOWSKI, GENE. "It's Fiesta Time for Schnellenberger : Louisville: Controversial bowl situation puts his rebuilt program in the spotlight." Los Angeles Times. November 30, 1990. http://articles.latimes.com/1990-11-30/sports/sp-5608_1_fiesta-bowl.

33. Bianchi, Mike. "Schnellenberger hindsight What if he hadn't made fateful USFL decision." NewsOK.com. September 2, 2001. http://newsok.com/article/2753792.

WHAT IF THE METRO CONFERENCE BECAME THE FIRST SUPERCONFERENCE?

1. Dienhart, Rivals.com September 14, 2011, Tom. "WAC a Cautionary Tale for Superconferences." Rivals.com. September 14, 2011. http://www.realclearsports.com/2011/09/14/wac_a_cautionary_tale_for_superconferences_93568.html.

2. *Raycom Super Conference Report.* Charlotte, NC: Raycom, 1990.

3.   *Raycom Super Conference Report*. Charlotte, NC: Raycom, 1990.

4.   Zedalis, Joe. "In a Changing World, Rutgers' Future Uncertain ." *Asbury Park Press*, August 28, 1990.

5.   Dawson, Barrie. "Rutgers Listening To Metro." *The Courier-News Journal*, June 30, 1990.

6.   *Developing the Super Conference*. Working paper. Charlotte, NC: Raycom Sports, 1990.

7.   Dawson, Barrie. "Rutgers Listening To Metro." *The Courier-News Journal*, June 30, 1990

8.   Le Batard, Dan. "Metro Conference Sweets Bid to Lure UM." *Miami Herald*, July 4, 1990.

9.   *Developing the Super Conference*. Working paper. Charlotte, NC: Raycom Sports, 1990.

10. *Developing the Super Conference*. Working paper. Charlotte, NC: Raycom Sports, 1990.

11. Hardesty, Abe. "Quick Metro Changes Unlikely." *The Greenville News*, May 31, 1990.

12. Zedalis, Joe. "In a Changing World, Rutgers' Future Uncertain ." *Asbury Park Press*, August 28, 1990.

13. *The Metro Athletic Conference: A Study of Expansion*. Report. Charlotte, NC: Raycom Sports, 1990.

14. "Survival May Be A Topic At Metro Meetings." *The Courier Journal*, May 6, 1990.

15. Bozich, Rick. "It's High Time U Of L Found Itself A Truly 'Metro' Conference." *The Courier Journal*, May 11, 1990.

16. AP. "Metro Target Date October 15." *The Index-Journal*, July 18, 1990.

17. D'Angelo, Tom. "UM, Florida State, Studying Metro 'Super Conference'" *Palm Beach Post*, June 30, 1990.

18. Gay, Nancy. "Metro's Appeal Expanding With Planned Changes." *Orlando Sentinel*. July 13, 1990.

19. Connelly, Bill. "1991: 2 champions, 1 great team." Football Study Hall. April 28, 2016. http://www.footballstudyhall.com/2016/4/28/11511002/1991-college-football-season-washington-miami.

20. Cavanaugh, Jack. "Will Huskies Embrace Big Time Football?" *The New York Times*. October 25, 1997. http://www.nytimes.com/1997/10/26/nyregion/will-huskies-embrace-big-time-football.html.

21. "Temple Voted Out Of the Big East." *The New York Times*. March 2, 2001. http://www.nytimes.com/2001/03/03/sports/plus-college-football-temple-voted-out-of-the-big-east.html.

22. Teel, David. "Orange Bowl Shows Interest in ACC Champ." *Daily Press*, October 3, 1990.

23. "Smith Would Take Vandy For Membership In The ACC." *The Tennessean*, August 22, 1990.

24. Woody, Larry. "VU In The ACC? No, Says AD." *The Tennessean*, December 19, 1990.

25. "Will Push Be A Shove For Vandy?" *The Tennessean*, August 25, 1990.

26. Thomas, Jim. "College Big Wheels Play the Realignment Game." *St. Louis Post-Dispatch*, August 12, 1990.

27. Si. "The oral history of the birth of the Big 12." SI.com. August 16, 2016. https://www.si.com/college-football/2016/08/16/big-12-expansion-oral-history-big-8-swc-merger.

28. Dunnavant, Keith. *The fifty-year seduction: how television manipulated college football, from the birth of the modern NCAA to the creation of the BCS.* New York: T. Dunne Books, 2004.

29. Si. "The oral history of the birth of the Big 12." SI.com. August 16, 2016. https://www.si.com/college-football/2016/08/16/big-12-expansion-oral-history-big-8-swc-merger.

30. Si. "The oral history of the birth of the Big 12." SI.com. August 16, 2016. https://www.si.com/college-football/2016/08/16/big-12-expansion-oral-history-big-8-swc-merger.

WHAT IF WEST VIRGINIA BEAT PITT IN 2007?

1. Sports, Nicole Auerbach. "Appalachian State's win at Michigan helped legitimize Big Ten Network." USA Today. December 5, 2016. https://www.usatoday.com/story/sports/ncaaf/bigten/2016/12/05/appalachian-state-win-at-michigan-helped-legitimize-big-ten-network/94997288/.

2. Outsiders, Football. "Football Outsiders." Football Outsiders Everything. http://www.footballoutsiders.com/stats/ncaa2007.

3. Thamel, Pete. "Fitting End to a Tumultuous Season." *The New York Times.* December 1, 2007. http://www.nytimes.com/2007/12/02/sports/ncaafootball/02mountaineers.html.

4.	"The Backyard Brawl, A Brawl to Remember." Pittsburgh Sporting News. November 29, 2012. http://www.pittsburghsportingnews.com/the-backyard-brawl-a-brawl-to-remember/.

5.	Outsiders, Football. "Football Outsiders." Football Outsiders Everything. http://www.footballoutsiders.com/stats/ncaa2007.

6.	Talty, John. "Looking back at what really happened between Alabama and Rich Rodriguez 10 years ago." AL.com. December 08, 2016. http://www.al.com/alabamafootball/index.ssf/2016/12/looking_back_at_what_really_ha.html#incart_river_index?platform=hootsuite.

7.	Rivals.com. https://n.rivals.com/content/prospects/2008/terrelle-pryor-10121.

8.	"Pryor drops West Virginia from list, adds Michigan." *Pittsburgh Post-Gazette*. December 17, 2007. http://www.post-gazette.com/sports/2007/12/17/Pryor-drops-West-Virginia-from-list-adds-Michigan/stories/200712170183.

9.	Look, I don't care what the NCAA says. I watched all of these games. Ohio State won 12 of them.

What if UAB hired Jimbo Fisher?

1.	Robbins, Danny. "Bartow Was in Fear of UCLA Booster : Basketball: Former Bruin coach believed an NCAA investigation of Sam Gilbert would have endangered his life." *Los Angeles Times*. August 4, 1993. http://articles.latimes.com/1993-08-04/sports/sp-20220_1_sam-gilbert.

2.	Robbins, Danny. "Bartow Was in Fear of UCLA Booster : Basketball: Former Bruin coach believed an NCAA investigation of Sam Gilbert would have endangered his life." *Los Angeles Times*. August 4, 1993. http://articles.latimes.com/1993-08-04/sports/sp-20220_1_sam-gilbert.

3.   Solomon @JonSolomonCBS Nov 14, 2014 • 16 min read, John. "Is the Alabama board of trustees finally ready to kill UAB football?" CBSSports. com. June 2, 2015. http://www.cbssports.com/college-football/news/is-the-alabama-board-of-trustees-finally-ready-to-kill-uab-football/.

4.   Watson Brown quits as UAB coach, heads to Tennessee Tech." ESPN. http:// www.espn.com/espn/wire/_/section/ncf/id/2692132.

5.   Scarbinsky, Kevin. "Jimbo Fisher glad Alabama trustees nixed his deal to become UAB's head coach (Kevin Scarbinsky)." AL.com. January 04, 2014. http://www. al.com/sports/index.ssf/2014/01/jimbo_fisher_glad_alabama_trus.html.

6.   Scarbinsky, Kevin. "Jimbo Fisher glad Alabama trustees nixed his deal to become UAB's head coach (Kevin Scarbinsky)." AL.com. January 04, 2014. http://www.al.com/sports/index.ssf/2014/01/jimbo_fisher_glad_alabama_ trus.html.

7.   Scarbinsky, Kevin. "Jimbo Fisher glad Alabama trustees nixed his deal to become UAB's head coach (Kevin Scarbinsky)." AL.com. January 04, 2014. http://www.al.com/sports/index.ssf/2014/01/jimbo_fisher_glad_alabama_ trus.html

8.   Guilbeau, Glenn. "LSU's Fisher to interview at UAB." *Monroe News-Star*, December 14, 2006.

9.   Doyel, Gregg. "'Little Bear' Bryant crosses line again in denying UAB." CBSSports.com. December 26, 2006. http://www.cbssports.com/college football/story/9891201

10. Schad, Joe. "Source: Garrick McGee to be UAB coach." ESPN. December 3, 2011. http://www.espn.com/college-football/story/_/id/7309851/source-uab-blazers-hire-garrick-mcgee-arkansas-razorbacks-football-coach.

11. Irvine, Steve. "UA Board of Trustees stop UAB on-campus stadium proposal before it starts." AL.com. November 1, 2011. http://www.al.com/sports/index. ssf/2011/11/ua_board_of_trustees_stop_uab.html.

12. Cantrell, Tyler. "#UAB's Clark misled about potential of in-door practice facility when he was hired." Underdog Dynasty. January 7, 2015. http:// www.underdogdynasty.com/2015/1/7/7505253/uab-in-door-practice-facility-was-almost-a-reality-with-funds-at-hand.

13. Scarbinsky |, Kevin Nsky |. "UA trustee Finis St. John killed plan to put artificial turf on UAB football practice field, boosters say." AL.com. January 09, 2015. http://www.al.com/sports/index.ssf/2015/01/ua_trustee_finis_st_john_kille.html.

14. Solomon, Jon. "Death of UAB football: Anger remains, but study banks on healing." CBSSports.com. December 23, 2014. http://www.cbssports.com/college-football/news/death-of-uab-football-anger-remains-but-study-banks-on-healing/.

15. Solomon, Jon. "Sources: C-USA won't change bylaws to keep UAB without football." CBSSports.com. April 29, 2015. http://www.cbssports.com/college-football/news/sources-c-usa-wont-change-bylaws-to-keep-uab-without-football/.

16. Ellis, Steve. "Jeff Bowden gets $537,000 severance." *Florida Today*, November 16, 2016.

17. Raby, John. "Terry Bowden Lobbying For West Virginia Job." December 18, 2007.

18. Maiocco, Matt. "Jameis Winston regrets not attending Stanford." CSN Bay Area. October 20, 2016. http://www.csnbayarea.com/49ers/jameis-winston-regrets-not-attending-stanford.